The Unwritten Rules of PhD Research

The Unwritten Rules of PhD Research

Second edition

Marian Petre and Gordon Rugg

 Open University Press

Open University Press
McGraw-Hill Education
McGraw-Hill House
Shoppenhangers Road
Maidenhead
Berkshire
England
SL6 2QL

email: enquiries@openup.co.uk
world wide web: www.openup.co.uk

and Two Penn Plaza, New York, NY 10121-2289, USA

First published 2004
Reprinted 2011 (twice)

A catalogue record of this book is available from the British Library

ISBN-13: 978-0-33-523702-9 (pb)
ISBN-10: 0335237029 (pb)

Library of Congress Cataloging-in-Publication Data
CIP data applied for

Typeset by RefineCatch Limited, Bungay, Suffolk
Printed in the UK by Bell & Bain Ltd, Glasgow

The McGraw·Hill Companies

Contents

Preface to the first edition

I know just where the sea-elephants are stored.[1]

One of the most frequent laments of the postgraduate researcher is: 'Why didn't someone tell me that earlier?' There are innumerable things which nobody bothered to tell you, or to write in the books, and which could have saved you from large amounts of confusion, depression, wasted effort and general tears and misery if only you had been told them earlier.

The authors have spent more than their fair share of time with desperate beginners, explaining the basic principles of research over cups of coffee. This book is an attempt to cut down their caffeine overload. It explains the basic craft skills and ground rules of the academic world in general, and research in particular. Its focus is the vitally important things that the standard textbooks don't bother to mention on the sweet assumption that they can be left to the readers' lecturers and supervisors.

If you are doing a PhD or an MPhil then this book is intended to help you to do the best research possible with the minimum of wasted effort. It is also intended to help you use your research as part of your career development and self-development so that you don't end up on graduation day, certificate in hand, wondering just what the hell to do next and realizing that you've just spent several years moving painfully in the wrong direction.

The authors' backgrounds are varied. Their academic credentials include PhDs, publication of various journal papers and encyclopaedia articles, advanced research fellowships, a couple of journal editorships, refereeing for major journals and fund-giving bodies, and raising between them over a million pounds of research funding. Their students still talk to them, and sometimes say nice things about them.

---

[1] O'Brian, P. (1996) *The Fortune of War*. London: HarperCollins, p. 225.

Preface to the second edition

By popular demand, in this second edition we've made some changes to reflect feedback from readers, and developments in the world that affect students, such as the growth of open access journals. We've tried to keep the best bits, tighten the others and add things that will be of use.

About this book

What it is, what it's not, and how to make best use of it

. . . I had said much, but found that my words had been given scant attention. [1]

We've spent a lot of time helping PhD students with problems, and advising potential PhD students who want to avoid problems. Most of these people have read books with titles like *How to get a PhD*; most of them have been given good advice by supervisors and potential supervisors. The problems don't come from the books and the advice – most of the books on this topic range between good and excellent, and most of the advice we've heard reported to us has been sound. The problems usually come from what's absent from the books and the advice. This book is intended to fill at least part of that gap.

Most of the problems we've dealt with involve what's known as tacit knowledge in the broad sense – things that nobody bothers to tell you explicitly, either because they assume you know them already, or because they are so familiar to them that they completely forget that other people don't know them, or because they don't think they're worth mentioning. Book writers usually assume (correctly, in our opinion) that these things are better dealt with informally by supervisors. In an ideal world, this would happen, but in practice supervisors are human (i.e. overworked, forgetful, distracted and imperfect). What we've done is to write down an overview of these unwritten rules, so that the situation makes more sense to you. You can then ask your supervisor about how things work in your discipline, and (with luck) get some solid, specific guidance.

For PhD students, the main problems in our experience fall into two main categories. One is 'big picture' knowledge about how the academic system works, and why it works that way. For instance, what are some classic career paths in academia? Why is academic writing so dry? Why do some people get lectureships in good departments before they've finished their PhD, whereas others are still struggling to find any job ten years after their doctorate? What counts as a 'good' department anyway, and why? Many students are too embarrassed to show their ignorance by asking questions like these; more

---

[1] Lovecraft, H.P. ([1917] 1985) Dagon, in *Omnibus 2: Dagon and Other Macabre Tales*. London: Grafton Books, p. 17.

students are too focused on the immediate problems of the PhD to think of asking them until it's too late.

The second category involves what are known as 'craft skills'. These are usually low-level skills, normally viewed as not sufficiently important to be worth mentioning in textbooks – tricks of the trade which are usually taught informally by supervisors or other mentors. These range from quite specific information (e.g. 'How many references should I have in the first paragraph of something I write?') to quite general rules of thumb (e.g. 'How can I get a reasonable brief overview of this topic that my supervisor's advised me to read about, without spending six months wading through the literature?') The specific skills, and the specific answers, vary across disciplines; however, once you're aware of the basic concept of craft skills, you can then find out what the craft skills are in your chosen area, and learn them.

Each chapter of this book deals with an area of tacit knowledge which is important to PhD students. Some fairly specific topics, such as how to handle criticism, are relevant in more than one place (for instance, handling criticism is relevant to writing, to presentations and to the viva). Some more general topics, such as writing, manifest themselves in different ways at different stages of your PhD (which is why this book is structured around topics, rather than in chronological order of what will happen to you in your PhD). Each chapter begins with a description of the topic, and is illustrated with examples and anecdotes. Where an anecdote is dubious or apocryphal, we've said so; the others are true, even when improbable. These verbal descriptions are intended to help you understand what the issues are, and why things are the way they are; the anecdotes are there to illustrate the underlying points and to help you remember them. Many of the chapters end with a table that summarizes some useful tips. The tables are offered as *aides-mémoire*, not to be confused with complete summaries.

Understanding is all very well, but isn't much consolation when it's the day before your first seminar presentation and you're worried about whether there's something blindingly obvious that you've forgotten. We've therefore included a fair number of checklists, bullet points and the like, so that you can check that you've remembered the key things.

That's the main body of the book. Our advice is to read it first from start to finish (since you'll do that anyway, and there's not much point in giving advice which will be ignored). The best thing to do next is to read it in more detail, starting with the topics furthest away from you in time – first, the section on what to do after the PhD, then the sections on the viva and on writing up, and so on. The reason for this is that most students are so focused, understandably, on the immediate problems surrounding them that they rarely look more than one step ahead. This is all very well in the short term, but it usually stores up long-term problems. What happens, for instance, if you're in a discipline where you need to be the author of at least two journal papers, and to have at least two years of part-time lecturing experience, to be shortlisted for a full-time lectureship? If you don't discover this until the last six months of your PhD then you'll have problems if you want to go straight on to a lectureship; if you know about it early, then you can start getting the right things on your CV in good time.

One important thing to keep in mind when reading this book is that disciplines vary. This is why we use words such as 'usually' quite a lot. The precise indications of quality in a CV will be different between, say, history and geology, but the underlying concepts usually remain the same – for instance, the concept of a strong CV as opposed to a weak one. This book is intended to help you understand what these underlying concepts are, so that you can find out what form they take in your discipline, and then make sure that you have the right indicators of quality in your written work, in your presentations and in your CV.

On the subject of informality, we have deliberately used an informal style throughout this book. This is not the style which we use for other venues, such as when writing journal articles, so don't be tempted to use this style in your own written thesis. For example, we have used the short abbreviation for a doctorate (i.e. PhD), as opposed to the full abbreviation (i.e. Ph.D.). The shorter abbreviation is a lot less fiddly when writing a large document like this book, but in formal contexts you need to show that you know the correct version, and to use that consistently.

We've deliberately omitted a variety of other things, such as how to use statistics, on the grounds that these are well covered in other books, and this one is quite long enough already. We hope you find it useful and enjoyable.

Acknowledgements

. . . it were insidious to particularize; but I must acknowledge the politeness of Mons. La Hire, of the royal French artillery, who volunteered his services in setting and firing the train to the magazine, and who was somewhat bruised and singed. [1]

We would like to thank all the people who helped us with the writing and publishing of this book – they know who they are.

We thank John Oates for permitting us to use his material on ethics. We thank the Research Councils UK and Vitae (a national programme incorporating the UK GRAD Programme) for permitting us to use material pertaining to research skills. Inevitably, the book draws on material we have been amassing and rehearsing over time in a variety of contexts, and so inevitably parts resemble material presented or published in other contexts. We have done our level best to indicate cases where this is so and to seek permission in good faith.

We would also like to acknowledge our gratitude to our own PhD supervisors, from whom we learned much, much more than we realized at the time. Our remaining sins are our own faults, not theirs. Finally, we would like to acknowledge the students who have, directly and indirectly, brought colour to our lives, and wealth to coffee manufacturers round the world . . . without them, this book would never have been written, and our lives would have been much less fun.

---

[1] O'Brian, P. (1990) *Master and Commander*. London: W.W. Norton & Company, p. 225.

1

So you want to do a PhD?

What is a PhD? • Cabinet-making – the PhD as a 'master piece' • Cabinet-making skills • Instrumental and expressive behaviour • Necessary skills • Criteria for a PhD: some reassurance

> *You can't imagine, even from what you have read and what I've told you, the things I shall have to see and do. It's fiendish work, Carter, and I doubt if any man without ironclad sensibilities could ever see it through and come up alive and sane.* [1]

There are two classic ways of doing a PhD. One involves knowing just what you are doing; you will then go through a clearly defined path, suffer occasional fits of gloom and despair, emerge with a PhD, unless you do something remarkably silly or give up, and then proceed smoothly with the next stage of your career. The other way is the one followed by most PhD students, which involves stumbling in, wandering round in circles for several years, suffering frequent fits of gloom and despair, and probably but not necessarily emerging with a PhD, followed by wondering what to do next in career terms. This book is written for those who find themselves following the second path.

There are many good books out there for people wanting to do a PhD. If

---

[1] Lovecraft, H.P. (1919) The Statement of Randolph Carter, in *Omnibus 1: At the Mountains of Madness* (1989). London: Grafton Books, p. 356.

you're thinking of doing a PhD, you should read at least one of them. They give much good advice about what you need to do, and are a good start. We have spent a lot of time helping students who have read those books. The reason that we needed to help them was not because there was anything wrong with the content of the books; the problem was the things that the books didn't cover. One set of things involved the 'big picture' of doing a PhD; the other set involved low-level skills that the books typically didn't cover, probably on the grounds that their writers assumed these skills would be taught either by supervisors or by the training courses which most PhD students now undergo. This book is intended to fill at least some of that gap.

There are different reasons for undertaking a PhD, ranging from the pragmatic (e.g. acquiring a research credential for academia or for industry) to the idealistic (e.g. aspiring to deep scholarship). Students have many reasons in between, including things like curiosity, a drive to chase a long-held question, an avoidance of abject drudgery or the need to prove oneself. More important still are the reasons for *finishing* a PhD, the drivers that keep students going when the going gets tough. Students often don't admit those reasons readily, but when they do they're usually personal and potent: doing something your big brother didn't manage, laughing in the face of that disparaging infant school teacher, avoiding conscription, escaping the family business, getting a dreamed-for job. Your reason for finishing is important to your success, and you need a reason compelling enough to take you through the obstacles and frustrations of the process.

What is a PhD?

Entering students often think of a PhD as a 'magnum opus', a brilliant research project culminating in a great work. This is rather a demanding model and few students win Nobel Prizes as a result of their doctoral studies. As one colleague phrased it, a PhD is less like hacking through the jungle with a machete, and more like crawling around on the ground with a magnifying glass – less major discovery of new lands, more painstakingly detailed investigation of familiar ones.

More realistically, a PhD is a demonstration of research competence. There are certain things that you are demonstrating through your dissertation:

• Mastery of your subject
• Research insight
• Respect for the discipline
• Capacity for independent research
• Ability to communicate results and relate them to the broader discourse

These reflect competence and professionalism, rather than greatness. Importantly, they are as much about comprehending others' work as about doing one's own.

So, a PhD is research training leading to a professional research qualification. A PhD can be a deep, specific education in a discipline, preceding a post-doctoral period of on-the-job training (note: there is no implication that the PhD is the *end* of your education or training). It involves you doing a substantial chunk of research, writing it up and then discussing it with professional academics. You have a supervisor (or two, or more) to help and advise you, but in theory at least the PhD is something for which you take the initiative, and so it is a demonstration of your ability to do proper research independently. The process is rarely smooth; along the way you are likely to learn a great deal about how *not* to do research as well as about how to do it effectively.

At a sordidly practical level, the PhD suggests that you are good enough at research to be appointable to a university post. A PhD is highly advisable for a career as an academic, or helpful for a career as a researcher in industry. PhDs are recognized around the world and tend to have pretty good quality control, so a PhD from one country will be recognized in another without too much snobbery. Still at the practical level, if you have a PhD, you usually go onto a higher pay scale.

There are other views of a PhD, as well. It can be viewed as an initiation rite, in which you undergo an ordeal and, if you come through the ordeal in a creditable manner, are admitted to membership of the academic clan. Continuing the analogy, having a PhD will not be enough to make you a clan elder, but it will mark the transition to full adulthood. You are treated differently if you have a PhD – there is a distinct feeling of having become 'one of us'.

The 'rite of passage' is not just a snobbery thing; the ordeal (and the education) give you a different way of thinking about things. A PhD can be viewed as one's entry into the research discourse (which equates roughly to the research community's dialogue about what it believes it knows and has a good basis for knowing). What it should do is prepare you to consider and debate what you know and how you know it. This means that you'll have developed your critical thinking, that you'll have learned about weighing evidence and questioning assumptions. You will gradually notice a different way of thinking about things – for example, when you start making administrative decisions in your subsequent career. A good example of this is undergraduate student projects: in many departments, staff with PhDs typically want to use the projects as a way of teaching the students how to conduct research, and staff without PhDs typically want to use the projects as a chance to give the students an industrial placement. The PhDs' view is that the students need to learn critical thinking skills valuable for later life; the other view is that the students need to be equipped to find jobs. Which is right? This is a good question, and one which would take us on a lengthy diversion. The main point is that doing a PhD *does* change you.

So, a PhD can be many things: research training, springboard for specialist expertise, rite of passage, job credential . . . what it means for you depends on which opportunities you seize, whether you keep an eye on 'the Big Picture', what sorts of relationships you form and so on. So, how can you make it into what you need it to be?

The next sections describe some concepts which we have found invaluable, but which don't usually appear in other books. These provide a useful structure for (a) what you are trying to do in a PhD and (b) understanding how things work in the big picture. The first of these is the cabinet-making metaphor; the second is the distinction between instrumental and expressive behaviour.

Terminology: a brief digression

There are various types of research degree; what they have in common is that they involve research by the student as a core component. This is different from a taught degree where there may be a research project (for instance, an MSc project), but where this research project is only one component among many on the course.

Strictly speaking, a research degree involves a *thesis*, which is the argument that you propose as a result of your research. Again strictly speaking, the *dissertation* is the written document which describes your thesis. In common usage, the dissertation is often referred to as 'the thesis'. It's worth knowing about the distinction in case you have a particularly pedantic external examiner – it helps you get off to a better start.

Cabinet-making – the PhD as a 'master piece'

Doing a PhD has a lot in common with traditional cabinet-making. Back in The Past, an apprentice cabinet-maker would finish his apprenticeship (back in The Past, apprentice cabinet-makers had to be 'he') by making a cabinet which demonstrated that he had all the skills needed to be a master cabinet-maker. This piece of furniture was known as the 'master piece'. A successfully-defended PhD dissertation fulfils a similar role. It demonstrates that you have all the skills needed to be a researcher in your own right. The issue of *demonstration* is essential. The basis of the PhD examination is the dissertation, together with the subsequent *viva voce* examination. It doesn't matter how brilliant or well-informed you are – if the brilliance and erudition isn't visible in the dissertation, then you're going to fail.

You therefore need to know what the required skills are for your branch of academia (since different disciplines require different skills) and make sure that you demonstrate mastery of each of these somewhere in your thesis. If you're a methodical sort of person, you might go so far as to draw up a list of the skills required and tick off each one as it is represented in your thesis. For a cabinet-maker, the skills required would be things like making various complex joints, fitting hinges neatly, applying veneer, achieving a high polish and so forth. For an academic, the skills are things like mastery of formal academic language, familiarity with the relevant literature in the discipline, knowledge of the main data collection techniques, adherence to the standards of rigour and so on. (We talk more about research skills in Chapter 3.)

Things which do not normally appear on the list include personal interest in the area and the ethical importance of the topic. There is no point in going on about these at length in your thesis – you are awarded a PhD as an acknowledgement that you can make cabinets at master craftsman level, not an acknowledgement that you find cabinet-making fascinating, or that cabinets make the world a better place. In practice, few people would spend several years of their life doing a PhD on a topic which held no interest for them, so personal interest is usually taken for granted by examiners. Ethics is a more interesting question. One reason why examiners tend not to take account of claims about the ethical importance of a question (e.g. finding a cure for cancer) as a criterion for assessing a PhD is that bad research can actually impede the search for an answer to the problem by leading other researchers in the wrong direction. Bad research into a highly ethical question is still bad research. Back to the main theme.

Different disciplines have different required skills. Most experienced researchers are so familiar with these that they take them for granted, and would be hard pressed to produce a list from memory over a physical or metaphorical cup of coffee. However, other experienced researchers (especially those who teach research methods courses) will be able to give you some answers. In addition, it is worth having a look at the contents section of research methods books in your discipline, which will cover most of the main topics. The PhD regulations for your institution should also help.

An illustrative list of typical skills is given below. It's illustrative rather than definitive – your discipline will almost certainly have a different list. However, many of the skills will be the same, and the list will give you the general idea. A pragmatic recap of our top tips is gathered in Table 1.1 at the end of the chapter.

Most of the skills below assume that your work will be located within a single discipline. There is a reason for this. Interdisciplinary PhDs can be extremely interesting and useful. However, they need to be handled with care, since otherwise there is the risk that they will 'fall between two stools'. This can be a problem in terms of practical matters such as finding an external examiner, and in terms of theoretical issues such as deciding which approach to follow when the different disciplines involved have very different ways of doing things. It is usually much wiser to decide on a 'host' discipline, locate the interdisciplinary PhD within that, and then import the concepts from the other discipline into the host discipline.

Cabinet-making skills

Most disciplines require most of the following skills, although individual cases will vary.

Framing an appropriate and useful research question

At the heart of any research is the research question. The quality of output hinges on the quality of the question: why it is asked, how it is asked, how it relates to other questions and knowledge and what might constitute an answer. Hence, one key skill is the demonstration of the ability to develop a well-formulated question. You'll need to provide evidence of:

- Articulation of the motivation and significance of the question
- Situation in existing literature: coverage and limitations of existing and competing research, awareness of where your work fits in relation to the discipline and what it contributes to the discipline
- Identification and critique of alternative approaches

Use of academic language

An important part of research is engaging in the discourse: communicating research ideas, processes and results so that they may be scrutinized and discussed. Good communication relies on understanding the conventions of the community. Hence, one key skill is the demonstration of competent academic language. This includes:

- Correct use of technical terms
- Attention to detail in punctuation, grammar etc.
- Attention to use of typographic design (white space, layout, headings styles) to make the text accessible
- Ability to structure and convey a clear and coherent argument, including attention to the use of 'signposting' devices such as headings to make the structure accessible
- Writing in a suitable academic 'voice'

Knowledge of background literature

Research is not conducted in isolation; it happens in a context of prior thinking, prior knowledge, prior evidence, prior practice. One key skill is the demonstration of an awareness of that context and of how it shapes your own research. This includes:

- Seminal texts correctly cited, with evidence that you have read them and evaluated them critically
- References accurately reflecting the growth of the literature from the seminal texts to the present day
- Identification of key recent texts on which your own PhD is based, showing both how these contribute to your thesis and how your thesis is different from them
- Relevant texts and concepts from other disciplines cited
- Organization of all of the cited literature into a coherent, critical structure, showing both that you can make sense of the literature – identifying conceptual relationships and themes, recognizing gaps – and that you understand what is important

Research methods

Any established discipline has a tradition of practice, in the sense of how things are done. Many disciplines have established methodologies which prescribe the selection, combination and sequencing of the methods and techniques to be employed. Others select methods and techniques less prescriptively and borrow more broadly across domain boundaries. All disciplines require an appropriate application of methods in order to ensure rigour. Hence, one key skill is the demonstration of appropriate knowledge and competence in choosing and using research methods. This skill includes:

- Knowledge of the main research methods used in your discipline, including data collection, record-keeping and data analysis
- Knowledge of what constitutes 'evidence' in your discipline, and of what is acceptable as a knowledge claim
- Detailed knowledge – and competent application – of at least one method
- Critical analysis of one of the standard methods in your discipline, showing that you understand both its strengths and its limitations

Theory

Again, research is conducted in a context of existing ideas, evidence and thinking. One key skill is the demonstration of cognizance of the theoretical context and of how it shapes your own research, including:

- Understanding of key theoretical strands and theoretical concepts in your discipline
- Understanding how theory shapes your research question
- Ability to contribute something useful to the theoretical debate in your area

Researcher maturity

Part of a PhD is confirming your 'research independence'. You need to demonstrate your:

- Ability to do all the above yourself, rather than simply doing what your supervisor tells you
- Awareness of where your work fits in relation to the discipline, and what it contributes to the discipline
- Mature overview of the discipline

Instrumental and expressive behaviour

In fairy tales, you sometimes encounter a magic book. This is usually a book which appears once, in time of need, and which contains the information needed to solve the crisis at the heart of the tale; when the hero or heroine returns afterwards to look for further wisdom, the book has vanished from the place where it was left, never to be seen again. In the tales, finding the book is something which happens once in a lifetime, when you most need it.

Real life isn't quite like that. As we can testify from personal experience, the book can appear more than once in a lifetime, and not always at the immediate point of need. On the first occasion, the book was an anthology of writings about new religious movements, in which an article appeared at the time to be very interesting, but of no immediate relevance to anything that Gordon was doing. On the second occasion, the book was an extremely good encyclopaedia of psychology, which provided the key information needed for a successful large funding bid. Gordon neglected to note the full bibliographic reference for either book, and no amount of detailed searching of the relevant libraries (both on the shelves and in the online and printed catalogues) subsequently produced anything quite like those books. These experiences are (a) one of the reasons why we go on at such length about the need for proper bibliographic references for everything you read, and (b) the principal reason for the lack of a proper bibliographic reference for the article discussed in this section. If you'd like to track down the original article, it's a chapter describing the de Leonist political movement in the United States, in an edited anthology of writings about new religious movements, which was in the University of Nottingham library sometime between 1986 and 1992 and, no, Gordon never did manage to track it down again, though he did find the background literature from which it had come.

The author of the said chapter was a sociologist who was studying the de Leonists. Some of their behaviour made little sense to him – for instance, they once spent a lot of time putting up posters around the city advertising a talk which had already happened. Eventually he realized that they were engaging in what he called expressive, rather than instrumental, behaviour. Instrumental behaviour consists of actions leading toward a stated goal; for instance, the goal of learning to drive a car might involve the instrumental behaviours of booking driving lessons, buying a copy of the *Highway Code* etc. Measured against this criterion, the de Leonists' behaviour appeared senseless. Expressive behaviour, on the other hand, consists of actions demonstrating to other people what sort of person you are; for instance, sitting in the front of a lecture theatre and taking copious notes in a very visible manner to show that you take your studies very seriously. Against this criterion, the de Leonists' behaviour made a lot more sense; much of it was intended to demonstrate group loyalty, and was intended for other members of the group to see. Sticking up large numbers of posters publicizing an event which had already happened could therefore be a good way of demonstrating that you were a committed member of the group and, in consequence, of increasing your standing within the group.

Instrumental behaviour and expressive behaviour are both important. In our experience, students are normally good at some types of instrumental behaviour and woefully bad at the sensible sorts of expressive behaviour, usually because nobody has explained to them which signals they need to send out.

An example of this is the use of bibliographic referencing. At an instrumental level this is important, because inadequate referencing can lead to your being unable to relocate a key text which you read earlier; it is also important for other people who might want to follow up one of your points, or to check one of your assertions (external examiners for PhDs, for instance, often want to do this). At an expressive level, good referencing is also important: it sends out signals saying that you take core academic values seriously, that you are familiar with the core craft skills, that you are thorough and professional, and so forth.

More often, however, students engage in expressive behaviours which send out signals such as 'look how hard I'm trying' – for instance, spending all day every day in the library, regardless of whether what they are reading is particularly useful or not. The usual sequence of events is that the supervisor sooner or later notices that the student is not making any progress, and points this out; the student reacts by even more expressive behaviour sending out the same signal; the supervisor notices continuing lack of progress; and so on, until an ending occurs which is usually unhappy. What students in this situation need to realize is that the problem is not how hard they are trying, but what they are omitting to do. One large part of this book is about the instrumental skills which are needed to do a good PhD, and another large part is about the signals of skilled professionalism which you need to send out via the right sort of expressive behaviour. (There is also yet another large part which is about identifying the wrong sorts of expressive behaviour, and about what to do to rectify them.)

Necessary skills

Those readers who are familiar with *1066 and All That* will be pleased to know that skills are currently viewed as a Good Thing. This is especially the case with skills which can be described as 'transferable skills'. You can therefore treat them as a positive asset, to be added to your CV, rather than as another cheerless obligation. Your institutional training course will probably wax eloquent on skills of various sorts – transferable, generic, project-based, discipline-based (though readers with an interest in BDSM may be disappointed to hear that this does not normally involve whips and leather) and doubtless many others. Transferable skills are particularly favoured by The System because they are allegedly usable in areas other than just academia. They include (depending on whose versions you receive) writing, public speaking and coping with prejudice.

We'll talk more about the wonderful world of research skills in Chapter 3; the rest of this section describes skills which may not be included on your institution's training programme.

Tact and diplomacy

As a PhD student, you need to accept that you are not exactly at the top of the academic pecking order; as a new PhD student, you are also the new kid on the block. There is therefore a time for being right and a time for using the quiet word that gets you what you want. PhD students tend to do a lot of complaining about how The System treats them (often with some justice on their side), but tend to forget that they are in a system which dates back to the Dark Ages, and which has learnt a thing or two about dealing with complaints. An important skill is to learn when to let something pass and when to stand up (tactfully and politely, but firmly) for an issue. Otherwise, you are likely to find yourself winning the battles and losing the war. For instance, you will probably have complaints about the shortcomings of the library; PhD students almost everywhere have complaints about the library, usually ill-founded, so if you get stroppy about this issue you are unlikely to get a huge amount of sympathy. ('The library doesn't have many books on my area of interest' usually translates into: 'I haven't learnt yet that I should be reading journal articles at this stage' – not the strongest position for winning an argument.) A second example: you may have grave reservations about the quality of the research methods training course that your institution puts on for PhD students. Bear in mind that PhD training courses are still in their early days, and that a tactless confrontation with the professor responsible for the course is unlikely to produce the result that you need; some suggestions, phrased in a face-saving manner, are more likely to achieve this. Remember also that most PhD students know what they *want*, not what they *need*; there is sometimes an enormous difference between the two. This leads on to another important skill.

Having the right cup of coffee

Probably the most important research tool you will encounter is the cup of coffee. Successful students know this; unsuccessful ones tend to wonder why we're wasting time with jokes, and then wonder why the world is so unfair to them. Knowledge is power; rare knowledge is greater power. The best way of finding out what you really need to know is usually to have a cup of coffee with the right person, and to ask their advice (tactfully and diplomatically). Who is the right person? Someone with the knowledge, which for most situations means someone who is not another PhD student – if they're still a student, then no matter how helpful and friendly they are, you can't be sure whether their advice is sincere and right, or sincere and mistaken, since they haven't yet got successfully through a PhD. There are a lot of folk myths in circulation among PhD students. Fellow students are a good source of social support, and of help with tasks like blind judging for data analysis, or with babysitting; they're not a good source of advice about what your thesis should look like, or where to find the equipment you need for your next bit of fieldwork. The right person is someone who has a successful track record in the relevant topic – for instance, supervisors whose students usually have happy endings, chief technicians with a reputation for producing the right bit of kit out of a cupboard when all hope seemed gone, librarians who have helped your friends to find obscure but essential references. Show them due appreciation and treat their advice as confidential unless they specify otherwise. The most useful knowledge is often the sort that people will not want to be quoted on – for instance, hints about good or bad people to ask for help.

Asking the right research question

Once you learn this skill, life becomes very different. We have an entire section on this elsewhere because it's so important; we mention it here because it's well worth mentioning twice. So is the skill of asking the *next* question. The real insights often come in the follow-up and validation – by not being satisfied with the first result, but by investigating its implications and limitations.

Academic writing

Writing is indeed a transferable skill; you can transfer academic writing skills from one academic setting to another, and you can transfer business writing skills from one business setting to another. It is quite possible that there are areas where you can even transfer academic writing skills appropriately to industry or vice versa.

Most students know that a PhD requires good science, or good archival research, or good engineering or good disciplinary research of whatever flavour. Many forget that it also requires good 'story-telling'. Getting the form and voice of the dissertation right is just as important as getting the content right in showing mastery, rigour and insight – indeed, they are essential to conveying the content. The dissertation is the 'highest form' of academic writing, requiring content, precision, substantiation and mastery of context beyond what is normally required in individual published papers. It is a 'master piece', not in the sense of an 'ultimate work', but in the sense of a piece that qualifies an apprentice to be called a master through its demonstration of techniques, skills, form and function.

Filling in forms

Forms are a sort of tax you pay for belonging to (and being supported by) an organization. Academia has an insatiable appetite for forms, which it associates with quality control and due process (and which students associate with racks and thumbscrews). 'Doing' forms well and promptly can make you many friends – the sort of friends (administrators, budget-holders, tutors and deans) who can smooth your way when it comes to really getting things done. So come to terms with forms as an easy way to show goodwill, and learn to deal with them with dispatch.

Some useful habits, in no particular order:

- Read every form through to the end before starting to fill it in
- Know the audience – knowing who is going to read the form and with what purpose can help you complete it efficiently and avoid pitfalls
- If the form is important and you only have one copy, photocopy it, and fill in the copy as a practice run before filling in the final version
- If you're not sure what a particular section means, then refer to the notes – most forms have accompanying notes which most people don't bother to read
- If you're not sure what sorts of answers are required, then see if you can get an example of a successfully completed form to use as a model (e.g. from another student)
- Complete internal administrative forms as minimally as possible – imagine someone reading 50 of them and you'll understand why concise bullet lists are generally preferable to wordy narratives for standard forms like expenses claims, stationery requests, progress reports and travel reports
- Know the exceptions to the previous tip (such as grant proposals, fellowship applications and cases for awards) – but keep narratives concise
- Read over the completed form (you'll be surprised how many stupid slips you can make)
- If you find forms terrifying, ask someone to help you; if your fear is intense,

then consider asking for help from someone who deals with phobias – the process is usually fast and surprisingly pleasant
- Photocopy every form that you fill in, after you have completed it, and keep the copies neatly filed – they can be useful reminders for how to fill in the forms, as well as a record of what you claimed last time

Criteria for a PhD: some reassurance

PhD students often worry about whether their research will be good enough for a PhD. It's useful to remember the criteria which most universities have at the core of their PhD assessment: 'original work' which makes 'a significant contribution to knowledge'. It is no coincidence that most refereed journals and conferences use similar criteria – such publications are notionally how the research community communicates and continues to build knowledge. Therefore, you can provide evidence of 'significance', 'originality' and 'contribution to knowledge' in advance of submission of your thesis by publishing your work in refereed journals or conferences. There is more on this at various places later in this book. You don't need to make a major discovery to get a PhD – you just need to show that you're able to do good enough research independently.

Key dissertation ingredients

A number of ingredients are essential for a satisfactory dissertation:

- A thesis: one coherent over-riding 'story' or argument that embodies a research insight
- Situation in existing knowledge: a critical review of prior research which motivates and justifies the research question
- Contribution of something new (the 'significant contribution to knowledge')
- Appropriate voice and argument: the provision of clear and explicit evidence, substantiation and chain of inference

More hangs on the student's ability to demonstrate intellectual maturity and critical depth – and through them to provide insight – than on the scale or scope of the research findings. A good PhD is based on an honest report of research that reflects sound practice and well-articulated critical thinking.

What is a 'significant' contribution?

Most students, when they hear the phrase 'significant contribution', think in terms of a new theory, crucial experiments, technological breakthroughs – the stuff of Nobel Prizes. For a PhD, the truth is that 'significant' need not mean 'revolutionary' or 'major' or even 'large'. The phrase might be more accurately read as 'significant – albeit modest – contribution'.

Characterizing your contribution means answering 'So what?', which means articulating:

- The importance of the question (Why is it worth asking?)
- The significance of the findings (Why should anyone care? Why do they matter?)
- Their implications for theory
- The limitations to generalization

Making a 'significant contribution' means 'adding to knowledge' or 'contributing to the discourse' – that is, providing evidence to substantiate a conclusion that's worth making. Research is not something done in isolation; it is a discourse among many researchers, each providing evidence and argument that contributes to knowledge and understanding, each critiquing the available evidence. Research is about the articulation and analysis of phenomena observed and investigated through a variety of techniques. It's about 'making sense' of the world: not just describing it, but also analysing and explaining it. As more evidence is presented, the analysis and explanations are re-evaluated. Knowledge claims can be small and still have a role in the discourse.

What sorts of contribution are typically made in dissertations?

- Re-contextualization of an existing technique, theory or model (applying a technique in a new context, testing a theory in a new setting, showing the applicability of a model to a new situation): showing it works – or that it doesn't – and why
- Corroboration and elaboration of an existing model (e.g. evaluating the effects of a change of condition; experimental assessment of one aspect of a model)
- Falsification or contradiction of an existing model, or part of one
- Drawing together two or more existing ideas and showing that the combination reveals something new and useful
- Demonstration of a concept: showing that something is feasible and has utility (or showing that something is infeasible and explaining why it fails)
- Implementation of theoretical principle: showing how it can be applied in practice; making concrete someone else's idea, and hence showing how it works in practice and what its limitations are
- Codification of the 'obvious': providing evidence about what 'everyone knows' (possibly providing evidence that received wisdom is incorrect)
- Empirically-based characterization of a phenomenon of interest (e.g. detailed, critical, analytic account of the evolution of an idea; detailed analytic characterization of a crucial case study or a novel chemical compound, or a new planet)

- Providing a taxonomy of observed phenomena
- Well-founded critique of existing theory or evidence (e.g. correlating the results of a number of existing studies to show patterns, omissions or biases etc.)
- Providing a new solution to a known problem (and demonstrating its efficacy) – even an obscure one; conceiving and justifying a new explanation for a problematic phenomenon
- Filling a small technical gap (e.g. showing that a 'tweak' to an algorithm or technique is more effective or developing a novel methodology)

The key is that, although the dissertation must stand alone in presenting your research, the research doesn't exist in isolation. Doing research means contributing to the discourse – adding knowledge that moves the discourse along. We say that 'research proceeds by baby steps' and that 'researchers stand on each other's shoulders'. A 'significant contribution' is a baby step, one that combines with the baby steps of others to produce progress. A decent PhD should yield at least one sound paper in a strong, peer-reviewed journal.

Table 1.1 Ten top tips for research students

Read, read, read	Seasoned researchers typically have an evolving 'reference set' of around 100–150 papers which forms the core of the relevant literature in their specialty, and with which they are conversant. Students need to read enough to form an initial reference set.
Write, write, write	• Writing is a skill that requires practice: the more you write, the easier it gets • You should aim to write up as you go; this will both make it easier at the end (when you rewrite it all) and give you something to show people who are interested in your work • Don't throw writing away; date it and store it in an 'out-takes' file; that material can be useful • Revising is often easier than writing new
Keep an annotated bibliography	This is the single most powerful research tool you can give yourself. It should be a personal tool, including all the usual bibliographic information, the date when you read the paper and notes on what *you* found interesting/seminal/infuriating/etc. about it.
Form an 'informal committee'	Try to find a small set of reliable, interested people who are willing to read for you, comment on ideas, bring literature to your attention, introduce you to other researchers and so on. They may be specialists who can provide expertise on which you can draw, or generalists who ask tough questions.
Expose your work	Make your work public in technical reports, research seminars and conference papers. The best way to get information is to share information; if people understand what your ideas are, they can respond to them. Making your work public exposes you to questions and criticism early (when it can do you some good), helps you to 'network' and gather leads and gives you practice articulating your reasoning.
So what? Learn to ask the other questions	Students often get a result and forget to take the next step. 'Look, I got a correlation!' *'So what?'* Learn to go beyond your initial question, learn to invert the question in order to expose other perspectives and learn to look for alternative explanations.
Never hide from your supervisor	'Hiding' is a pathological behaviour in which most research students indulge at some point. Communicating with your supervisor is a prerequisite to getting the most out of your supervisor.
Always make backups (and keep a set off-site)	More than one student has had to start writing from scratch or to repeat empirical work because he or she neglected this most basic of disciplines.
Read at least one completed dissertation cover to cover	Reading something that has 'passed' is an excellent way to reflect on dissertation structure, content, and style – and on 'what it takes'.
A doctorate is pass/ fail	Part of the process is learning when 'enough is enough'.

2

The many shapes of the PhD

Phases • Milestones • Different models of study • Different models of supervision • Different models of theses • About processes and procedures

> ... *Candia said: 'You'll all attend lectures, you'll attend seminars; most of all you'll attend the practical classes. Punishments for absence vary from stocks to whipping.*[1]

We've already said that a PhD is not just one thing, and that institutions, disciplines and departments vary widely in their norms. Variation is a familiar feature of the world; there are more metaphors about different ways of doing things than you can shake a stick at. Below the surface variations, though, there are a lot of commonalities in the things that masters of a given discipline do, which make them different from apprentices. Masters share repertoires of skills and are able to recognize and appreciate skills in others, whether or not they learned those skills in the same ways.

This chapter is about these similarities and differences: different models of PhD study, different models of supervision and different models of theses, and about the commonalities behind these. We'll begin with phases and milestones.

---

[1] Gentle, M. (1991) *Rats and Gargoyles*. London: Corgi, p. 15.

Phases

A modern PhD can be viewed as having three key phases, each of which contributes a necessary element of mastery.

1 Orientation

The first phase, 'orientation', concerns mastering the literature (including existing theory and existing evidence), formulating your research problem (and relating it to existing theory and evidence), identifying an appropriate approach for addressing the problem and specifying a plan of work, including a clarification of how 'success' is recognized. In some cases your research question may have already been specified in a proposal drawn up by your supervisor to secure funding for you. But, even if this is the case, you must become familiar with the literature and able to discuss the relevance of your research question within the context of your discipline.

2 Intensive research

The second phase, 'intensive research', is concerned with conducting a programme of research (whether evidence-gathering or theory development), reasoning accountably and explicitly to reach conclusions, critiquing, iterating and validating your work, and reasoning about generalization and limitations.

3 Entering the research discourse

The third phase, 'entering the discourse', involves exposing your work to discussion and scrutiny, which means presenting and defending your work both orally and in writing. This takes the form of making paper submissions to conferences and journals, giving research seminars and conference presentations, responding to referees' comments, and ultimately producing, submitting and defending your dissertation.

Strangely enough, the three phases correspond to three key requirements for a PhD:

- Mastering the discipline – knowing what's already out there
- Planning and conducting sound, informative research
- Communicating research

You need all three elements in order to earn a PhD, because all three are necessary to making significant contributions.

Milestones

In addition to the intellectual phases, PhD programmes have a number of administrative steps, basic milestones common in some form to just about all programmes.

Induction

When you sign on as a prospective PhD student, the whole process is phrased in terms of your having to make active moves from one stage to another, rather than a default assumption that once you have started a PhD you will automatically end up being examined for one. The earliest phase of a PhD is figuring out the ground rules: orientation to the literature, introduction to expectations and norms, training in basic research methods, figuring out who makes which decisions, coming to terms with The System: the politics, procedures and structures of the institution. Some institutions have a formal induction period, others leave students to work it out for themselves. Students who arrive thinking they know it all are always surprised – either because they pay attention at induction and ask lots of questions of students who have been around a while, or much later, when they discover the cost of their arrogance (and ignorance).

Research proposal

At some point, whether during the application process, as part of probation, in discussion with your supervisors or five minutes before writing up, you'll have to convince your supervisors, department and institution that you have identified a topic worth pursuing. You'll have to formulate your research proposal: specify a research question to answer or a research problem to solve, justify why it's important enough to bother with, set it in the context of What Other People Know and propose a specific method for addressing it. The research proposal is rarely contractual and is likely to change over time – research rarely goes strictly to plan (otherwise it wouldn't be research). The significance of the research proposal lies in demonstrating that you know what it means to pose research questions and propose rigorous ways of answering them.

Transfer, or passing probation

Passing probation and transferring to registration as a PhD student is an important step, both academically and administratively. Contrary to pessimistic folklore among students, institutions do care about whether their PhD students survive or fail, if only because their completion rate (the proportion of students who actually complete PhDs in a timely manner) reflects on the institution and can affect its funding. One simple and effective way of reducing the number of students who fail at the submission and viva stage is to re-route the problem cases before they reach that stage – if they don't reach it, then they can't fail it. The point at which this is done is 'transfer', somewhere between the end of your first year and halfway through the PhD, when you should have done enough work for The System to have a fair idea of your ability. (If you haven't done enough work, or it doesn't give a fair idea of your ability, then this suggests that you should be re-routed on grounds of cluelessness.) Transfer is considered an active process, not a 'rubber stamp': students need to demonstrate their suitability and earn the approval to continue.

Transfer normally involves genuine academic assessment of how you are doing, rather than an administrative convenience. It can take the form of 'qualifying exams' or other formal assessment, a substantial document such as a 'research proposal' or 'probation report', a live performance such as a department seminar or oral examination, a practical demonstration of research skills – or some combination of these or other elements. By amazing coincidence, these things can be viewed as useful practice for proposing and conducting research, writing the dissertation and undertaking the viva. The purpose is to demonstrate your competence – not to demonstrate perfection, nor to set your research plan in concrete.

Some students decide, around transfer or probation assessment, that doing a PhD is not for them. An honourable withdrawal, or an informed choice to undertake an MPhil, is actually a success for the student, the supervisors and The System. It's a much happier option for everyone than years of anxious and often unsuccessful toil.

Annual report

Each year during your doctoral studies, most institutions require your faculty, department, postgraduate tutor or supervisors to submit an annual report outlining your progress during the year, assessing your continuing potential for PhD completion and making a recommendation about whether or not to continue your registration. Some institutions engage the student in this process, some require the student to engage in a form of interim assessment (e.g. by writing and defending a report, or by giving a seminar), some involve academics outside the supervisory relationship, such as a research degrees committee. The process can be more or less formal, but it involves documentation that Goes On File. A sensible strategy is to view the annual report as a chance to reflect constructively on your progress, not just as an administrative hurdle.

Candidate declaration form

Before you can submit your dissertation, you will have to notify your institution formally that you are ready to do so, using a form called something like the 'candidate declaration form'. This form has two major purposes:

- It requires your supervisors to vouch for the quality of the work, because in signing the form they must declare both that they have read a complete draft and that the work is worthy of examination
- It sets the machinery in motion to appoint your examiners, a process which may take some time, because it requires the provision of CVs, completion of forms and approval by relevant committees

Submission and viva

The PhD is a long process that culminates in one document and one discussion. The document is your dissertation; the discussion is the *viva voce* examination, when you are asked penetrating questions by a panel of formidably bright and knowledgeable examiners. When the academic system decides whether or not you should have a PhD, it does this only by assessing your performance in the dissertation and viva; any other work not represented in them is irrelevant.

Different models of study

Back in The Past (when we were earning our PhDs), a typical PhD went something like this. You sought out a potential supervisor, told them about your brilliant ideas and then, if they thought you were worth taking on, you would start a PhD with them, quite probably on a totally different topic from the one you originally proposed. You would potter around with whatever level of supervision your supervisor felt like providing and be left pretty much in peace until you either submitted your dissertation (quite probably on a topic different both from your original brilliant idea and from the one you changed to) or gave up and did something else instead, like becoming a mushroom farmer in Devon. An alternative model was for the department to show a student into a closely packed office, shut the door, open it in three years and demand: 'Are you finished yet?'

Days long past; times long changed. While there are still institutions that operate such 'throw them in the deep end' models of PhD study (and why not, we got PhDs didn't we?), PhD programmes have become far more varied. The models are shaped by the expected place of study (e.g. in an ivory tower, on a university campus, in an industry laboratory, at the kitchen table), by the intensity of study and focus (e.g. full-time, part-time), by the number of influences on the research (e.g. student-directed, part of a larger research project, part of an industry research programme), by the level of intended guidance (e.g., taught introduction, supervision-as-collaboration, largely independent working with infrequent supervision), and by who takes responsibility for skills training (e.g. research-only focus, taught component). We'll discuss some of the most common models.

The essential PhD

The essential PhD – focused on the PhD research, shaped largely, if not exclusively, by the supervisory relationship, with minimal structure and judged only by the final output – is at the core of every PhD, because every PhD student ultimately needs to find his or her own path up the research mountain. In some places (such as the UK), this is the dominant PhD model, making the supervisory relationship the most important feature of the programme. It is the least specified, and certainly the least structured, of any of the models, but nevertheless includes the basic procedures and milestones common in some form to all. Some institutions, unwilling to just 'throw them in the deep end', augment the essential PhD with training and development programmes: group supervision and research groups, seminars, courses on research methods and specialist topics, and so on.

Project-based PhD

One of the ways to fund PhDs is to embed them in funded research projects. This has advantages and disadvantages. It has the advantage of creating studentships where there may have been none (or not enough). It has the disadvantage of tying the PhD into the project goals – and project politics. It has the advantage of giving the studentship structure and focus. It has the disadvantage that the student has to shape his or her interests to the project specification. It has the advantage of providing the support of a project team and project management. It has the disadvantage of making the PhD one of the project deliverables – and possibly of making the PhD subordinate to the project priorities. It has the advantage of providing momentum and accountability. It has the disadvantage of reducing flexibility for the student. And so on. The biggest challenge for a project-based PhD is to maintain a clear sense of identity within the project; and so students undertaking project-based PhDs must continually ask: What is my PhD research and how is it distinguished from the project as a whole? Can I specify clearly where my individual contributions lie?

PhD with taught components, or masters plus PhD

This model is commonplace in North America, where students spend a year or two 'qualifying' for PhD study by demonstrating mastery of their discipline. This initial period is structured by advanced courses in their specialist topics and punctuated by advanced examinations. Some institutions make this phase explicit through the award of a masters degree, however some only award the masters degree as a sort of consolation prize to those who do not continue into PhD study. The taught component can be very useful, ensuring that all PhD students demonstrate a comparable degree of competence and sophistication in their discipline before they are sent off into the wilds of research, and reassuring students that they indeed have that competence.

In other formulations, evident for example in recent practice in Europe, students spend a year or two earning a taught masters degree as a pre-requisite to a PhD programme, sometimes before they even apply for a PhD. The masters provides either specific research training or advanced study in a topic relevant to the proposed PhD. The subsequent PhD programme can then focus on independent research.

Professional doctorate

Designed for people who wish to combine research with professional practice, these degrees recognize that domain expertise can contribute to research expertise, and that professional practice itself provides a relevant (although perhaps not sufficient) skill set and a context for research in that domain. The degrees are structured to incorporate and exploit that professional activity. They typically include a taught (and assessed) component – filling in the research perspectives and research skills that are not part of the profession – and draw explicitly on the professional practice for examples and data. Although professional PhDs typically rely on the dissertation and oral examination as the summative assessment, they are often satisfied with a shorter, more specific thesis, that links to professional experience.

Industry-based study

These schemes are designed as an academe-industry handshake: academics get to collaborate with non-academic organizations that do cutting-edge research, and organizations that cannot themselves award degrees get academic recognition for their personnel. The students work and research in the organization and draw on its resources, and their doctoral research is embedded in or associated with the organization's research. The organization directs the work, but the university sets the academic standards. There is usually an industry-based supervisor as well as a university-based supervisor. The two perspectives can create conflicts in terms of practical matters such as priorities, deadlines and intellectual property, and the student can feel isolated, but the richness of the environment and the opportunities it holds can be mighty compelling advantages.

PhDs by publication

This is an umbrella for many different practices. It can be a mechanism for giving academic recognition for a body of published professional work, such as a series of scholarly biographies, or a series of patented or published technological advances, or an implemented, innovative pedagogy. In that case, the dissertation makes the overall case for the significance of the body of work and its contribution to knowledge. The PhD by publication can be a mechanism for exposing doctoral research to peer review before examination, by requiring that the dissertation consist largely of material accepted for publication by high-quality, peer-reviewed journals or conferences. In that case, the dissertation binds the published papers together with a narrative that draws out the resonances and overarching themes between them and locates them in existing knowledge and theory. The PhD by publication can be a minor variant of the monograph dissertation. In many disciplines it is normal to publish conference and journal papers during PhD study, and the resulting dissertation chapters may owe a great deal to those publications. The PhD by publication just uses the papers explicitly (rather than rewriting them as chapters), weaving them together with an overriding narrative.

Part-time PhDs

Part-time PhDs are a lot like full-time PhDs, only harder, because they must compete with the day job, and they typically receive less support. At best, there is a sympathy between the day job and the PhD, which means that each can benefit from the other. Such examples may bear some resemblance to professional doctorates or industry-based PhDs. But even in this case there are two masters – the market and academe – with different characters, different languages and different priorities. Something like sharing a flat with flatmates from different countries, who don't speak each other's languages, have different eating and cleaning habits and each think they're in charge. At worst, the day job and the PhD compete for the same resource: you.

Whatever the model of study, the culmination is always the dissertation and defence, and the outcomes are arguably comparable. Models of study are influenced by national and institutional culture.

Different models of supervision

Supervision is utterly individual and varied. Every supervisory relationship is unique. Students of a given supervisor may have very different views of the person and very different experiences of supervision, just as different children in a given family can sound as though they were raised in quite different households. And yet, there are some common models.

The sole supervisor

There was a time when the supervisory relationship was a closed world. One supervisor 'owned' a student, and others dared not intrude nor interfere.

This worked very well when the supervisor was excellent. Unfortunately, supervisors were not always excellent, with predictable results. There are still many cases when there is a 'lead' supervisor who oversees day-to-day work and is the primary mentor and contact for the student. However, these relationships are rarely exclusive, and nowadays supervisors are typically accountable to other supervisors or other forms of oversight – and can draw on other experience and expertise.

Joint supervision and its variants

Along the way, The System recognized that supervisors are only human (although some appeared to have come straight out of a horror movie), and that joint supervision can be a good way to compensate for variation among supervisors, distribute responsibility and provide some accountability. Joint supervision can take a variety of forms.

- 1 + 1: in effect, there are two (or more) supervisors who act independently, meet the student separately, and leave the student to negotiate between them. The student potentially receives twice as much input. This has all the hazards of sole supervision, multiplied by the number of supervisors. The more often the student can negotiate the supervisors into the same room for a joint discussion, the better. A degraded form of this variant is the 'absentee supervisor'. In effect, there are two supervisors on paper only, and the student experiences sole supervision.
- **Specialists:** the supervisors take particular roles relating to their expertise and availability. One may be the generalist and the other the domain expert. One may handle experiment design and the other statistical analysis. One may be the theorist and the other the pragmatist. And so on. This can work well, as long as the roles and decision-making processes are agreed by all, and communication is effective. It helps if all parties meet together at regular intervals.
- **Lead and support:** one supervisor may act as lead supervisor, with other supervisors in supporting roles – for example, providing specialist expertise or acting as readers/reviewers. This can provide clarity for the student: the lead supervisor has the greater voice. But supporting supervisors can become detached and disaffected, leaving things to the lead supervisor even when they might have contributions to make.

Supervisory panels or committees

Supervisory panels or committees can be thought of as combining sole and joint supervision. Most supervision is layered in formal and informal interactions; supervisory committees tend to embody this layering. A committee of experts oversees the research, with the big decisions (the design and direction of the research) made or ratified in formal meetings with the committee.

The day-to-day supervision, however, is provided by an adviser, who tends to manage the activity more informally. This model is common in North America. The advantage is the assembly of expertise – as is the disadvantage. Lots of input may mean lots of opinions, some of which are likely to compete. On the other hand, when the whole committee signs off on something, the student can feel well-founded confidence.

The key to all supervision is *communication*, assisted by clear lines of responsibility and decision-making. At its best, joint supervision is a profound advantage: the assemblage of supervisors provides a more complete portfolio of expertise and talents, and the redundancy takes the pressure off any individual supervisor, compensating for absences and distractions. The student may appreciate the educational dialogues between supervisors, especially when they argue different perspectives. Clever students can manage the supervisory relationship, using supervisors for what they're best at and enlisting one to help resolve issues with another. We talk more about managing supervisors in Chapter 4. Sinful students try to play off one supervisor against another, and then blame everyone but themselves when the PhD goes horribly wrong. Joint supervision can work very well, but only if you allow it to work and help it to work when it hits problems.

Different models of theses

There are various models of theses, in terms both of the structure of the document and its content, for example:

- The scholarly book, drawing on a host of existing or discovered evidence, discussed thoroughly and woven into a pattern of insights in a compelling narrative
- The collection of publications, threaded together by a unifying discussion
- The engineering model, which solves a problem, often by building a tool, implementing a solution, creating an algorithm or designing a process or method
- The empirically-driven model, in which the thesis is justified through (or may emerge from) a series of empirical studies
- The science model, in which a research question is addressed via the application or generation of theory supported by experimental evidence
- The theory-driven model, which presents a new theory, or extends an existing one, and may rely on argument, analysis and illustrative examples, or may draw on empirical evidence
- The mathematical proof, which rests on the importance of the insight and the correctness of the proof

Clearly, this list is neither definitive nor complete.

Different models are normally associated with different disciplines, with different expectations in, say, maths and fine arts, biology and history, archaeology and computing. The differences lie, not just in the length and structure of the dissertation, but more importantly in the expectations about what sorts of knowledge claims are permitted and what counts as evidence. Differences are reflected in how existing knowledge is presented and discussed, in what sorts of arguments are made, in the balance of theory and evidence, in the nature of evidence presented and in the scope of the thesis. All of these parameters have different disciplinary interpretations – so, know your discipline.

About processes and procedures

Academia is what it is, and that is bureaucratic. Processes and procedures are what they are, and that is persistent – they'll still be around when you're not. The result is that you will probably have to go through procedures that, however well-intentioned and important they might be, appear cumbersome and pointless to you. Our advice is to cooperate with them, however much or little sense they seem to make. If they don't seem to make much sense, cooperate with them all the same and save your energy for other battles. Or ask gentle questions and perhaps discover that there is a point and purpose of which you were simply unaware. If nothing else, you might learn something about the arcane mechanisms of institutions. Fill in the forms neatly, hand them in before the deadline and, essentially, show the skills that you need to show.

Keeping processes and procedures in perspective is a form of 'research hygiene', and more tips for maintaining a healthy research life are offered in Table 2.1.

Table 2.1 Research hygiene – or 'good research practices' to preserve your intellectual and mental health

There are a number of practices you can adopt to help yourself. These practices are reasonably easy to maintain and have demonstrated benefits. If they're just a chore, you're going about them the wrong way.

Accumulate ideas	A big component (perhaps the biggest part) of doctoral research is the accumulation of ideas, both the acquisition and organization of a core repertoire of ideas that represents the discourse surrounding the topic, and the identification and development of one's own ideas for one's own research. Ideas come from many sources – from the literature, from empirical work, from practice, from impromptu conversations on the bus.
	What distinguishes a good researcher is the organization and filtering applied to the collection. Important ideas must be distinguished. Competing ideas must be understood. Ideas that are pertinent and useful to one's own research must be selected for attention. One part of making sense of a literature is to notice which ideas repeat. One way to figure out where you want to focus is to notice which ideas repeatedly catch your attention.
	Once you have some grasp of which ideas (or questions) you find interesting, fun or compelling, you need to prioritize them, in terms of their interest (to you), their feasibility within the constraints of your research resources and their importance (potential impact).
Keep a progress record	One useful form is just a page of bullet lists of accomplishments and activities within a period. You can use categories such as 'insights and research developments', 'publications and talks', 'empirical work or other research steps', 'knowledge of the literature', 'skills development' and so on, if they help. Whenever you accomplish something, just note it in the record. Most academics keep such lists in some form or other; they're a good reality check, and they make it really easy to compile reports such as annual progress reports (and hence to reflect on how you've been doing), without having to rely on memory or scrounge through pages of notes and other documents.
Keep an annotated bibliography	• Keep it up-to-date – seems time consuming now, but it will save you much more time (and spare you anxiety) in the future • Read as though refereeing: make notes as though for a critical review • Recognize that reading changes as one's own knowledge and context change • Keep notes that can reflect that evolution of perspective • Read deliberately from different perspectives (e.g. your research goal, meta-level analysis of structure and rhetoric, examine research methods, critiquing) • Keep track of papers that aren't relevant so that you know you've seen them and made a judgement • Keep electronic copies of papers in your own file store

Email weekly updates to your supervisors	Good updates tend to be short, just a couple of lines to say what you did in the past week, note any concerns and set out the plan for the coming week. They are a way of 'staying honest' with yourself and your supervisors and they provide really useful information that can help your supervisors help you. They are especially important for part-time students.
Draft your thesis outline and abstract once you've passed probation, and update them regularly	Updating your outline and abstract is a great means of reflecting on your 'great overall scheme of things', and the successive versions give you a powerful record of how your thinking develops over time.
Keep an ordered to-do list	Sort your to-do list (e.g put each item on a Post-it and sort them into groups): prioritize what is *urgent* and *important*. Specify your targets; establish what 'success' looks like. 'The trick to finishing is to keep starting things': start with something easy to achieve.
Make backups regularly	Does this really need explanation?

3

The route to research independence

What does it mean to be an 'independent researcher'? • How skills are embodied in the research programme and dissertation • Developing and documenting skills • How to become an international researcher

> *Rest is good, but for a man who has always led an active life too much of it is very bad, for then he begins to think, and thought in large doses is depressing.* [1]

So, back in The Past, when we were doing our PhDs, the 'throw them in the deep end' model was the norm, and students lingered in the halls of academe trying to look as if they knew what they were doing. PhD supervision was traditionally arcane and inviolable, and the supervisory relationship was strictly private to the supervisor and student. Supervisory practice was learned implicitly, with new supervisors usually drawing on their own experiences as students and their own observations of supervisors and supervision. Some supervisors were highly effective mentors, guiding their students to become highly skilled and independent researchers who moved gracefully on to their own careers. Others were less adept, stumbling along with their students through an implicit process. Others ran PhD factories, cranking the handle to produce dissertations that were the academic equivalent of flat-pack assembly rather than cabinet-making, without giving their students any true independence, consigning their students to subordinate roles until

[1] Haggard, H.R. (1960) *She and Allan*. Dublin: Arrow Books, p. 51.

someone else managed to develop them further. Still others were absent or inept. Some students with such supervisors somehow struggled to completion. Others didn't.

Then times changed.[2] Politicians started asking unpleasant questions about the amount of money being spent on funding PhDs which were never completed, and started making noises about quality of research and value for money. Funding bodies started insisting on 'best practice'. Employers started lobbying for graduates with usable skills. Motherhood and diversity were praised. Procedures were implemented which, to paraphrase the classic quotation, gave the appearance of progress while often producing other things.

The result was that the unwritten agenda for PhDs and PhD supervision changed, as summarized in Table 3.1: the intended output of a PhD is an independent researcher, as demonstrated by research leading to a satisfactory dissertation and defence.

Table 3.1 The unwritten agenda for PhDs, old and new – a flippant summary

Old agenda	New agenda
Output = thesis	Output = competent researcher
Emphasis on product	Emphasis on 'student experience'
Single supervisor (hidden)	Team supervision (scrutinized)
No guidelines	Code of practice
Supervisor = island	Supervisor = part of network
Recruitment 'by smell'	Recruitment governed by institutional code
Content idiosyncratic	Skills training content prescribed
We do it in our 'spare time'	We allow a bit of time in our workload plan
Minimal documentation	Reports, audits, monitoring
Goal = education	Goal = employability

[2] The sea change in the UK was driven by the Roberts Agenda, in turn arising from the 'SET for Success' review chaired by Sir Gareth Roberts and published in 2002. The report reviewed the supply of graduates in science, engineering and technology ('SET') skills throughout the education system and set an agenda of personal, professional and career training and development for PhD students and postdoctoral research staff. The Roberts Agenda was largely driven by the need for researchers to develop skills that would make them more marketable to industry. The skills were defined by the UK Research Councils in collaboration with the UK GRAD Programme and the higher education sector in their 2001 'Joint Statement of Skills Training Requirements of Research Postgraduates'. One of Roberts's recommendations was that major funders of postgraduate researchers should make all funding conditional on postgraduate researchers' training meeting stringent minimum standards, and that this should include the provision of at least two weeks' dedicated training a year, principally in transferable skills.

But it's still all about the dissertation

Regardless of the agenda, the PhD is a long process which culminates in the dissertation and *viva voce* examination. The decision about whether or not you should receive a PhD is based only on assessing your performance in the dissertation and the viva, which is meant to embody and represent all your other endeavour. There are three main ways in which people tend to view this:

- You still need to concentrate on each stage and do each properly, because otherwise you won't get to the submission and viva stage
- All that really matters is the dissertation and the viva, as long as you get through the previous stages somehow
- All of this is preparation for what you do after you get through the PhD

The first of these views is popular among administrators and among nervous students (who probably constitute the majority of PhD students), since it reduces the risk of people crashing into early hurdles because they didn't aim to jump high enough. The second is less popular, but is more accurate, though it's open to misinterpretation which can cause you needless grief (for instance, failing to realize that knowing how to deal with procedures is an essential skill). The third is the least popular, but is actually the one which will stand you in best stead both for the PhD itself and for life afterwards. The third view is what this chapter is about: understanding that underpinning your ability to produce a passable dissertation and defence is a collection of research skills that you need to learn – and to learn to demonstrate.

Here's a classic story about what's wrong with the second view. A student focuses clearly, submits the dissertation and starts looking for a lecturing job, only to discover that they need two years of lecturing experience and preferably a journal publication as well if they are to be appointable for a job in a good department in their field. If they had known this two years previously, they could have started doing some part-time lecturing and submitted a paper or two to a journal. Here's another one: another student, the notional twin of the first, also focuses on dissertation and defence alone and starts looking for a job in industry, only to find that they need team-working experience, people skills and practice with some different research methods. Again, had they spotted this earlier, they could have found opportunities for appropriate experience and perhaps an industry internship. The dissertation and viva are the things that get you the PhD, but it's also wise to think about ways of doing a PhD which simultaneously set you up to get the job or career that you want.

That's what the skills agenda is about. If you insist on looking at it bureaucratically, it's about filling out forms and ticking boxes. If you look at it constructively, it's about adopting a Big Picture perspective on your development as a rounded, independent researcher. It's also about remembering that life doesn't end with the successful viva – the day of your successful viva is the first day of the rest of your life. There is a life after the PhD, one worth considering in advance.

What does it mean to be an 'independent researcher'?

Being an 'independent researcher' means having the knowledge, skills, critical thinking and initiative to design and conduct rigorous research (as rigour is understood in your discipline). We've already outlined a basic skill set – those 'cabinet-making' skills you'll demonstrate in your apprenticeship. You can compare it to the skill set compiled by the UK research establishment in the table at the end of the chapter, or you can just sit down and brainstorm a list of skills you think you'll need to conduct a research career. If you were to compare the three, you would find important commonalities among them; it's not a surprising sort of list to make.

But independence doesn't mean working alone, it means having the competence to initiate, design and lead a research project. Technical skills are only part of the picture. Most research is done in social settings, and so part of the skill set has to do with knowing the 'rules of the game' in the academic or industrial research community you hope to join, and having the social and organizational skills to operate effectively within that community.

Independence does *not* mean doing everything yourself, without reference to anyone else or anyone else's work. In fact, working in determined and persistent isolation is almost an anti-skill. It suggests a lack of key competencies. It may seem poetic to imagine oneself cloistered in splendid isolation in an intellectual nest atop an ivory tower, but even mathematicians have to emerge and discuss their proofs, and the history of science is fuelled by the rich written correspondence conducted by scientists separated geographically. There's a reason why we keep talking about 'research discourse'. Students who shut themselves away from dialogue and interaction tend to end up out of touch with the research community. Yet it is the community, ultimately, in the form of examiners, reviewers and referees, that assesses the research, and learning how to express one's ideas and findings and get them into that community's discourse is a fundamental research skill. Communication is a necessary component of research, and like all skills it needs practice.

It's not 'cheating' to consult other people, debate ideas and get expert advice – it's competence. It's an important part of the process of reflection that is essential to becoming expert.

How skills are embodied in the research programme and dissertation

You might not be surprised to know that researchers developed research expertise in the days before research skills were taught explicitly. The development of the knowledge and skills necessary to become an independent researcher is a natural outcome of good supervision – the real 'change of agenda' is not the introduction of skills training, but just the explicit attention to it. For example, we've done an implicit initial skills audit at first meetings with our own students for years. It goes something like this. Can the student read (and report accurately what they read)? Can the student write (preferably in grammatical English sentences)? Can the student answer back intelligently? We used to think of it as 'sizing a student up', and if we noticed any deficiencies we'd structure the early supervision accordingly, guiding the student through reading, writing and argumentation tasks. We just never talked about it.

So what's different? Just making it explicit. Asking students to reflect periodically on what they need, then laying plans to address those needs, and finally documenting some evidence that skills have improved sufficiently. The key part is getting students to pay attention, and to reflect periodically on themselves as rounded researchers.

If you consider it, the dissertation and viva are two of the most important pieces of 'evidence of skill' that students accumulate. Like 'master pieces', they are explicit demonstrations of necessary skills: posing well-formed questions, encompassing and making sense of existing knowledge, theory and practice in the domain, critiquing that existing knowledge, theory and practice, building on it and relating one's work to it, formulating a plan of research appropriate to the questions, conducting that research rigorously and effectively, analysing outcomes, discussing limitations and implications, generalizing from that research to propose enhancements to theory, articulating and defending one's reasoning, communicating research clearly, and so on.

As for all those annoying bureaucratic milestones, like transfer/probation assessment, seminars and annual reports, these are also pieces of evidence, like a benevolent conspiracy to make students show that they know what they're doing. And that is why a PhD is not just a 'significant contribution to knowledge'; it is also a demonstration of research competence.

Developing and documenting skills

Skills are not just one thing. There are different levels of skills, such as generic or transferable skills (meant to cut across all disciplines), discipline skills (relating to norms and practices within a given discipline – for example, not everyone needs to know about the finer points of rubber gloves and lab coats as part of their health and safety competence) and project skills (those needed specifically to conduct a given piece of research – e.g. not everyone needs to apply structuration theory or program Java applets).

And of course time plays a role. Not only do skills change and (hopefully) develop over the course of PhD study, but also the threshold for 'competence' varies for different roles and different projects. Skills development is not something you do once and are done with, like inoculation. It's something you do iteratively over time, with small steps and activities which gradually accumulate and consolidate into an embedded skill – which then continues to be developed and refined. If you want to do it consciously and reflectively, then you'll be looking at both short-term and long-term targets, tailored to your personal goals and your research project. It helps if you prioritize a small number of targets at a time, and if your targets are concrete, with specified outputs and deadlines.

Skills tend to be expressed in fairly abstract terms. We've included the list prepared by the UK Research Councils at the end of the chapter – have a look at it and you'll see what we mean. But it's not hard to reflect on them more concretely. Consider the first skill in the list at the end of the chapter: 'The ability to recognize and validate problems'. What might that look like in the wild?

- Can you identify the research questions addressed in the research papers that you read?
- Have you clearly defined the research question(s) you will pursue in your PhD?
- Can you develop valid research hypotheses from your research question?
- Can you:
  - give examples from the literature of problems which have been addressed by others?
  - explain why those researchers addressed the problems as they did?
  - discuss advantages and disadvantages of those approaches?
- Can you explain the sorts of evidence and/or arguments that are seen as valid in your field?
- Can you design a research study which addresses one of those research questions?

If you can do all that, you can probably claim some competence in 'The ability to recognize and validate problems'. And, in doing so, you'll probably generate evidence of that skill in use, such as notes from a discussion with your supervisor about gaps in the literature or a written analysis of problems addressed in a selection of studies, with a description of how the problems were addressed, and a discussion of the benefits and limitations of those approaches.

Take another example, one that entails lifting your head from your desk and looking around a bit: 'Show a broad understanding of the context, at the national and international level, in which research takes place'.

- Do you know how research is funded in your country? Do you know how your own studentship is funded?
- If you need extra funding (for instance, to travel to a conference), do you know where you could go to get it – both inside and outside your university?
- Can you outline the organizational structure for research in your university – at university, academic unit and department levels?
- Can you describe how research in your field is organized in terms of the key professional organizations, conferences, societies, publications and funding bodies?
- Can you describe the administrative processes for submitting papers for publication in your field?
- Do you attend research seminars regularly and discuss them with your peers and supervisors? Do you attend research seminars outside your discipline? Do you attend inaugural lectures?
- Have you ever refereed or reviewed someone else's research paper? Have you read other referees' comments?

As you can imagine, having an awareness of the research environment – and finding out the ground rules by which the research community operates – can be very useful both during your PhD studies and afterwards.

Thinking about what skills mean concretely not only gives you an idea of what they might mean and how they might be relevant for you, but it also suggests the kinds of activities you might undertake to develop those skills. And, in turn, doing some of those activities gives you a way of documenting a degree of skill. This process emerges seamlessly in good supervision, complementing the development of the doctoral research with minimal intrusion. If it's a chore, then you're probably going about it in the wrong way. A crucial part of the process is reflection and discussion – considering which skills to prioritize and how to go about developing them gives you something concrete and achievable to talk about with your supervisor.

Actually, most people do this implicitly. Most academics have a 'portfolio of evidence' of skills, albeit almost certainly not by that name. In some form, they'll have a file of the papers they've published (and some they haven't); a collection of slides and notes from talks they've given, a record of the grant proposals they've submitted, a CV they keep up to date, and so on. And it's typical in job interviews to ask for examples: Can you give me an example of when you've worked in a team? Can you give me an example of research you've designed and talk about how you made the design decisions? Can you give me an example of a project on which you took the lead? And so on. Documenting your skills is itself a generic skill.

A word on standards and norms

It's always good to know the 'tools of the trade', 'the rules of the game' and 'the standards of engagement'. It's like learning a vocabulary and grammar for a language, or the tools and repertoire for a trade. Methodology, standards and norms are your working vocabulary as a researcher in your discipline. It's unlikely that one could be a brilliant violinist without a comprehensive grasp of the mechanics of the instrument and of music theory. But methodology, standards and norms are not your only vocabulary, and like any language they can change. Methodology, standards and norms evolve as researchers find compelling reasons to change them. Creativity suggests that sometimes we warp standards and stand outside norms. However, if you're going to be radical you need to be able to couch your innovation in terms the community will recognize, and relating it intelligently to standards and norms may well make it easier for the community to accommodate it.

How to become an international researcher

Why stop at independence? If you want a research career, then you'll want to build an international research reputation. This isn't something you'll necessarily achieve during your PhD studies, but you can certainly lay the groundwork and orient yourself to take a strategic view of your research.

Know the tools of your trade in detail

Most researchers learn enough about the tools of their trade to get started. This isn't good enough. The more you know about them, the better the work you can do.

Study a role model

Find someone in your field whose position you admire. Investigate that person's publications. Where do they publish? Where did they publish when they were first rising to prominence? Investigate that person's activities. Which activities? Which projects, funded how? Which conferences? Which meetings? Investigate that person's collaborations. With whom do they co-publish? With whom do they share projects? Where do they visit? Use their model to inform your priorities.

Keys to success

If you do study role models, you'll find that international researchers have certain qualities in common:

- **Quality:** (although cynics would argue this is optional, it does help sustain passion, see below): as a wise colleague once phrased it, 'Do damned good work, and tell a damned good story'
- **Visibility:** not just doing good research – but also joining the discourse; engaging in the community
- **Passion:** you need to really want to do it
- **Vision:** identify your territory, and have a coherent story about your work 'as a body'
- **Collaboration:** work with excellent people who motivate you and extend your knowledge and thinking
- **Honesty:** you can't win long-term any other way: saying 'I can't this time' won't stop the next invitation, saying 'I don't know' and then responding intelligently lends authority
- **KISS (Keep It Simple, Stupid):** don't try to do everything at once; one good work leads to another

Cultivate your personal research agenda

Choose the 'right' area. First, it needs to be something that really interests you, or even better, inspires you – you're looking at the long term. Then, it needs to have the right characteristics: you need an 'open' topic that hasn't peaked yet, something acceptable to mainstream conferences but with a small research population. (Hybrid and cross-disciplinary topics are often good for this.) Identify your territory. Identify a variety of issues/questions within it that interest you. Choose sub-topics that accumulate to contribute to a 'bigger picture'. Maintain a coherent story about your work as a whole.

Ask yourself before you start any new work: how does this contribute to my agenda? Identify short-term targets and milestones that serve your agenda. Identify publication targets of international calibre that serve your agenda. Remember that 'science (or other research) proceeds by baby steps'.

Work 'smart'

You can't do everything. Working hard is a pre-requisite, but working even more or even harder won't always be the answer, because you are a finite resource. Instead, choose high-yield activities that serve your agenda.

- Learn to say 'no'.
- Target international conferences and journals and make the best possible use of your material.
- Find out who the 'gatekeepers' are, and figure out what rules they follow.
- Publish iteratively, advancing from small conference papers to cumulative journal papers, and building up a body of material.
- Re-use content: use components like ideas, theories and literature reviews for different purposes (e.g. turn grant proposals into papers, and vice versa)

and re-cast material for different audiences (e.g. an empirical study of requirements elicitation can be reported with a requirements engineering focus, or with an empirical studies of software development focus). An important skill is to learn the difference between this and 'self-plagiarism'. If you re-use material where you've already assigned copyright to a third party, such as the journal publishing the article containing that material, you can get into horrible legal problems. If in doubt, ask someone knowledgeable.

- Only accept invitations if they are strategic. That goes for talks, publications, collaborations, refereeing and so on. You needn't do everything you're asked to do, just because you're invited. Consider whether the invited contribution will further your agenda, or whether it has a role in making you visible and valuable in a research community – or whether it's just more work without particular strategic benefit to you. Focus on the invitations that serve your agenda.

Join the community

- Be visible: get out and talk to people.
- Give seminars at relevant institutions, making sure that you have appointments for individual conversations afterwards with the key researchers there. Follow up on particular interests with email or other conversations.
- Join the programme committee for a key conference. (Subsequently, referee for a key journal. Eventually, join the journal's editorial board.)
- Host a workshop or tutorial. Invite key researchers and make sure you find opportunities to talk to them.
- Do good work in public. Ask good questions at conferences. Make constructive suggestions in 'birds of a feather' sessions.
- Be a 'good citizen': be fastidious about citing other people's work and giving credit. Pass on references to other people's work in discussions; when appropriate, follow up by sending copies of papers. Keep your promises. This sort of activity establishes you as a useful, knowledgeable 'good egg'.

Collaborate with excellent people

Accumulate a broad network of contacts – research acquaintances that you might contact on particular topics or with whom you might correspond. Select a core network of 'advisers' – research colleagues you trust and respect, who are knowledgeable, and with whom to exchange manuscripts and explore work-in-progress, including early ideas. Seek contacts and collaborators outside your department, outside your university and outside your country. Don't limit yourself to academic researchers in your area: look for industry contacts and collaborators, for interesting thinkers in other domains. Concentrate on the excellent ones, and on people with whom you get along comfortably.

Making contacts, even international contacts, isn't hard, if you've practised networking as part of your PhD (see Chapter 5). International conferences and research visits are good ways to identify like-minded researchers and build relationships. Various funders offer overseas travel grants to promote collaboration. Even without travel funding, you can correspond with other researchers about their work. Scan the appropriate discussion lists, journals, conference proceedings and newsletters in order to keep track of who's active and influential in your community.

How to join a programme committee

For many conferences, this is a gradual process: you start with a small 'apprentice' role, and then advance over a couple of years into a larger one. In effect, you're asking to join a particular community, so you need to engage with the community and show that you can contribute to it. Go to the conference. Attend the 'business meeting' or 'feedback session' and make constructive suggestions. Meet members of the current programme committee and express interest. Follow up on those meetings with an email confirming your interest. If you are asked to review papers, then do a good job (write objective, constructive, informative reviews that identify virtues of papers as well as deficiencies), and do it on time.

Have a good website

Make sure that your agenda is evident and stated with enthusiasm. Put an attractive, upbeat photo on your homepage. Include nifty, useful things, like a good annotated bibliography in your area, or some nifty software, or a compilation of specialist research techniques, or up-to-date pointers to other relevant websites.

Table 3.2 Skills for research postgraduates, adapted from the 'Joint Statement of Skills Training Requirements of Research Postgraduates' established by the UK Research Councils and the UK GRAD Programme, and available from the Vitae (a national programme incorporating the UK GRAD Programme) website: www.vitae.ac.uk/policy-practice/1690/Joint-Skills-Statement.html.

(A) Research skills and techniques – to be able to demonstrate	1 The ability to recognize and validate problems 2 Original, independent and critical thinking and the ability to develop theoretical concepts 3 A knowledge of recent advances within one's field and in related areas 4 An understanding of relevant research methodologies and techniques and their appropriate application within one's research field 5 The ability to critically analyse and evaluate one's findings and those of others 6 An ability to summarize, document, report and reflect on progress
(B) Research environment – to be able to	1 Show a broad understanding of the context, at the national and international level, in which research takes place 2 Demonstrate awareness of issues relating to the rights of other researchers, of research subjects and of others who may be affected by the research, e.g. confidentiality, ethical issues, attribution, copyright, malpractice, ownership of data and the requirements of the Data Protection Act 3 Demonstrate appreciation of standards of good research practice in their institution and/or discipline 4 Understand relevant health and safety issues and demonstrate responsible working practices 5 Understand the processes for funding and evaluation of research 6 Justify the principles and experimental techniques used in one's own research 7 Understand the process of academic or commercial exploitation of research results
(C) Research management – to be able to	1 Apply effective project management through the setting of research goals, intermediate milestones and prioritization of activities 2 Design and execute systems for the acquisition and collation of information through the effective use of appropriate resources and equipment 3 Identify and access appropriate bibliographical resources, archives and other sources of relevant information 4 Use information technology appropriately for database management, recording and presenting information

(Continued overleaf)

Table 3.2 Continued

(D) Personal effectiveness – to be able to	1 Demonstrate a willingness and ability to learn and acquire knowledge
	2 Be creative, innovative and original in one's approach to research
	3 Demonstrate flexibility and open-mindedness
	4 Demonstrate self-awareness and the ability to identify own training needs
	5 Demonstrate self-discipline, motivation and thoroughness
	6 Recognize boundaries and draw upon/use sources of support as appropriate
	7 Show initiative, work independently and be self-reliant
(E) Communication skills – to be able to	1 Write clearly and in a style appropriate to purpose, e.g. progress reports, published documents, thesis
	2 Construct coherent arguments and articulate ideas clearly to a range of audiences, formally and informally through a variety of techniques
	3 Constructively defend research outcomes at seminars and viva examination
	4 Contribute to promoting the public understanding of one's research field
	5 Effectively support the learning of others when involved in teaching, mentoring or demonstrating activities
(F) Networking and teamworking – to be able to	1 Develop and maintain cooperative networks and working relationships with supervisors, colleagues and peers, within the institution and the wider research community
	2 Understand one's behaviours and impact on others when working in and contributing to the success of formal and informal teams
	3 Listen, give and receive feedback and respond perceptively to others
(G) Career management – to be able to	1 Appreciate the need for and show commitment to continued professional development
	2 Take ownership for and manage one's career progression, set realistic and achievable career goals, and identify and develop ways to improve employability
	3 Demonstrate an insight into the transferable nature of research skills to other work environments and the range of career opportunities within and outside academia
	4 Present one's skills, personal attributes and experiences through effective CVs, applications and interviews

4

Supervision
Or, PhDs, marriage and desert islands

The role of the supervisor • The role of the student, or managing expectations • Getting the most from supervisory meetings • Effective debate • Establishing a good relationship • Prevention is better than cure • Strategies for when things go wrong • Cardinal rules

Could that fellow have me whipped?[1]

When you become a PhD student, you embark on what is likely to be an intense relationship, both personally and professionally, with your supervisor(s) – for simplicity, we'll refer to 'the supervisor' in the singular from now on, but the same principles apply to a supervisory team. It's likely to be different from your previous academic relationships, because as a research student you'll take up much more of your supervisor's attention and time. You can't hide among the other students the way you could on a taught course; you're a visible individual as a PhD student.

Similarly, your supervisor is going to be a lot more important to you than your undergraduate project supervisor, who was only one member of staff among many.

A good relationship between student and supervisor needs work by both parties. It isn't your supervisor's responsibility to make everything all right; it's up to both of you to work together. Many doctoral students encounter

[1] O'Brian, P. (1990) *Master and Commander*. London: W.W. Norton & Company, p. 122.

unnecessary problems because they make classic mistakes in dealing with their supervisors. Unfortunately, our experience is that most students don't think this relationship through, and that most supervision problems are predictable and preventable. So, it's time to start thinking things through ... If you've already thought these things through, then you will be much more likely to be viewed as an asset to your supervisor and the department, and to finish with a happy ending.

Most PhD horror stories have their origins in the supervisory relationship rather than in the research topic or the external examiner. The most common cause is that the student didn't take the supervisor's advice. Less common, though not unknown, is horror due to an incompetent supervisor. The current trend is for PhDs to be supervised by more than one supervisor, which reduces the risk of your having a rogue incompetent supervising you; in addition, departments normally pay keen attention to students' performance at stages such as transfer, where incompetence is usually spotted and subsequently investigated.

The relationship between student and supervisor is about as close as many marriages, and lasts as long as many marriages. It's a fairly good analogy in several ways. One important issue is compatibility. Nobody in their right mind would expect to have a happy marriage if they married the first single person they met; similarly, you can't expect that your relationship will be equally straightforward with every potential supervisor you might meet. Likewise, it's not your supervisor's job to put up with every unpleasant idiosyncrasy of every idiot who wants to do a PhD with them. As a student, you are an apprentice, not a customer who is always right.

Also on the subject of rightness, there isn't a single type of 'right' student or 'right' supervisor, any more than there is a single type of 'right' partner. There are various types of supervisor, and various types of student; each type of supervisor will be well suited to some types of student, and less well suited to other types of student. At this point, the marriage analogy starts to become somewhat strained. In the old days, a high proportion of students signed up to do a PhD with a specific supervisor. Now, it's increasingly common for students to sign up with a department, and then to be assigned a supervisor or, more often, a supervisory team. A closer analogy for this situation is two or three survivors shipwrecked on a desert island and having to learn not just to get along with each other but also to work constructively together, regardless of whether they would have chosen each other as companions if they had had a choice. Sitting on the beach complaining that the other survivors aren't perfect human beings isn't going to get a fire lit; similarly, sitting at your desk expecting your supervisor to be perfect isn't going to get your dissertation written.

You have to make the most of what you've got, unless the situation is completely pathological (discussed in more detail below). Note that this is an active process, not a passive one; you don't simply put up with the situation that you first encounter, but instead you identify the resources you've got and then put them to the best use you can. With this in mind, it's a good idea to assess yourself in relation to your personality and your needs as a student, so that you can assess what you would like from your supervisor and how to set about obtaining those things in a way which suits you both. Relevant factors usually include your need for technical support; your need for emotional support; your need for guidance and structure in planning the work; your ability to handle criticism; and your ability to deliver on time, to the agreed standard.

It's also a good idea to ask yourself which of your characteristics (a) will make you awkward for anyone to supervise and (b) are likely to lead to problems with a particular type of supervisor. You should then think about which of these things you are willing to improve and what the implications are for how you approach your supervisor and your PhD.

The role of the supervisor

Another fruitful area for misunderstanding involves what services supervisors are supposed to provide. Students seldom think much about this.

One common misconception is that the supervisor is a purely technical resource, there to provide expertise in (for instance) the obscure area of Unix programming that you are studying for your PhD. Students with this misconception typically encounter problems when their supervisor doesn't have the answer to an obscure technical question. Such students typically complain loudly that the supervisor is incompetent, and then wonder why they receive so little sympathy from the department. The purpose of the PhD is to demonstrate that you can operate as an independent researcher and uncover new knowledge; if you expect your supervisor to know more than you about every aspect of your PhD, then you have missed the whole point.

There are many different ways to supervise a PhD, and many different roles which a supervisor can have. Each student is different and will require different support. At one extreme is the student who can be pretty much left to get on with it, with supervisory meetings being something that both parties enjoy, and where each party learns from the other. This is rare, but it does happen. Such students don't always have brilliant academic grades from their first degree. What they tend to have in common is a willingness to learn for themselves and good judgement about when to stop and ask for feedback. At the other extreme is the student who doesn't take the initiative about anything, who needs constant feedback and active encouragement, and who appears to expect a worrying degree of spoon-feeding. For students at the willing end of the spectrum, supervisors will often be very busy behind the scenes, trying to find funding for the student after they graduate; for students at the needy end of the spectrum, the supervisor may have different priorities.

The minimum supervisory role involves filling in the relevant forms as you progress through The System, writing annual reports, liaising with the organization where you are doing your fieldwork, etc. Beyond that, there are numerous possible roles, which may or may not be relevant to your case, and which will probably be invisible to you.

Other roles include:

- **Specific technical support:** for instance, skills training in using the library or specialist software; pointers to relevant literature; providing contacts with other researchers; guidance on structuring the thesis; training in critical reading.
- **Broader intellectual support:** for instance, helping you develop skills in discussion and critical thinking; providing high-level knowledge about the field and about research issues in the field; providing specialist expertise in conducting studies in the field.
- **Administrative support:** for instance, finding funds; finding other resources; protecting you from political and administrative difficulties within the institution; publicizing your work.
- **Management:** for instance, providing a structure (meetings, deadlines, goals); deadline creation and enforcement.
- **Personal support:** for instance, career advice, emotional support and counselling.

If you're feeling cynical about this, it's worth remembering that the student's performance reflects on the supervisor who has to undergo, among other things, institutional procedures and reports (including scrutiny of PhD failure rates); supervisors' meetings; peer scrutiny at transfer/probation assessment; research assessment exercises; and scrutiny from funding bodies.

Why do people become supervisors? It's certainly not for the money, as supervision is almost never remunerated. And it's not for release from other tasks, since workload planning almost always underestimates the time supervision takes. There are many reasons, ranging from a direct order from the head of department, via a feeling of duty, on through mercenary self-interest (such as using the students to further the supervisor's career), to idealism and a love of working with students.

Whatever the supervisor's motivation, it's in both your interests to get along. Whatever the moral rights and wrongs of a particular issue, it's very much in your interests to make the relationship work; failing your PhD is a greater disaster for you than it is for your supervisor, so expecting your supervisor to do all the running in your relationship is not an advisable strategy. It is, as usual, a good idea to try seeing things from their perspective. If you were asked to supervise an undergraduate project, what sort of student would you want to supervise and what sort would you not want to supervise at any cost? Once you've thought about that for a while, try looking long and hard at your own behaviour from that point of view: how often have you missed a meeting, turned up late, turned up unprepared, expected your supervisor to do all the thinking, and so forth?

You are ultimately responsible for your work; your supervisor is not. Taking your share of responsibility in the supervisory relationship is good practice for the dissertation and viva, where the burden is on the student to communicate – if the thesis is unclear to the examiner, it's the student's problem, not the examiner's. So practise on your supervisor. Decide what you want from the PhD and from the individual meetings, and communicate this to your supervisor.

As with marriage, it's worth putting the effort in, because the relationship is likely to last at least three years, and a good supervisory relationship will benefit you for the rest of your career. Also as with marriages, it can be useful at times to remember that supervisors are human too – they'll have bad days and human failings. Be realistic and forgiving in your expectations and the chances of a happy ending for you both are much better.

The role of the student, or managing expectations

You may think that the student's role is simply to get a PhD. The reality, however, is somewhat different. The student's *goal* is to get a PhD, and in pursuit of that the student has a number of *roles*: keen apprentice, contributing member of a research community, junior employee of an institution and so on. Strangely enough, your PhD is not just 'about you'; it's also about your supervisor, your department, your university. It's not all take – you have to give, too.

Whatever your expectations about your PhD, others have expectations, too. It's worth finding out what they are. Some of them have to do with meeting your contractual obligations: attending specified training sessions, completing forms on time, showing up in the office, etc. Some of them have to do with behaving sensibly: attending meetings on time, keeping your supervisor informed, being aware of ethical issues, etc. Some have to do with engaging with the research environment: attending research group meetings, attending research training, attending seminars by external speakers, etc. Some have to do with taking an active role in your research community: talking to other researchers, trading favours (like reading each other's papers), offering moral support, etc. Some of them have to do with making it worth your supervisor's investment: showing enthusiasm, being responsive, bringing ideas and evidence to the table, following through and so on. There's usually a student handbook and code of practice that gives some clues about expectations, but nothing beats a frank conversation with your supervisor.

Getting the most from supervisory meetings

As usual, try looking at it from the other person's point of view – most of the answers will then become pretty obvious. Supervisors are research-active academics, and research-active academics are hideously overworked. PhD students take up time, which is the supervisor's scarcest resource, and are in that sense a liability. A sensible student will reduce their liability rating; a good student will find ways of being a positive asset.

Reducing the liability rating mainly involves basic professional courtesies. It's your PhD, not the supervisor's; if you can't be bothered to work on making it happen, why should they? Making it happen includes making supervision meetings work: you should take the initiative in setting up the meetings, circulating relevant information in advance, drafting an agenda and coming with a clear set of things to report and questions to ask. Something which is easily overlooked is that you should also minute the meeting, recording decisions and actions, and circulate those minutes afterwards, then check that the actions are in fact taken. A related issue in many organizations is keeping logs of meetings for The System.

Running meetings properly is a rare skill, so we've summarized the key points in Table 4.1 – this particular skill is valuable in most walks of life.

There are different types of meeting, suitable for different purposes. The description in the table relates to formal meetings, but PhDs also require informal meetings when you explore ideas or discuss your longer-term career plans, or work through a problem which is bothering you. These usually take place over the legendary cup of coffee.

Table 4.1 Running meetings

Several days before the meeting, the organizer of the meeting should	• Circulate the agenda • Check that the venue is still available, if it isn't the supervisor's office • Remind people of the time and place of the meeting • Circulate any briefing material, including minutes of the last meeting
During the meeting, the chair of the meeting should	• Record the date and the parties present • Check that everyone agrees with the minutes of the last meeting • Check that actions from the last meeting have all been done • Record any decisions made, including milestones and deliverables (and check that everyone agrees with this record) • Record any actions agreed (and check that everyone agrees with this record) • Fix the time and place of the next meeting
After the meeting	• The organizer should write up the minutes and distribute them • Everyone should do what they have agreed to do

Insight after the event

There is a delay effect that beleaguers many a supervisory discussion, which may arise from disparities between supervisor and student: experience, authority, speed of processing, familiarity with debate and so on. It's the 'insight after the event' phenomenon, rather like thinking up a witty riposte after the party has ended. Often, students leave supervisory meetings and *then* make sense of the supervisor's point, or what their reply should have been, or which question they should have asked, or what they wished they'd said instead of what they did say.

That's what email was invented for. Take the time to capture the delayed insight, preferably clearly, and send it to your supervisor promptly.

Behaviours to avoid

Students have classic ways of sabotaging meetings and irritating supervisors.

- Failing to take deadlines seriously
- Failing to respect the supervisor's time pressures (you are but one demand among many)
- Dumping demands on the supervisor at the last minute instead of allowing them time for reading, thinking, enquiring etc.
- Expecting the supervisor to read every draft, usually by the next day
- Expecting the supervisor to organize everything
- Organizing things without consulting the supervisor (independence is good up to a point, but you need to check you're being independent in the right way)

Table 4.2 (at the end of the chapter) offers some constructive alternatives and sets out a scheme for effective meetings.

Effective debate

Too many students sit silently when they should speak up. Some supervisors (including us) find this infuriating; they like students who can answer back and defend their position. After all, that's what they'll need to do in order to defend their thesis.

Debate thrives in an atmosphere of respect. Too many students are too ready to say: 'My supervisor is an idiot' or: 'I don't want to do it that way'. They're usually wrong, often because their vision is clouded by their arrogance. If your supervisor critiques your ideas or opposes your proposal, there's probably a reason. Rather than drawing harsh conclusions about your supervisor's intellectual ability, it's safer to assume that your supervisor knows something you don't, or has experience that you don't, or is looking from a perspective that's obscure to you. It's your job to elicit that knowledge, experience or perspective. It's also worth remembering that the supervisor is criticizing your ideas or proposal, not criticizing you: that's a very important difference.

On the other hand, students from cultures with deeply ingrained values about respect for elders are often reluctant to question or challenge. In the West, telling your supervisor your ideas, and showing your understanding of your supervisor's ideas through discussion, is actually a form of respect. It shows that you're doing your job, meeting your responsibilities, respecting your supervisor's time and offering your own intellectual investment.

Debate thrives on evidence. Do your homework and marshall your evidence. Be prepared to make claims or suggestions and to back them up. Follow up conjectures or proposals with 'because' statements: 'I think we should check the reliability of the instrument, because our readings are all over the place'; 'I think we should restructure the framework because the new structure does away with an unused category and clarifies a useful distinction'; 'I would rather not rely on Bloggs, because his study is deeply flawed in the following ways'; 'I think we should get someone else involved in the discussion because I need to hear it in different words'. Then be prepared to analyse and critique your ideas and the evidence on which they're based – and possibly to alter them or to let them go.

You are not the same thing as your ideas. Understand that, when your supervisor probes or questions an idea, that constitutes engagement with the idea – not a personal attack on your intellect. Feel the compliment.

Ask questions. 'The only stupid question is the one you didn't ask.' Most misunderstandings arise from miscommunication – and from unexplored assumptions. Human beings have developed all sorts of glosses and shortcuts that help them to think quickly – useful when facing immediate danger like a saber-tooth tiger, but sometimes problematic in a supervisory discussion. Asking questions about what things mean, underlying reasons and apparent assumptions can be the key to insight: yours about the subject, or your supervisor's about your thinking.

Ask a question, rather than making a statement. One of the skills of effective debate is to learn non-aggressive forms of speech. Rather than making an outright challenge, ask for clarification or explanation. This can save you profound embarrassment when you discover that you're the one with the erroneous assumptions or misconceptions. Instead of 'What idiot thought that germs could heal?' try 'Why would someone think that germs could be a way to cure?' Instead of 'That doesn't make sense' try 'Why does that make sense?' Develop a repertoire of elicitative forms of speech: 'Can you show me an example?'; 'Why this and not that?'; 'May I repeat that back to you?'; 'I'm not sure I've understood accurately . . .'

Managing the supervisory relationship and offering effective debate are how you stay 'in the driver's seat'.

Establishing a good relationship

There are various strategies which students can use to make life better for all parties in the PhD, but which are not as widely used as they should be. These include:

- Exchanging favours, such as tracking down an obscure reference for your supervisor in exchange for some advice about a job application (but make sure that the exchange is agreed explicitly, so you both know where you stand)
- Showing passion and enthusiasm
- Showing explicitly that you value your supervisor's knowledge and experience
- Trying to do something the supervisor's way, but setting criteria and a date for evaluation of the success of it (especially if you're reluctant)
- Not just refusing to do something you don't like, but offering an alternative instead
- Being scrupulous about giving credit where credit is due (e.g. when you publish papers)
- Finding out about your supervisor's research – surprisingly few students do this, even though their supervisor's research is probably one of the most valuable resources available
- Allowing your supervisor to be human – tolerating human weaknesses and making the most of your supervisor's strengths.

What to contribute

The supervisory relationship is a two-way one; you are supposed to be actively learning, not passively waiting to be told all the answers.

At the most academic level, you should be actively finding things out and actively generating ideas. One sign that you're doing a proper PhD is that you're finding out things which are new to your supervisor; another is that your supervisor finds at least one of your ideas sufficiently interesting to merit genuine engagement and discussion. It's useful as well as courteous to give your supervisor a *précis* of what you've found, and to offer full copies of any material that the supervisor would like to read in more detail.

At the implementation level, you should be generating ideas about specific research questions to ask and specific research methods to investigate them. You should be doing this increasingly as the PhD progresses and you learn more. Your supervisor will probably advise against most of these ideas; what you need to do is to assess the reasons for this advice, rather than going into a corner and sulking. One thing which most students never consider is that a good supervisor will be generating ideas about their own research all the time, and discarding the vast majority of them on various grounds. If you expect to have a higher hit rate than your supervisor while you're still an apprentice, then you're being a bit silly.

At the motivation level, you should be generating passion and enthusiasm. If you're bored, that will make your supervisor bored too; give them a reason to look forward to your next meeting instead of planning an escape to Acapulco.

What to ask for

There are various things that you should ask for, with appropriate courtesy, at various stages of your PhD.

From an early stage, you should ask for appropriate training, both in research methods relevant to your research and also in other areas which will help you – for instance, many students would benefit from assertiveness training and relaxation training, as well as time management and numerous other ancillary skills. You should ask specifically for skills advice if you need it (e.g. what is the form of a conference paper; how does one read a paper and make notes about it?). It's particularly helpful if the supervisor can work through an example with you, rather than just telling you how to do it. A lot of students are embarrassed to ask for this sort of advice on the grounds that they think they should already know it. That's a faulty assumption. The point of the PhD is that it's about learning these skills; if you had them already, there wouldn't be much point in doing the PhD.

When you're at a later stage and have some findings to discuss, you can ask your supervisor to recommend (or introduce you to) other experts who might help. This needs to be done with discretion. Your supervisor will probably not introduce you to someone who will steal and publish your ideas (a frequent source of generally unfounded nightmares for PhD students), but you do need to have enough knowledge of academic etiquette to handle such encounters properly.

What to tell your supervisor

You should keep your supervisor informed:

- About the state of your work
- About what interests you and what concerns you
- About outside opinion: report feedback from talks and papers accurately and promptly; be specific about both compliments and criticisms
- About decisions and turning points (the supervisor can often provide helpful insight and forestall hasty misjudgements)
- About life circumstances: let your supervisor know about personal or practical matters that are affecting your work, preferably before they turn into a major issue

Things you can do for yourself

There are also various things you can do for yourself. You should keep your supervisor briefed about all of these, in advance. This is partly common courtesy and partly practical self-interest (so that the supervisor can stop you if you're about to do something remarkably stupid on your own initiative).

Another thing worth doing is to assemble an informal 'committee' of people (both staff and students, both in the department and external) who are able and willing to help with your PhD. The key thing to remember is that this is to complement your supervisor, not as an alternative to your supervisor. The informal committee can be helpful for things ranging from low-level logistics (e.g. babysitting) and low-level practical skills (e.g. learning how to use your computer properly) up to general emotional support and specific academic advice on topics complementing your supervisor's advice (e.g. help translating foreign language articles about your area of research).

Another thing you can do is to give seminars and/or circulate draft papers (again, with your supervisor's approval). This both gives you experience and provides you with feedback.

Destructive behaviours to avoid

Students do stupid, suicidal things, especially during PhDs. Here are some of the most destructive, which can sabotage your relationship with your supervisor.

- Hiding (yourself, or real or imagined problems)
- Ignoring (advice you don't understand; advice you don't like)
- Mixing (business with pleasure or with personal issues)
- Gossiping (about your supervisor or colleagues)
- Denigrating (your supervisor, department or institution)
- Bypassing (your supervisor, by making decisions without due consultation)
- Assuming (what something meant; what you're entitled to do)
- Sinning (illegal or unethical acts – these are in a different league from the failings listed above)

In our experience, all students hide at some time or other. So keep an eye on yourself: do you really need to postpone your supervision meeting again to give you that third week to write that pesky paragraph, or would you be better off admitting that you're stuck and asking for help?

If in doubt, ask. This is particularly important in relation to assuming and sinning. Students often don't check that they really understand something that they're not quite sure about, and then end up with serious misunderstandings and serious problems. Similarly, students often have mistaken understandings of what is considered reasonable; for instance, is it reasonable or not to phone your supervisor at home without explicit prior agreement?

Illegal acts are usually fairly easy to identify, but unethical ones may require much more knowledge. For instance, thanking respondents by name in the acknowledgements section may be intended as a sign of genuine appreciation, but may breach their anonymity and lead to significant professional and legal problems. Commercial sensitivity is another problematic area, as is publication of draft material. If in doubt, ask . . .

Prevention is better than cure

In any relationship which lasts as long as a PhD, and which involves learning new skills and exposing one's ego and intellect to scrutiny, something will inevitably go wrong. The key questions are what that thing will be and what you're going to do about it.

Most difficulties in the supervisory relationship are 'cock-ups' rather than 'conspiracies'. Always start from the assumption that all parties are acting in good faith. As is often the case, prevention is the best cure: if you have good work habits (e.g. networking effectively, keeping good records, letting other people know what you're working on, publishing internal and external reports promptly, communicating clearly and promptly), then many difficulties can be avoided altogether. Good habits will also make early diagnosis easier. Good communication can usually sort problems out before they become serious.

A classic example is dealing with the supervisor who is never available. Make friends with your supervisor's secretary; get to know your supervisor's schedule; and make sure your supervision meetings are on that schedule. Discuss the problem with your supervisor. Explain your needs. You may not be able to reduce the travel schedule of an international expert, but you can probably work out means for remote communication, so you can still get advice when your supervisor is away. Use your informal committee to fill in when your supervisor is otherwise occupied – and keep your supervisor informed about developments.

Strategies for when things go wrong

If you are convinced that you have the wrong supervisor and you can articulate exactly what quality or problem is irredeemably fatal to the supervisory relationship, then you'll need to find a new supervisor. It's crucial that you find the replacement before rocking the boat, otherwise you'll destroy the relationship you have, and you'll have ruined your reputation with everyone else. The point is to find a better match, not to throw verbal rocks at your present supervisor. So find positive reasons for the change (different research specialism, better personality fit). The more diplomatically you handle the transition, the better it will be for you and for everyone else involved.

There are some classic problems that are usually fatal to the supervisory relationship, sometimes immediately, sometimes late in the PhD, when change is most difficult. These are in a different league to the inevitable misunderstandings, arguments, disagreements and suchlike that occur in any PhD.

The really serious problems include the following.

- **'isms:** sexism, racism, anti-Semitism etc. Most institutions have procedures for dealing with this. Whether or not you want to become embroiled in formal procedures, you should find a new supervisor.
- **Intellectual property issues:** 'absorption' or theft of work, obstruction of research, suppression of results. Good habits (like letting people know what you're working on, writing up results promptly) can help here, but sometimes they are not enough.
- **Non-communication:** when no matter what you try, you can't get through.
- **Harassment:** sexual harassment, bullying, damaging insensitivity. Again, most institutions have procedures for dealing with this, or at least a trained person to help you deal with it.

If you find yourself in any of the above situations, you must proceed with extreme care and diplomacy. You will need to:

1 Find out exactly how supervision is coordinated in your department; there will be a procedure for changing supervisor. The bottom line is that, once it has accepted you, the university has an obligation to find someone to supervise you. There may be a bullying and harassment policy which is applicable. Go about this investigation discreetly.
2 Establish the paper trail: write things down, keep all emails, etc. Write down the facts, with dates and details, as dispassionately as you can. If there really is a problem, the facts will speak for themselves.
3 Consult a third party, confidentially. There is often a designated third party, a 'third-party monitor' (whose job it is to review the progress of the supervisory relationship), a postgraduate tutor (who oversees all research student supervision), a professor or director of research, an equal opportunities officer, a research dean. Sometimes there is an accessible Wise Person in the department, often one of the professors, someone who has been around and knows the ropes and who is kind and sympathetic. Sometimes it will be easier to speak to someone outside your department. In any case, choose an academic who is experienced and respected as well as compassionate. Speak as calmly and dispassionately as you can, bring along your documentation, ask for advice and listen.

4 Call in a third party (not necessarily the same one that you consult for advice). It may be appropriate to ask someone – usually someone senior – to act on your behalf. This person can sit in on your supervision, in order to see what's going on, can intervene with your supervisor or can help you through the procedures. Choose your third party carefully and listen to the advice this person gives you.

It's usually better not to get into this situation in the first place; a cup of coffee in a tactful way can make an enormous amount of difference (for instance, a cup of coffee with someone discreet who can give you some hints about your potential supervisory team). Assertiveness training can also help prevent some situations arising.

Cardinal rules

In brief, there are a few cardinal rules about dealing with your supervisor. They should be blindingly obvious, but a surprising number of students seem to need to be reminded of them.

- Be honest
- Be articulate (say what you mean and ask for what you need)
- Be informative (keep the supervisor informed)
- Be respectful (remember, your supervisor holds that academic position for a reason, even if the reason is obscure to you, and you're asking for your supervisor's time and input)
- Be adult (i.e. take responsibility for yourself)

Table 4.2 A simple scheme for effective supervision meetings

Provide a discussion document	Send something to your supervisor(s) a week before the meeting (this can be a progress report, a study plan, a critique of the literature you've been reading, an annotated bibliography, data, a draft conference paper – whatever represents what you're working on). Having something concrete to discuss always helps, and preparing something can be a good way to focus your thinking. Bring copies to the meeting.
Provide key publications	Send copies of papers you consider to be seminal to your supervisor(s) in advance of the meeting, particularly If you wish to discuss them. Make sure the full citation is marked on the copy. Providing papers is a courtesy you can do your supervisor(s), and having them on hand can facilitate discussion.
Show up on time	If you're late, bring cookies.
Write down your objectives	Know what you want to get out of the meeting, whether it's technical, administrative or emotional. Give yourself a prioritized checklist in advance. It helps to have something interesting to discuss when you enter the meeting – if you don't have ideas, then prepare questions.
Check the agenda with your supervisor(s)	Find out what your supervisor(s) want to get out of the meeting. Agree an agenda.
Behave well	• Listen and consider before you speak • Be prepared to give a candid account of your progress • Ask stupid questions – they may seem stupid to you, but they rarely are • Focus on ideas, not emotions; trust your supervisor(s) and don't take things personally • Make counter-proposals if you don't like what your supervisor(s) are advising because this can help expose discrepancies in your thinking and help you understand the rationale for the guidance
Take notes	*Always* take notes!
Book the next meeting	Set a date for your next meeting before you leave and set a preliminary agenda.
Email an action-item summary	Immediately after the meeting, write a list of agreed action items (both yours and your supervisors'), with deadlines if possible, and email it to all concerned, asking for confirmation that you've summarized correctly. Include the date of the next meeting.

5

Networks

*Building a network • Tools for networking • First contact – cold calls •
People you should remember to include in your network*

> *The first horrible incident of our acquaintance was the greatest shock I ever
> experienced, and it is only with reluctance that I repeat it.*[1]

Contrary to a widespread belief among the general public and among depressed
second-year PhD students, you don't complete a PhD in gloomy isolation.
There are lots of people who help you, not just through your doctoral research,
but also throughout your subsequent career; there are more who can help you,
if you find them. This network won't be confined to eminent academics who
are noted experts. It will more usefully also include lesser mortals whom you
find good for conversations, who are good readers and commentators, who
may have insight into theories, literatures and methodologies with which you
are less familiar, who themselves have good networks and are happy to introduce you to useful people, who understand The System and so on. Some students have good networks; others don't. This chapter describes networks and
how to create a good one for yourself.

One common misconception is that networks involve cliques of people
doing morally dubious favours for each other, at the expense of more virtuous
but less well-connected ordinary people. That's only one type of network.
We're using the term in the different sense of normal, ethical support networks
and normal, ethical professional networks – people you know and can turn to
for advice.

---

[1] Lovecraft, H.P. (1921–22) Herbert West – Reanimator, in *Omnibus 2: Dagon and Other Macabre Tales*
(1985). London: Grafton Books, p. 158.

Building a network

Networks don't just happen; they're something you build, whether consciously or without thinking about it. Even if you're normally good at building networks without conscious effort, PhD networks will by definition be new to you, so it's worth knowing about a network structure which most students find useful.

At the heart of your network, of course, are your supervisors.

A second important component of your network is your informal 'committee' (i.e. people who will help you to ensure that your research is of good quality). For this, you need a small set of reliable, interested academics who are willing to do some work for you: to read, to comment, to advise, to critique, to provide pointers, to introduce you to other researchers and so on. They may be specialists who can provide particular expertise, or they may be generalists who can ask incisive questions.

A third main component is your personal support network (i.e. people who give you encouragement and moral support, who help you manage your work, keep life in perspective and bring you pizza when you're in the throes of inspiration). They may be family, or fellow students, or old friends. They may be academics in your department who are good at bringing you to your senses.

In addition, you need people who can be called on occasionally for specialist help, or people you can visit once or twice to pick their brains. They may be leading researchers in your specialist field, or they may be technical experts who know about things like laboratory instruments, running databases and formatting documents.

Targeting

Most networking is opportunistic: if you meet someone that you happen to like, or find a useful contact, then you stay in touch with them. Sometimes, however, you need to find particular kinds of help or expertise, and for that you need a strategy. Three particularly useful starting points are:

- The writers of particularly relevant papers
- People you saw or met at a conference who had pertinent and interesting things to say
- People recommended by someone reliable (e.g. your supervisor, or a member of your informal committee)

Once you've identified some possible leads, you need to do some initial work and then make contact. The initial work consists of some homework. There's a reason why you've identified this person as someone to contact, but don't forget to find out what else you can about the person before you make contact, since there may be other ways in which they can help you. It also makes the contact easier if you know something about the person you're contacting. Here are some things you can do.

- Check their website
- Ask people who know them
- Check with the person's secretary about when would be a good time to call, and whether the person is in the country

Another useful bit of preparation is to consider what it is that you want to ask them. It's not enough to say that you're working in the same area as they are – they might justifiably react to this news by thinking, 'So what?' You need to say whether you want to clarify something about their work, or want a chance to discuss ideas, or want them to review your work. The more focused and informed the question you ask, the better the chances of things going well. Remember that anyone with enough stature to be worth approaching is probably also approached by other students. A surprising number of these students will ask vague, lazy questions which amount to, 'Can you tell me everything I need for my literature review, to save me the effort of finding it out for myself?' This is why we stress the need for tact and courtesy when asking someone for an overview of something over a cup of coffee – there's a world of difference between a cup of coffee with a well-read, hard-working student and a cup of coffee with an ignorant, idle one.

It's usually easier to make contact with someone local, because it's feasible to 'just drop by' their office and take them to coffee. However, just because they're local, that doesn't guarantee that they're available or friendly; you still have to do the homework first.

Tools for networking

Two of the main time-honoured tools for networking are shameless flattery and bribery. Shameless flattery usually takes the form of shameless flattery; bribery usually takes the form of coffee, chocolate biscuits and practical favours such as unearthing obscure references. (Just in case of misunderstanding, real bribery via monetary or sexual favours is unethical and illegal, and we emphatically disapprove of it.) There is a short table of tools and tips for networking at the end of the chapter.

Flattery

The secret of effective flattery is that it is barefaced, precise, economical and accurate. That is, it has to flow easily and openly from the flatterer, it has to relate specifically and accurately to the flatteree, you mustn't overdo it and it must bear some relation to reality. One well-informed, well-placed compliment on a recent publication will do more good than ten vague generalities. It also reduces the risk of your compliment being mistaken for the opening line in a seduction attempt – attractive women researchers at conferences apparently have more than enough unwanted attention of this sort.

Coffee

Eminent people are human too, and at venues such as conferences they can be very glad of a break and a decent cup of coffee paid for by someone else. Coffee can be used in various ways. One is as the setting for unofficial advice of one sort or another – career prospects, organizational politics, the future of a research field. Another is as a chance to unwind a bit at a gruelling conference or similar occasion. Treating someone to a cup of decent coffee as a break from a long admin session can be a real act of kindness, especially if you behave with tact and consideration during the coffee (for instance, by not talking about work, if your guest wants to get away from it for a while).

Chocolate biscuits

These are a surprisingly useful incentive. If you offer someone some cash to be a subject in your experiment, it might motivate them to some extent. If you offer them an upmarket chocolate biscuit and real coffee, then this is likely to motivate them considerably more, and make them more cooperative and friendly into the bargain. There is a literature on the reasons for this (it involves 'currencies', 'strokes', and 'judgement and decision making', if you feel inclined to follow it up, not to mention 'cognitive dissonance').

Not many people believe in the efficacy of chocolate biscuits, which is probably just as well, because if everyone adopted this approach then it would devalue the currency, and the shrewd researcher would need to find a different incentive (which would be a double annoyance to those researchers who happen to like upmarket chocolate biscuits).

Trading favours

People are busy. Interesting people are often very busy. One way to borrow some of their precious time is to offer them an exchange – to do something of value for them which allows them to free some time for you. For example, you could offer to do some administrative work or library searching in exchange for half an hour of discussion over coffee (you still buy the coffee).

First contact – cold calls

'Cold calls' (contacting someone who doesn't know you) outside your own institution can be awkward both for the caller and the person being called. It's hard to establish the basis for a conversation in a sentence or two, but you can make it easier if you prepare in advance. Cold calls can succeed if you can establish quickly that the exchange can be of mutual benefit. So think through in advance what you want, and what you have to offer in exchange.

Your best chance is to establish an immediate connection with the person you're contacting (e.g. through an introduction by a mutual acquaintance such as your supervisor or through reference to that person's publications). Having made that link, you need to say who you are and what you want.

Smart researchers like students with interesting ideas, and so they generally respond well to them, especially ones who have potential as named candidates on future grant applications. But sometimes active researchers already have as much work as they can handle, so you shouldn't assume that they'll have time for you – or that a lack of response necessarily means a lack of interest.

Be prepared to follow up your initial contact with some substance, for example a good, one-page *précis* of your research or a well-constructed conference paper reporting some of your early findings. Make sure what you send represents you well: ensure that it is clearly written, free of major and minor errors and clear it with your supervisors and other experienced readers first.

Via phone

Phoning works best if you have a 'hook' for the person you're calling, for example if you've been referred to them by someone they know, or if you've already emailed them and suggested that you will call. You need to establish quickly who you are and why you're calling, and then you need to ask if this is a convenient time for, say, a five-minute conversation. Often, it won't be – be prepared to call back at another time. Also be prepared to follow up via email or post.

Via email or post

Published researchers, especially well-known ones, are inundated with requests from random research students wanting favours. Requests that run 'Dear Professor Haagen, I am a graduate student in Budapest researching ice cream and I wonder if you could offer me any advice about a choice of research topic' are tediously uninformative and suggest that the student, being incompetent, is not worth the bother of answering. On the other hand, concise requests that give substantive information about the student's research and ask specific questions are far more interesting and usually attract a response, though perhaps not an immediate one. It might well take the researcher six months to find time to read your message, decide to think about it, lose it in the crush of work and eventually find it again and reply. Maybe the researcher won't reply but will remember a good message when you meet at a conference and introduce yourself. Think about it from their point of view: if you had 50 emails about a research bid with a budget of several million pounds, and a deadline next Tuesday, would you defer answering them until you'd read every word of an email from a PhD student you'd never heard of before? If anything, it's surprising how many positive responses you can get to a well-constructed cold call.

If the researcher does reply to your message, be sure to send a thank-you message immediately. If you have a good summary of your research, or of a piece of it, then you might attach it to the follow-up message.

We have deliberately not included examples of good cold call emails, since we don't particularly want to be lynched by eminent colleagues who receive large numbers of identically worded requests for help in the weeks following publication of this book, but some things to think about include the following.

- Did you get their name and title right?
- Does your question show that you've done some homework?
- Does your mentor/supervisor think that your question looks interesting?
- How long would it take a reasonable human being to write a reply to your question? (If it's more than ten minutes, then consider rephrasing the question.)
- Is your message so long that it scrolls off the page when the addressee opens it? (If so, shorten it.)
- Does the message show you in a good light, as someone who can spell, write clearly, think and generate interesting questions?
- Does the message offer them anything (e.g. access to data), and if so, can you deliver on that promise?

At a meeting or conference

Have something interesting and relevant ready to say. A compliment is handy, but be prepared to follow it up with a question, otherwise the conversation will die. (Even the most eminent researchers can be embarrassed by compliments, especially if they're too gratuitous.) It's best to have a question prepared that requires a multi-word response: for instance, 'Professor Katz, I was intrigued by your paper in *Nature* on semi-stochastic systems. I wondered whether you had tried applying that approach to trade networks?'

Use the opportunities that the meeting provides. If your person asks a good question during a session, you might catch them after the session and remark on the question and its implications. If you see your person talking to someone you know, you might ask the person you know to introduce you. If you see your person in a loosely arranged group, you might stand visibly on the periphery until you get a chance to make a contribution (a short question or a joke is good) or ask if you may join the group. A good time to catch people is as a session breaks up, before they've found their way to coffee or lunch. But don't keep them from refreshment – offer to walk with them.

Have a business card to hand, and perhaps a copy of a summary of your research (previously read and approved by your supervisor).

Don't assume that you are beneath notice, or, worse, beneath interest. Here are some home truths about Great Researchers to help you put them in perspective.

- They are usually great because they love ideas and asking questions – so they usually have an appetite for nifty ideas and good questions
- They are usually just as susceptible to deft flattery as the rest of us
- They were once research students and many of them still remember that

People you should remember to include in your network

Most of the section above refers to contacting researchers about research. There are other categories of very useful people that it's easy to overlook, so we've included a short section about them here.

Mentors

Mentors are Wise People who take an interest in your personal, professional and intellectual development. They're the people who teach you the 'unwritten rules' and who can see the 'bigger picture'. In theory, your supervisor should be a mentor, but it doesn't always work out that way. A mentor is a more experienced researcher who will show you the ropes from this perspective of success and informedness. A mentor can show you the things you don't know how to look for. This is particularly useful for the things that you don't *know* that you need to look for or do, such as getting the right things on your CV as early as possible – a friend won't always know what the right things are, and some of the right things are counter-intuitive. Other students are often good at identifying things actively wrong with your institution, but bad at identifying things which are passively wrong (i.e. things not being done which ought to be done). Mentors are useful for this, among many other things.

Secretaries and other support staff

Always treat support staff – secretaries, technical support, custodians of facilities – with respect. *Never* underestimate their value. *Never* confuse salary

level with worth. Support staff are the keepers and collators of useful information – they are the ones holding together the department, they are the pro-
viders of services and assistance, they are often the gatekeepers to things you
need. Consider: if you really wanted to know the inside story about govern-
ment policy, would you ask the prime minister or the civil service? Journalists
know all about this, and successful journalists always get on well with the
secretaries of the people they investigate.

Wonderful People

One invaluable resource is Wonderful People. There are a few people who have
invaluable skills such as improbably excellent social or professional contacts,
or encyclopaedic knowledge of one or more literatures, and who are helpful
and pleasant. Such people should be cherished and appreciated. As a new
researcher you will probably not know any people fitting this description (or
more probably, not realize that you know them). When you do start meeting
them, treat them well; they should be declared living national treasures.
Librarians and secretaries are also often wonderful, and friendships with them
are almost always well worth cultivating.

Table 5.1 Useful tips for networking

Aim to be genuinely nice to people	It makes the world a better place and it pays off in the long term – people will remember you and put things your way. This is not the same as being silly or a victim, or as being mercenary.
A cup of coffee with a knowledgeable, supportive person can be the best investment you ever make	Asking advice from the right person at the right time (usually before you get started) can save you a lot of tears and a lot of wasted effort. Remember to ask someone knowledgeable about the relevant area – a fellow lost soul, or someone knowledgeable about a different area, may be comforting but is unlikely to be much help in getting you out of the problem.
If you have any choice at all, only work with nice people whom you respect	You achieve much more this way and you have a nicer time along the way.
If you don't know what you're doing, then stop and find out	Another cup of coffee can help at this point.
Do good work in public	Ask good questions at conferences. Make constructive suggestions in 'birds of a feather' sessions. Phrase commentary as questions rather than statements.
Trade favours	Don't just ask for things – offer useful services in return. One way to borrow time from busy people is to offer them an exchange – to do something of value for them which allows them to free some time for you. Engage in constructive forms of 'you scratch my back; I'll scratch yours': swap papers with other researchers, participate in each other's studies, help each other with reliability tests and so on.
Be a 'good citizen'	Like it or not, you're a member of a research community, and it helps if you pay tax. Offer a bit of your time to contribute to that community: sitting on appropriate committees, reading other people's papers, helping to organize selected research events, exchanging leads with other researchers. Keep it under control, but the occasional bit of strategic volunteering can introduce you to interesting and helpful people, increase your exposure in the community and generally encourage people to think of you as a 'good egg'.
Follow up	Carry the dialogue on past the conference or initial contact. Keep track of who you meet, where you meet them and what their interests are. Keep your promises; send the citations or copies of papers that you offered to send. Email other leads that you think might be of interest.

6

Reading

Why read? • *Finding the right references: where do I start?* • *Online searching* • *Other sources of information* • *Reading between the lines of a paper or dissertation* • *Literature reviews* • *Using material from the literature* • *Keeping an annotated bibliography*

> *. . . those frightful parts of the Pnakotic Manuscripts which were too ancient to be read.* [1]

PhD students are painfully aware that doing a PhD involves doing a lot of reading. By the time you get onto a PhD, you'll already be well aware that doing a lot of reading is hard work. By the time you're a few weeks into a PhD, you'll also be worrying about how to decide what to read. There's an enormous amount of material out there, far too much for any human being to read in a lifetime: how do you know which parts of it to read and which parts to ignore? What happens if the examiner in your viva starts asking about a literature that you've never heard of, let alone read, but which sounds horribly like something that has fatal implications for the thesis that you've spent years painfully assembling? Where do you start with your reading, how do you decide where to go with it and how do you know where to stop? That's what this chapter is about.

We have included a fair amount of detail about how to search for relevant literature. If you're going to be a good professional researcher, you need to be aware of the differences between sources of various kinds and able to use the tools of your trade efficiently and well. Few students are strong in this area

---

[1] Lovecraft, H.P. (1921) The Other Gods, in *Omnibus 2: Dagon and Other Macabre Tales* (1985). London: Grafton Books, p. 149.

(although many believe they are), but it's a valuable skill which will both improve the quality of your work and save you effort.

Why read?

Why does doing a PhD involve so much reading? Because reading is the road to mastery: it's how you come to acquire and understand existing knowledge and existing techniques; it's how you come to know the research community; it's how you come to understand the tools of your trade. So, while you're reading, you're doing a number of things, including:

- **Mastering the literature:** discovering what has been discussed and what hasn't, what is known and what isn't, what the major strands of thinking are and how they have evolved
- **Mapping the community:** identifying who the key researchers are and how they interrelate
- **Identifying your niche:** finding the gap that you hope to fill, understanding its relationship to the rest of the literature and identifying the publications most relevant to your project

Students' use of the literature usually matures and focuses during the course of their research in a way that corresponds to the development of their research question. The development goes through several phases, as shown in Table 6.1.

Table 6.1 Development of students' use of literature

Entering student	Later student	Still later student	Completing student
Knows which research area	Knows which research topic	Knows what research question	Knows what research evidence
Reads to find what's already known			Reads to know what isn't already known
Surveys, collects, reports	Organizes information	Selects information relevant to research question	Judges information (quality and gaps)
Wonders how to organize sources	Wonders how to identify problem	Wonders what has been already said about the problem	Wonders what has not been said about the problem

Literature surveys versus literature reviews

Students typically begin by surveying the literature, and gradually learn to review it. As one colleague phrases it, they go from reading to discover 'What's there' to reading to discover 'What isn't there'. The difference between a literature survey and a literature review is the difference between report and critique. A report just lists things which the report writer considered worth listing. A review says what happened, and why, and how, and also says why the review has focused on the issues it did and why it treated other issues as less important. Ideally, the completing student should have developed a 'critical voice'. The literature review in the dissertation should 'make sense' of the literature in terms of the thesis. If the literature review is well-structured and appropriately critical, then, ultimately, the research question emerges as a logical conclusion of the literature review.

It's also worth pointing out that there's a difference between the sort of 'stand-alone' literature review published in a journal and the literature review that frames a thesis. The difference relates to the *purpose* of each: the former should provide an accurate overview of and introduction to the subject literature (and typically 'add value' by structuring it, critiquing it or providing an insightful perspective on it); the latter serves the thesis, providing a frame and focus for the research question.

The researcher's core literature

One tool that established researchers have is a working knowledge of the relevant literature. Most established researchers have a core repertoire of 100 to 150 works on which they can draw readily. (Of course, there's huge variation, but the numbers don't really matter – the idea of keeping a selection of pertinent literature accessible in memory does.) These are a useful selection from the hundreds or thousands of articles and books the researcher has digested over time. The repertoire gives a researcher a context in which to place ideas: the collection characterizes the major strands of thinking in the field, identifies the major researchers and provides research models and examples. Of course the repertoire evolves and must be updated. As researchers continue to read, the core adjusts, shifting to follow developments in the discipline or to follow a researcher's changing interests. But some of that core will persist for years. One of the things a good doctoral student will accomplish is to amass a first 'core' literature.

Reading a lot

You need to read a lot. You need to read a lot in your own discipline (so that you have a thorough grasp of what it is all about) and in other disciplines, both apparently relevant and apparently irrelevant. Much of the best work comes from cross-fertilization between apparently unconnected fields. Table 6.2 (at the end of the chapter) summarizes tips from successful people who read a lot about how they manage to do it.

In your own field, you should read in depth and in breadth and in *time* – you should have a detailed knowledge of the relevant literature in your chosen area, and a general knowledge of the main work in related areas, and of previous work in your area for as far back as possible. For your own area, you should be reading everything up to and including the most specialized journal articles. For other areas, you might find book chapters a more appropriate level (though be careful about the level of the book – don't even think about popular books for the lay public, and be wary of textbooks unless they are prestigious ones).

What you read, versus what you cite

A classic question that PhD students ask is: 'How many references should I have in my dissertation?' It's a sensible, simple question. So is asking: 'How do I repair a broken car?' In both cases, the sensible, simple question has a sensible but complex answer; in both cases, once you understand the complexity, then you're ready to be admitted to the ranks of the experts, whether with a PhD or as a qualified motor mechanic.

There are some 'quick and dirty' answers that can be useful for calming down a nervous student until they're ready for the more complex answer. One is: 'Look at some recent successful dissertations in your field; have about as many references as them; cite the same landmark texts as them.' This approach may well get you through, but it means that you're doing something simply because that's what other people have done, rather than because you understand the reasons for what you're doing.

The more complex answer is: 'You use as many references as you need: no more, no less. Once you know how many that is, you're ready for the PhD.' It sounds like a facetious answer, but it isn't. It sparks the obvious follow-up question: 'How do I know how many references I need?' When you stop to think about this question, you'll probably realize that you already know the answer. Every significant point in the chain of reasoning and evidence in your thesis needs to be linked explicitly to the relevant literature. If there are points which aren't linked to the relevant literature, then you haven't got enough references; conversely, if there are references in your thesis which don't link to the significant points, then those references may well be needlessly cluttering the text.

Once you start looking at the question this way, you soon realize what some of the other follow-up questions are, and what the answers are to those follow-up questions. For instance, there's the question of how you know what all the significant points are in your thesis, to which the answer is that you can't know that at the start of your PhD: your thesis will develop as you gain new insights from the literature, and those insights will in turn point you towards other reading that you need to do. It's a cyclic process that will go on through your PhD, until your thesis stabilizes. Another question is how to decide what is a relevant literature or reference, and what isn't. That takes you into some interesting issues about the sociology of research, where disciplines (and individual supervisors) vary in what they consider relevant and necessary, including how receptive they are to insights from other disciplines.

The implication is, of course, that what you need to read is a different matter from what you end up citing. For every paper that ends up in the reference list in your dissertation, there will be a number of others that do not. What you cite is a selection from what you have read – but determining what literature to cite involves reading a much larger literature.

You have to convey the right message when you're writing, and that involves some hard work beforehand, reading what you need to read so you can cite it at the appropriate point (the first golden principle: *don't lie*, in this case by pretending to have read things which you haven't read). However, there is no point in overkill. One of our usual examples of strong academic writing contains eight references in one paragraph on the first page. Do you think that page 24 of that thesis contains the same number of references per paragraph? It doesn't, because it doesn't need to – the writer has by then already cited practically all the references he or she needs to.

How do you know what the key references are that you need as a starting point? The next sections go through that and other issues to do with reading in more detail.

Finding the right references: where do I start?

So, where is a good place to start looking for references? Some students have a fair idea already because of writing their PhD proposal; others are taking up a studentship to work on a topic which has already been outlined by someone else. The easiest solution if you're unsure where to start reading is to ask your supervisor, politely, where to start. Your supervisor is likely to remind you about literature reviews in the papers you've already read, about review articles and about the literature reviews in passed dissertations in your area. You may also be pointed toward some online searching, with keywords either supplied by your long-suffering supervisor or included in the articles which you have already found.

You also need to develop an understanding of where researchers in your discipline publish. What are the key publishers, book series, journals, conferences, symposia, workshops or meetings? One way to find out is to ask your supervisor. Another is to identify a couple of researchers (such as your supervisor) whose work you respect, and investigate where they publish, and what events they attend (much of this information will be on their websites, in one form or another). In addition, find out if there are any important mailing lists, bulletin boards or blogs in your area, as any of those are likely to provide leads.

If your supervisor doesn't know, ask someone else, politely, and keep your supervisor informed, in case you start blundering in where angels fear to tread. You need to send out the signal that you're a hard-working individual who will make good use of the advice, rather than an idle brute who can't be bothered to do their own research (mentioning what you've already read and asking where you should go next is a good start). Your supervisor can be invaluable here.

If you're lucky and virtuous, your supervisor might say something along the lines of, 'The person to talk to about this is X; I've emailed them, and they're happy to give you some guidance. Here's their email address.' This is an encouraging sign and is academic shorthand for the following things:

- Here is something which will save you a lot of effort
- Here is a chance to make contact with a major player in this area
- I trust you enough to let you speak to important players in this area by yourself

It does *not* mean, 'I am too ignorant or idle to provide guidance on this by myself'. If your supervisor offers you this opportunity, then grab it with both hands and do some intelligent preparation before you meet or contact the person in question, so you don't look clueless – find out more about the person and their research, and do at least some background reading beforehand, so you don't look as if you're asking them to do your literature review for you; the rest of this chapter should help with this process.

Cynical supervisors have been known to give students explicit advice about which sources to read, but not quote, as an initial overview so that they understand the area. Alleged examples range from *How to Lie with Statistics* (almost certainly true) to *The Ladybird Book of Computers* (surprisingly, perhaps true to some extent).

Online searching

Although review articles and literature reviews in individual articles are a useful way into the literature, they are not infallible and were not written with your particular needs at the forefront of their writers' minds. You therefore need to do your own trawls through the literature to see what's out there and find bits of the literature that are relevant to you. You'll also need to take on the difficult task of deciding whether there's a significant gap in the previous literature – a gap which can act as the reason for the existence of your PhD (by making it a contribution to knowledge, plugging a previous gap). It doesn't need to be a big gap, for a PhD, but you do need to have taken reasonable precautions to ensure you're not just reinventing an old wheel, and making it square.

Supervisors and externals are not allowed to execute students who include in their literature reviews a sentence starting, 'A search on the internet found no previous work on this topic' or 'There were no books in the library on this topic'. They are, however, allowed to fail students and to write elegant, cutting comments on the offending page, which goes some way toward remedying this shortcoming in the legal system.

Why do supervisors and externals get so worked up about these sentences? Answer: because they're equivalent to writing in large letters, 'I am either ignorant or lazy or both'. That is not a signal that you want to send out to the reader.

Sending out the right signals

If you want to be treated as a professional, you need to send out the signals that show that you are a professional. Professionals know the tools of their trade – for instance, a brain surgeon should know about surgical instruments and about other relevant issues such as the physiology of the brain. If someone claimed to be a leading brain surgeon and then appeared to be unsure of the difference between a clamp and a retractor, that would not be an encouraging sign.

Anyone in the academic system ought to know the tools of the academic trade. The amount of detail required will vary with the academic level – for instance, undergraduates will not normally be expected to know as much as PhD students, who in turn will not be expected to know as much as leading professional researchers in the area. However, if you know more than you are expected to, this is usually viewed as a very encouraging sign.

Academics deal with knowledge and information and should know how to find, interpret and present knowledge and information. An important part of this is finding the best possible sources so that your assessment of the problem in question is based on the best information and knowledge available. The academic literature has a pecking order, ranging from publications which are accepted on sufferance through to publications which are treated with considerable respect. Some of this pecking order is quite possibly based on snobbery, but most of it is based on the quality control that the publication uses. The more rigorous the quality control that a publication uses, the more prestigious the publication is. It's a simple and sensible concept, and it makes life a lot simpler and more reliable for everyone involved. If you're about to spend months or years of your life, and perhaps sizeable amounts of money researching a topic, then it's very reassuring to know that your initial assumptions are as solidly based as they can be.

At the top end of the pecking order come encyclopaedia articles and the top journals. Encyclopaedias usually choose the leading international experts in an area to write their articles – it's a considerable compliment to be asked to write one. Anything submitted to a top-quality academic journal for publication will normally be checked in detail by several leading international authorities on the topic before being accepted for publication. Anything which is not of suitable quality will be rejected.

Further down the pecking order come the middle-range journals, which also use refereeing, but which normally use less eminent referees. Towards the bottom of the scale come specialist newsletters and professional trade magazines, where articles may be reviewed by the editor rather than specialist referees.

The precise status of a publication will be affected by individual factors – for instance, some specialist newsletters will be edited by very eminent authorities, have very high-level contributions and be higher in the pecking order than some journals. Books are also very variable in their status. As a fair rule of thumb, textbooks are low in the pecking order, because they usually present simplified accounts for students. Specialist books may be extremely prestigious.

The observant reader will by now have noticed that this description of the pecking order contains absolutely no mention of the internet, of newspapers or of popular magazines. There is a good reason for this. The internet has absolutely no quality control as regards the content of the sites accessible through it. If you find an interesting-looking site relating to your chosen area it may possibly have been written by a major authority, but it could just as easily have been put together by someone who believes that they are being controlled by devices put in their brain by aliens, and who has a degree from a college based above Joe's Pizza Shack in Peoria. Newspapers and popular magazines at least have some quality control, but if you think that reading a newspaper sends out the signal that you are a professional with considerable expertise, then you might be better advised to transfer your registration to that college based above Joe's Pizza Shack.

Back to online search

For a member of the general public, an online search generally involves typing 2.4 words into a search engine (the average length of query) and mis-spelling about 14 per cent of the words they type in. What this typically produces is URLs for websites, most of which have no quality control, as described above. This strategy doesn't send out a strong signal about its user's academic sophistication; it also misses enormous amounts of relevant literature which simply isn't accessible via that route.

As a PhD student, you need to know where the relevant literature for your PhD is actually located. A lot of relevant literature isn't freely accessible to the general public over the internet because of issues such as copyright law; for instance, the copyright of a journal article will usually reside with the journal's publisher, and the publisher will charge a fee for access to it. Some journals have soft copy of all their material available online, and will let you have access for a fee; many long-running journals are still in the process of putting old issues online, so there may only be printed copies of the article that you're looking for.

There are numerous online facilities available to registered university students via university libraries; it's no coincidence that the title 'library' is often being replaced by titles like 'information services' to make the point that they don't just provide traditional paper-based facilities. These online facilities include free access to a wide range of online articles, via Emerald, Athens and other systems that you may or may not recognize. It's highly advisable to find out as soon as possible which online facilities your university library offers you. If you need back issues of a particular journal for your literature search, most libraries pride themselves on the number of journals to which they provide access, and on being able to arrange access to more if students need them.

You need to know which online resources are the key ones for your field, and how to access them. You also need to know how to make best use of them once you do access them.

A key online resource is the bibliographic database. This may take various forms. It may be a database listing the bibliographic details of numerous articles (typically the names of the authors, the titles of the articles, the journal name, journal volume, journal issue and page numbers for the articles and a short list of keywords) but containing nothing more – it can help you find the bibliographic reference for a particular article, but you then have to find a physical copy of the article via something such as an inter-library loan request. It may be a database listing bibliographic details of articles, including the abstracts of the articles, so you can get a better idea of whether the article is relevant to you before deciding whether or not to obtain a physical copy. It may be a database which includes not only bibliographic details of the articles, and their abstracts, but also the full text of the articles themselves. There are numerous other forms and variations on these themes – for instance, giving you free access to the abstracts, but charging you for access to the full text. Open access journals offer free access to their contents, but charge the authors of those articles a significant publication fee after their papers have been accepted. Some traditional paper-based journals allow authors to put soft copies of their own articles onto their websites after a specified interval; others don't.

Once you know which online resources are relevant to you (a chat with your supervisor, and another with a friendly librarian, can be invaluable here) it's a wise idea to learn how to use them properly. The traditional '2.4 keywords with 14 per cent spelled wrong' approach isn't the most useful one at PhD level. It typically produces either far too many hits or far too few. For example, searching for the concept 'repertory grid' (a technique from psychology) will get huge numbers of hits about repertory theatre and enormous numbers of hits about city grids, power grids etc. which are completely irrelevant. Something as simple as typing in the two words surrounded by a pair of inverted commas will dramatically improve the percentage of relevant hits on most search engines.

It's highly advisable to find the 'advanced search' option for your online resource and to learn how to use it well. It will probably be one of the best investments of a couple of hours' effort that you ever make. Different systems offer different advanced facilities, but typical examples include an 'only show me records which have both this word and this other word' option and a 'don't show me records which include this word' option. These options make it much easier to prevent false hits (such as the repertory theatre example) and to broaden your search if you're getting suspiciously low numbers of hits (e.g. if there are several different names for the concept you're searching for and you've been getting low numbers of hits because you've only put in one of those names).

It's also advisable to be systematic about what you do during the search. One good strategy is to write down a list of keywords to try, before you start the search; another is to work through permutations of keywords and options systematically, keeping a record of which you've tried. Another useful tip is to update your list while you do the search. For example, if you were searching for 'repertory grid' and 'career choice' then you would soon notice that articles about repertory grids described them as part of personal construct theory, so you might consider using that as a search term (e.g. with the keywords 'career choice' and 'personal construct theory'). Technical terms and authors' names are usually good keywords (with obvious caveats if the author has a common name such as Smith or Brown), since someone who has published once on a topic is likely to publish on it again.

Searching the literature efficiently can save you a lot of wasted time, and can give you invaluable insights. It's an essential skill, but online searching isn't the only source of information: there are others.

Other sources of information

As usual, a cup of coffee with a friendly expert can save you an enormous amount of effort. It is also a good idea to get an overview from a textbook, which will list relevant articles in its bibliography, and an even better idea to get an overview from a review paper or from a recent encyclopaedia. Review papers and encyclopaedias are usually good things to quote in your bibliography; textbooks are usually not a good thing to quote in your bibliography, since they are saying to the reader: 'I've read the simplified account for beginners, not the professional account.'

It is also worth being pleasant to librarians – they have a wealth of information which they are usually happy to share with polite, appreciative people.

Review articles are an invaluable source of information. These are articles which summarize developments in a field, usually over the previous 10 or 20 years. They're typically written by people who are extremely knowledgeable about the field and they identify key issues and key papers in that field during that period. They're an excellent way of finding the key references to start your work; those key references will usually include references for earlier literature reviews, allowing you to work back through the years. They're also invaluable as supporting references for some key points which may otherwise be very awkward. For instance, if a review article says that there hasn't been enough work on a particular topic and you're doing your PhD on that topic, then the review article gives you an authoritative justification for your choice. Without that reference you'd have to make the claim yourself that there hadn't been enough previous work, and that's a difficult claim to substantiate without a very solid knowledge of the field, which a new PhD student is unlikely to have. How can you find review articles? Their title often includes the phrase 'review article' so a search on 'review article' and the name of the topic involved should find something useful.

Reading between the lines of a paper or dissertation

After you've found papers to read, you have the problem of evaluating the quality of what you're reading. This is not always easy for the average student. If you find a paper impossible to understand, is it because the paper is far too brilliant or because it's a pile of pretentious, obfuscatory garbage? This section describes some ways of reading between the lines of academic writing so that you are in a better position (a) to evaluate what you're reading and (b) to improve the quality of what you're writing.

The most interesting things in a paper are usually written between the lines. In the stereotyped picture of the Good Old Days, this was something which your supervisor would teach you over a glass of sherry (and a very pleasant way of operating it was too for both parties, as we can testify from personal experience). Nowadays you usually have to pick this up the hard way.

The sections below are arranged in roughly the sequence in which a seasoned professional might look at them. This is not the same as the sequence in which they would appear in a paper, which is different again from the order in which you would write them.

Abstract

What do the authors claim to have done, and what do they claim to have found? If it's not clear what they've allegedly done or found, is there any point in reading the rest of the paper? If it is clear, does it look plausible, or does it look like self-publicizing hype?

First page of introduction

Do the authors give a clear overview of what problem they're investigating, and why they're investigating it? Do the authors refer to the key literature and key concepts relating to this topic? If not, they might not be aware of it and may be clueless amateurs. How advanced are the references and concepts the authors use on the first page – are they just the standard undergraduate ones or do they include advanced, sophisticated ones? Do the authors give a reasonable-looking overview of relevant literatures and schools of thought or do they appear to be strongly biased in favour of one approach, either because they don't know about any others or because they're not prepared to listen to anyone else?

References

What sort of references are the authors citing? Really bad referencing will usually be caught by the peer review process, so you won't see much of it in the articles you read, but it's worth knowing what the people doing the peer review look for, so we've written most of this section from the viewpoint of a journal or conference reviewer. Reference sections consisting solely of URLs and/or popular books suggest that the author is an amateur, and possibly a crank with an obsession, who is completely unaware of the academic literature on the subject. (Note that for some purposes, URLs are fine but using nothing else is a worrying sign.) References to textbooks is also worrying: textbooks are generally simplified versions for students. References to specialist books, such as edited compilations by leading researchers in the field, are a completely different proposition and are usually fine. In most fields, reviewers would expect a high proportion of references to journal articles and conference proceedings – the proportions vary across disciplines and you need to know the usual proportions for your own discipline. What are the dates of the references? If almost all of them were more than a couple of years old when the paper was submitted, is this an old piece of work that's been dusted off and submitted, and which therefore may be out of date, or is it an article that's been rejected from other journals and then simply been resubmitted to the one that you're reviewing for? Do the references include the key articles relating to this topic or are there gaps? Do the references go back from the present to the earliest relevant literature or do they only go back ten years or so? If the references only go back a few years, the authors may be reinventing an ancient wheel because they are unaware that the issue was resolved long ago.

Main text

Is the main text reasonably clear? This isn't the same as asking if it's in 'plain English' – writing about technical topics without using technical language is a pretty pointless exercise. However, there's a difference between clear exposition using technical terms on the one hand, and verbal fog on the other. If you don't know the technical terms, then you'll need to learn them; unfortunately there are no shortcuts on this. If the text isn't clear to someone who understands the technical terms, is there any point in reading it? Note also that ambiguity is even worse than vagueness, since if something is clear but ambiguous, readers may follow the unintended meaning without realizing that it's different from the intended meaning.

Is the text complete? Does it tell you everything you need to know in order to make a reasoned assessment of what the authors did, and how much you can trust them? For example, if it's an empirical paper and the authors haven't told you things like how big their sample was, then this is a worrying sign. What are their conclusions? Have they used the most appropriate method for their work, with a sensible explanation of why they decided not to use other methods, or have they just used this method because they've never heard of anything else? Do their conclusions pass the 'So what?' test for whether you should bother reading this paper? Do their conclusions please you because they agree with your beliefs on the topic? If so, it's wise to re-examine the work on which their conclusions are based, because it's horribly easy to be uncritical about work which agrees with one's own prejudices. Are their conclusions justified by the evidence they present? If their conclusions are justified, are there other, very different, conclusions which are also consistent with the evidence they present?

This isn't a complete list, and disciplines vary, but it gives a flavour of the thoughts which pass through reviewers' minds, and of the reasons for those thoughts. A key, recurrent theme about academic practice is that usually there's a reason for things being done the way they are (even if it's not a great reason); the more you understand about the reasons, the better your experience on the PhD is likely to be.

Literature reviews

Academic papers and dissertations normally begin with a literature review. There are good reasons for this.

The ostensible reason for a literature review is to set the scene for the work described in the paper – explaining what has been done previously by other researchers. This is done via standard referencing conventions, so that interested or sceptical readers can locate the original sources and read them to check the alleged facts in the literature review, if they so wish. The second, and equally important, reason for a literature review is to demonstrate that you have done your homework thoroughly, so readers are assured that reading the rest of your text won't be a waste of their time.

The literature review needs to have a structure, since even the best academic prose is pretty hard reading at times. The structure is also a way of demonstrating that you have a clear understanding of what you're doing and why you're doing it. It is your responsibility to make your work understandable; it is not the reader's responsibility to make sense of a pile of references indiscriminately grabbed from the internet and then tacked together with semi-coherent prose.

The usual structure, and one with which we have no quarrel, is one which begins with the earliest work in this area and proceeds via the most important past work up to the present. Your references will therefore usually begin with old seminal references, then continue with more recent key references and assorted examples of less important references, and end with very recent foundational references.

Other structures can also be effective. Effective structures are based on an explicit organizing principle, such as chronology (as above), thematic threads, key issues and how they are addressed, or schools of thinking. Some topics draw on a number literatures and the review may be organized either in terms of those contributing literatures or in terms of themes that cut across those literatures.

One widespread source of confusion is the link between literature reviews and introductions. Institutions and people differ. Some favour a completely separate literature review and introduction; others favour a complete integration of the two. The best advice is to find out whether there is a specified formalism for your venue (including PhD regulations). If there is, follow it; if there isn't, use whichever approach you prefer. There's no point in getting into a war on this topic.

At the heart of your literature review is a good plot. The story should start with a problem of some sort (for instance, a dragon laying waste the land, in a good legend, or a practical or theoretical problem, in research). The literature review and/or introduction then follow the steps taken by previous work in an attempt to resolve the problem. The literature review and/or introduction ends at the point where you, the hero or heroine, enter the scene, armed with your enchanted sword/improved research methodology. The rest of the paper/dissertation follows your adventures, to the point where you emerge triumphant. If you do not emerge triumphant, then you should have got your experimental design right before you started, and it is your problem. This strand is known by various names, such as 'plot', 'red thread' and 'narrative spine', and is viewed as extremely important by most experienced and able writers.

Novices usually have a lot of trouble with narrative spine. The situation normally improves with practice, if you deliberately work at it, but will not automatically improve otherwise. There are various ways of helping yourself with this issue. One simple way is to use top-down decomposition. This involves starting with a very short list of key points in the story – half a dozen brief sentences at most. For example:

Elicitation of software metrics via card sorts
- Choice of metrics for software is difficult
- Card sorts should have advantages over previous methods for choosing metrics
- What happens if you use card sorts in this area?
- Card sorts do have advantages over previous methods in some ways

Once you are happy with this top-level structure, you then break down each part of it into smaller parts and keep on repeating the process as necessary (for instance, unpacking the ways in which card sorts have advantages and the ways in which they don't). You should end up with a set of section headings, subsection headings and so on which will give you the main structure.

In practice, readers tend to get lost quite easily, even in a well-structured paper, because of the sheer volume of information which should be in there. (If there isn't much information, this is usually a danger sign.) The wise writer therefore uses 'bridging text' and 'signposts'. Bridging text is used to join two sections of a paper or other document. It usually consists of a closing paragraph or two at the end of a section, summarizing that section, telling the reader what will be in the next section and explaining how the previous section leads on to the next section. A signpost is a piece of text flagging (i.e. indicating) something which will be mentioned later.

At this level, you should be making extensive use of journals as your main source of information. Although textbooks and the internet are useful starting places, they are usually not appropriate as main sources of information because they tend to present simplified accounts. (There's a big difference between textbooks and specialist books on a topic; specialist books are at least as appropriate as journal articles in most fields.)

Using material from the literature

You will never lose by giving credit. Indeed, you are likely to gain respect and trust by doing so fastidiously. Doing so shows not just that you behave with integrity, but also that your reading is broad and that you are clever enough to gather and synthesize information from a variety of sources.

Plagiarism

The interpretation of what constitutes plagiarism is subject to cultural variation. To avoid errors of interpretation it's worth adopting the strictest, which happens to be the interpretation used by academic journals and publishers in the UK, US and western Europe. Plagiarism is using someone else's ideas, words or material – directly or indirectly – without giving them credit. The rules are very clear.

- Any time you use ideas, words or material of any sort that relates to a specific source, you *must* attribute it to that source. Paraphrasing (restating) still requires explicit attribution.
- Any time you use someone else's words *verbatim*, you must put them in quotation marks and attribute them to that person.

Let's be absolutely clear. Plagiarism is academic suicide. In British academia, plagiarism is a 'mortal sin'. If your dissertation plagiarizes, *you will fail*. If you submit work for publication that plagiarizes, your work will be rejected and *you will be blacklisted*. So, if in doubt, attribute.

Incomplete or non-existent references: why they are sinful

Many – perhaps most – researchers have had the experience of stumbling quite by chance across a description of a piece of work in an unrelated discipline which has enormous implications for their own work. That has happened to us. If that happens, it is enormously frustrating to have to spend months or years trying to track down the relevant article because the person who mentioned it does not give an adequate reference. That has also happened to us.

Conversely, if you're a PhD examiner and you see that a substantial part of the candidate's thesis is based on a dodgy-looking claim without proper supporting references, one of the first things you will do is to question them in detail about the references behind that claim. An answer of 'I saw it in a book somewhere: trust me' is unlikely to lead to a happy ending.

References are functional, not decorative; good referencing is a sign of a good researcher.

Keeping an annotated bibliography

Part of doctoral study is acquiring one's own core repertoire. The annotated bibliography is an effective mechanism for facilitating this acquisition – and for keeping a record of the majority of papers that fall outside the core. The annotated bibliography is a powerful research tool. It should be a personal tool, keying into the way you think about and classify things.

What the annotated bibliography should include

It *should* include, as a minimum:

- The usual bibliographic information (i.e. everything you might need to cite the work and find it again).
- The date when you read the work.
- Notes on what *you* found interesting/seminal/infuriating/etc. about it. The notes should not just be a copy of the abstract; they should reflect your own critical thinking about your reading. They can be informal, ungrammatical, even inflammatory, as long as they retain meaning about your reading. If you read a paper more than once and get different things from it, then add to the notes – but do keep the original notes, which can prove useful even if you've changed perspective or opinion.

It *can* include many other useful things, such as:

- Location of the physical copy of the work is (e.g. photocopied paper, book borrowed from the library, book in one's own collection)
- Keywords, possibly different categories of keyword
- Further references to follow up
- How you found the work (e.g. who recommended it, who cited it)
- Pointers to other work to which it relates
- The author's abstract

The discipline

Keeping an annotated bibliography is a discipline. It is easiest to establish a discipline of writing notes about papers as soon as you read them and not going on to the next paper until you have done so. It's *much harder* to go back and try to catch up. Because keeping the bibliography is an 'overhead', and because the point is to maintain access to material, it's best to keep entries to under a page per paper.

Never delete things from the bibliography. 'Discards' can be re-categorized or filed away separately, but one year's 'junk' may be another year's 'gem' (and vice versa). There is also genuine value in keeping track of the changes in categorization: one way is to keep a list of working category 'definitions'. Don't discard the old scheme after a revamp; rather, file it as part of the record.

The discipline is to keep up a continual, accumulating record of your reading and thinking.

Other ways the bibliography can help

- It can help you to 'backtrack' on your own thinking
- It will reflect the evolution of your reading, of what you found important over time, and of your writing about what you read

- When you find a reference and can't remember the paper's particular perspective, the notes can give you the key
- When you re-read a paper just before your viva and say: 'Oh no, it doesn't say that at all, what could I have been thinking?' then the notes will be invaluable

The bibliography can help you to manage your reading effectively and keep accessible much more information than you can remember without aid. Always remember:

- Keeping a bibliography allows you to use a 'flat', unambiguous physical filing system (e.g. alphabetical by author) while being able to categorize, re-categorize and search fluidly
- The bibliography can help you avoid re-reading papers that are useless and forgettable but have interesting titles
- The bibliography can help you keep track of the physical form and location of materials

Mechanisms

There are different ways to keep a bibliography. The most common forms are card catalogues and electronic databases. Contrary to what many students believe, card catalogues are not an outdated relic of the past; there are a lot of things you can do with card catalogues which you can't do with an electronic database (for instance, spreading the cards into clusters on a flat surface to look for trends and patterns in the literature). You need to find the method that works for you; asking advice from experienced researchers can provide invaluable ideas. Examples of bibliographic software packages include:

EndNote: www.niles.com
Reference Manager: www.risinc.com
Zotera: www.zotera.org

Many people don't use specialist packages, preferring to adapt database, spreadsheet or word-processor usage. Many effective bibliographies are simply kept as very long text files.

That concludes this chapter on reading. A closing thought is that reading should be a source of pleasure to you, at least some of the time; if it isn't, it's worth asking yourself whether it's time to look for something outside academia as a career. Many students, though, feel guilty about reading for pleasure. It's worth remembering that there's usually no way of knowing in advance what will turn out to be useful reading, and what won't; unexpected discoveries in apparently unrelated literatures are a common feature in top-level research. So, read, read well and read happily.

Table 6.2 Reading habits of lifelong readers

- Steady consumption. The idea is not so much to read voraciously as to read regularly. Use a tortoise strategy, rather than a hare.
- Always carry reading with you – use the ten minutes on the train platform, or while you're waiting for your supervisor, or between seminars, or while dinner is cooking.
- Leave papers lying around where you're likely to pick them up and read them – in the bathroom, for some people, or the bedroom for others, or by an easy chair, or in your bag to read on the train.
- Keep an annotated bibliography – and keep it up to date.
- Find a regular reading time, about an hour a day. For many, this is first thing in the morning. Don't go straight to your office; go to the library first for your hour.
- Read books as well as papers; learn about the different types of books.
- Most great readers are a little obsessive and like to get a sense of 'completeness' when they're reading on a new subject. Many 'map' the key writers.
- Make sure all your photocopies of papers and your records of references have full citations on them, down to the ISSN or ISBN and page numbers – some publication venues require all of this, and having to track the full details down because you didn't record them the first time can be a real pain.
- Most great readers maintain more than one reading strand – so morning time may be technical reading, but bedtime is philosophy reading.
- Read a chapter every night before you sleep, no matter how tired you are.
- At conferences, carry the proceedings to the sessions with you and annotate the paper with your notes during the talk.
- Even when you find a paper uninteresting, cast your eye over the remainder, so that you have a portrait of the contents.
- Use your network to filter your reading, hence increasing the interest level of what you pick up.
- Join (or form) a reading group, or find a reading buddy.
- From Feynman (as recalled by Michael Jackson): when reading something difficult, if you get stuck reading something, start again from the beginning (this allows you to rehearse the early sections, correct misunderstandings that accumulate and benefit from elapsed time).
- Elapsed time can help: skim-read the material, then set it aside briefly before coming back to read it thoroughly.

7

Paper types

*Data-driven papers • Methods papers • Theoretical papers •
Consciousness-raising papers • Agenda-setting papers • Review papers •
Position papers • Conclusion*

Alien it indeed was to all art and literature which sane and balanced readers know . . .[1]

Why have we bothered to include an entire chapter on paper types? One reason is that becoming an expert in any field involves learning all about the tools of your trade – for instance, learning the difference between a tenon saw and a fret saw. Why do you need to know the tools of your trade? Because you can do things with the right specialist tool that would be difficult or impossible otherwise. What can you do if you know about different types of paper? That's what this chapter is about: for instance, when you can get a paper published in a good journal with a tiny data set, and when you can't, or what type of research you would need to do to get a paper published in a particular journal as part of your career plan. So, on to the categories.

Academic writing is not just an intellectual activity, but also a social one. It's about making your research available for scrutiny, critique – and use. Making a 'contribution to knowledge' entails communicating advances to the community of researchers, the ones you hope will read your papers. All academic writing requires certain ingredients:

• Context/situation

[1] Lovecraft, H.P. (1922) The Hound, in *Omnibus 2: Dagon and Other Macabre Tales* (1985). London: Grafton Books, p. 200.

- Justification of the content
- Substantiation of claims (evidence of rigour)
- A 'coherent and explicit chain of reasoning': appropriate structure, clear argument, a coherent overall vision
- Discussion of implications

Each type of writing has, in addition, a particular purpose and a particular social context – an intended audience. The purpose and content of a paper will determine what type of paper it is. The publication forum and intended audience will influence how long it is, what voice it should have and what elements should be prioritized.

There are different ways of categorizing papers. These ways are seldom described in writing; they are usually treated as craft skills, and also as a matter of personal choice. The categorization described here is a fairly standard one, and some of the paper types in it are recognized fairly formally (for instance, journals have an explicit category of 'review article'). Others, such as 'method-mongering paper', are less formal.

Data-driven papers

This is what most people tend to think of when thinking about papers. The data-driven paper reports on some form of empirical study, describing the study but concentrating on presenting and discussing the data (as opposed to the methods used to gather the data, for instance). The purpose of data-driven papers is to publicize the study and its finding (and ideally to provide sufficient information for replication and critique). Classic examples include survey reports, experiment reports, reports of benchmarking exercises that compare the performance of different systems on given tasks, reports of other sorts of empirical studies, such as observations and interviews, evaluations and case studies. The key ingredients of data-driven papers are: what question is addressed and why (and its theoretical context); a description of the study design, implementation and conduct (including justification, protocol, etc. – notionally in enough detail to allow another researcher to repeat the study); the results (data collected, analysis, findings); and a discussion (significance, limitations, claims to generalization, implications, further work).

Data-driven papers are important for several reasons, and the astute researcher using the 'cabinet-making apprentice' model of research will take care to have at least one data-driven study in their portfolio, if only to demonstrate that they know how to do them.

If the central focus of a paper is the data, then the data need to be good. This means (a) solid and also (b) interesting. 'Solid' means that the sample size, quality, representativeness, etc. need to be at a level where nobody sensible will even think of questioning them. Novice (and, often, less novice) researchers tend to spend a lot of time worrying about their sample size, on the grounds that more must be better. They also spend quite a lot of time worrying about representativeness, because representativeness is something they feel comfortable speculating about – anyone with an armchair and reasonable general knowledge can usually find several reasons for querying the representativeness of a sample without much effort. These scruples tend to be slaughtered on the altar of expediency the moment that the questionnaires go into the post (questionnaires are a favourite method for collecting large and dubious data sets). If you're doing this sort of work, you need to know about statistics. Unfortunately, novice researchers tend to spend less time considering the quality of their data (lest they talk themselves out of publishing at all).

The need for interesting data somehow tends to receive less attention among novices, though experts are well aware of it. This is probably because novices do not usually give much thought to what will be in their data until the questionnaires arrive in the post (again, questionnaires are a favoured tool for bad research in this area), and then fade out of public view when the full banality of their results becomes apparent. A more experienced researcher will probably take the view that the best way of conducting a fishing expedition is shooting the fish in a barrel (i.e. only doing a large data-gathering exercise when there is an extremely good chance that the data will produce an eye-catching result).

What catches attention is normally a surprising and useful finding, based on a sample so solid that the data can be treated as a safe foundation for further work. An example of this from computer science is the '5000-year fault' – i.e. the bug which might only be expected to materialize once every 5000 user-years of use. The classic paper on this topic used a very large data set to show what proportion of bugs could be expected to surface with what frequency, and showed that a surprisingly high proportion might only appear once every few thousand years. This has profound implications for the software industry, in areas such as debugging and the development of ultrasafe systems for safety-critical areas such as software for controlling nuclear power plants. An added attraction for the researcher who publishes such work is that it will be quoted in just about every subsequent paper on the topic, thereby boosting the researcher's reputation considerably.

How do you know when you're dealing with fish in a barrel (and therefore a suitable area for a big study) as opposed to an empty pond? This is where a good understanding of theory is useful, because it can lead you to predict a counter-intuitive finding. Another useful approach which complements theory is keeping an eye open for interesting effects while carrying out other research.

A classic data-driven paper can make a reputation. Most data-driven papers, however, do not break new ground; you need to have solid, interesting data to make a reputation from this type of publication. Or you need a series of solid, interesting data-driven papers that accumulate into a coherent body of work.

There are a number of variations on data-driven papers.

- **Meta-study papers:** data-driven papers also include meta-studies, which compile and analyse the data from a number of sources such as previously individually published empirical studies. Key ingredients are: a clearly-stated purpose; a selection of appropriate and well-understood source material (accurately cited); a clearly stated basis of analysis; and a good discussion.
- **Artefact papers:** the purpose of the artefact paper is to publicize the new artefact (tool, system, pedagogy, instrument, whatever) and to provide sufficient information for critique and application. Its key ingredients are: what it is (a thorough description); what gap the artefact fills (precursors, theoretical context if any, purpose); why it's novel; what key design ideas or innovations it embodies; evaluation (evidence of its effectiveness for its purpose); and where it leads.
- **Work-in-progress papers:** the work-in-progress paper is about 'making a stake' or 'marking a territory' by publishing a key idea or approach and having it associated with your name. It's a form of premature commitment, with publication preceding much of the research and most of the evidence, but it can involve you in early discussions in a new field. The key ingredients are: a strong idea; clarity about where the idea fits in the 'territory' and how it's distinguished; and speculation about its implications (if it works). It helps if there's also a description of the research programme and a demonstration of concept, but papers get published without them.

Methods papers

Methods papers describe a new method, technique, algorithm or process (or a new variant of any of these) to a given community for a specified usage. Good methods papers describe the method and explain how to use it in sufficient detail for a reader to apply. So the key ingredients are: what it is; how it works; what it's good for – both its utility and what distinguishes it from other related methods; and a discussion of any constraints on its use (e.g. level of resolution, conventions of use, limitations, costs). There are different subtypes of methods papers.

- **Method introductions:** these describe a new method, invented or developed by the author(s). Because the method is new, the justification is particularly important: the authors have to make the case for why the method is needed, what it's good for, how it's distinguished from other existing methods and how the authors know it works. Sometimes the authors are so busy justifying the method that they neglect to describe it fully, and readers are tantalized by the potential without the wherewithal to realize it themselves.

- **Tutorial papers:** these describe a method and explain how to use it. The method may not be original – it may be the full elaboration of a method introduced elsewhere, even by other authors. Good tutorial papers typically include worked examples. Such papers are invaluable, but journals are not fond of publishing them on the grounds that they do not normally involve original research, which is what journals are all about. However, if you do manage to publish the classic tutorial paper for a method, then people will quote it for years to come.
- **Method-mongering papers:** these describe a method with the aim of suggesting that it should be more widely used. The method may be original (i.e. developed by the authors) or may be an established method from another field which has not received sufficient attention in the field for which it is now being described. It is possible for a paper to be a method-mongering paper without being a tutorial paper. A common example of this is a paper which shows how a method can be applied to problems in the researcher's field, but which does not describe the method itself in great detail – instead, the author typically refers the reader to a suitable tutorial paper or textbook. One advantage of method-mongering papers is that if you are already familiar with a suitable method from another field, then you can put together a method-mongering paper fairly easily; all you will need are some nice examples of your method-cracking problems, traditionally viewed as difficult in the new field of application. You don't normally need a large sample size, since the point is made just as effectively with a small sample (or even a single example, if it's a good one).
- **Demonstration of concept papers:** these involve demonstrating that a particular concept (usually a method, but not always – it may, for instance, be a conceptual framework) is feasible, useful and interesting. This is a handy precursor to applying for funding. If you know what you're doing, you can get away with a single set of data from a single subject for a demonstration of concept paper. The tricky bit is finding a suitable concept in the first place . . .

Theoretical papers

Theoretical papers have a lot of kudos. The discuss theory from a variety of perspectives:

- Introducing new theory
- Explaining someone else's theory so that it makes sense
- Refining or extending existing theory
- Critiquing or debunking existing theory
- Setting the agenda for needed new theory (without actually proposing that new theory)

Or they may stop short of theory *per se* and offer theoretical constructs such as models, concepts or conceptual frameworks. The key ingredients are the theoretical insight and the argument that presents and justifies it.

Theoretical papers can also discuss theoretical issues such as the inherent limitations of symbolic reasoning, and can be highly influential. The published papers of this type are typically written by authorities in the area, and actually have quite a large component of review and methodology in them (it's difficult to tackle advanced theory properly without considerable reference to the literature and to the methods used in the area). The unpublished papers of this type are typically written by inexperienced new researchers who have not bothered to do the research equivalent of reading the FAQs first. It's advisable not to try writing theoretical papers until you're sure you're ready for the task and have evidence to support this belief.

Consciousness-raising papers

These are less psychedelic than they sound. They are intended to raise awareness of issues which have not previously received sufficient attention in a field of research; these issues often involve application of methods or concepts which are standard in another field, but not well known in the field where the consciousness-raising paper is written.

Good consciousness-raising papers can attract a lot of attention, and can change the viewpoint of an entire field. Bad ones can give the author a reputation as a pompous windbag. As usual in research, one of the touchstones is whether you're giving the reader some really interesting new tools to play with. Saying that (for instance) the methods of the physical sciences are not always directly applicable to the social sciences may well be true, but it doesn't really get us anywhere. Saying that (for instance) game theory can be used to provide a mathematical grounding for evolutionary ecology is the research equivalent of giving a small child the keys to a toy warehouse, and made John Maynard Smith the revered founding father of an entire new field of research.

A related type of paper is perspective papers, which are, at best, interesting or provocative essays about a topical topic. They present and justify a view of the topic, contrasting it to other perspectives. The key ingredients for both consciousness-raising and perspective papers are the same: a strong idea; a strong, rich argument, showing not just what the perspective is but also how it affects research and understanding; weight of experience, sufficient to provide a rich context for and instantiation of the perspective; and speculation about implications.

First-year students are fond of complaining that their field neglects various important issues. They are usually less fond of checking whether this is a standard complaint of first-year students and whether there is a good reason for these issues being neglected. Experienced researchers (a) have heard a lot of first-year students talking and (b) have reliable chums who can be used to see whether a promising idea will pass the giggle test or not, before going any further with it.

Agenda-setting papers

Related to consciousness-raising papers are agenda-setting papers, which are about pointing out new directions, mapping out journeys and generally playing navigator for a research community. There are two broad types of agenda-setting paper: stolid ones written by committees (the only sort in which it's acceptable to state the obvious) and visionary ones written by individuals. If the agenda is one to which enough of the community subscribes (or alternatively is the sort of 'straw man' a community can revel in disparaging), the agenda-setting paper is likely to be cited heavily.

Good visionary agenda-setting papers require (a) vision and (b) genuine authority, based in a comprehensive, up-to-the-minute knowledge of the field, a critical creative turn of mind and powerful insight into how fields develop. It really helps if the author also has a substantial reputation, lest the readers wonder 'Who is so-and-so, to set the agenda for us?' But it's not necessary, and an influential agenda-setting paper can gild an established reputation or create one for a bold and inspired young researcher.

Review papers

Thucydides would have approved of review papers. Every ten years or so, someone in a given field will decide that the time is right for a paper surveying the key research in that field since the last review paper was written. They will then survey all the main papers, and many of the minor papers, written over that period. This is a very substantial undertaking and can easily involve reading and assessing hundreds of papers and books, in addition to identifying and summarizing the main themes within that work.

Review papers are invaluable for ordinary mortals, since they provide an excellent way into a body of research, complete with overviews and key readings. But good review papers are more than just annotated bibliographies. They 'add value' to the reviewed literature by organizing it, either revealing the underlying structure or bringing structure to it, and by considering it critically and systematically. A few review papers take a particular, stated perspective. The key ingredients for a review paper are: specification of the focal topic; identification and description of the main strands of thinking (perspectives, approaches) and theory; honest, competent paraphrasing of seminal papers; genealogies of ideas (where they started, how they propagated and were developed); and of course comprehensive references.

Review papers are typically written by people so utterly familiar with a field that they will have read all the relevant papers anyway (and will probably have written quite a few of them as well). However, there is one useful exception to this generalization: if you have done the literature review for your PhD properly, then it should (pretty much by definition) provide the basis for a good review paper. However, there is a crucial difference between a review paper and the literature review in a dissertation: the former is a general, balanced overview of a field; the latter is a focused review whose purpose is to set the context for a particular programme of research. Therefore, although the reporting should be accurate in either case, the editorial and prioritization choices for the two reviews may be quite different. In practice, most people by this stage of their PhD are so sick of the topic and/or scared of being told that they've missed something vital that they find reasons not to go down the review paper road.

Position papers

Position papers are not so much about presenting research as presenting researchers. They usually arise in connection with a workshop or event, for which the organizers wish to assemble an interesting group of participants, and so they are always targeted to the event. The trick to position papers is distinctiveness; they are about portraying yourself as being interesting and having something to contribute. The key ingredients are: credentials (why I'm worth listening to); expression of interest (why I want to participate in the event); and position (what I can offer, and why I'm interesting). The trick is to express personality without excluding yourself. Position papers may include information about research, but usually in summary form, in the service of establishing the distinctive contribution the author makes to the community.

Conclusion

Looking at these categories, you should be able to map your existing and intended research onto different paper types. If your research involves importing an established method from one field into a field where that method isn't established, then you're in a good position to write a method-mongering paper about it (or several other types of paper) and will only need a small data set to illustrate your point. If you've just finished the literature review for your PhD, you may be in a position to write a review article, which will look very different from a method-mongering paper, and which probably won't use any data at all, other than the articles being reviewed. If you're trying to test the evidence relating to an evidence-based issue, you'll need to aim for a data-driven paper, with as large a data set as it takes (which may be very large). You may well be able to get two or more different papers out of the same piece of research, with each one focusing on a different aspect of the research.

So, different types of paper are useful for different purposes; you may find it a useful exercise, whenever you plan a piece of research, to ask yourself what type(s) of paper you intend to get out of it. That's it for papers; on to the next topic.

8

Research design

Designing empirical studies: three key steps • Types of research and research focus: machetes and magnifying glasses • Ethics • Tales of horror and how to avoid them • The three ignoble truths (with apologies to the three noble truths)

> *I have brought to light a monstrous abnormality, but I did it for the sake of knowledge.* [1]

Research design is a topic which requires a book in its own right. Excellent books exist on this subject, and we suggest that you read several. This chapter doesn't pretend to cover research design in detail. Instead, it offers an overview of the nature of the research endeavour and concentrates on the thinking and planning that precedes the choice of research methods.

Research involves finding something new. 'New' may mean 'new to everyone', or it may simply mean 'new to you'. That's a major distinction, and one which leads to a lot of misunderstandings. 'New to everyone' is known as primary research, and is what you need in order to earn a PhD. 'New to you (but not to everyone)' is a form of secondary research, and is what you need to do in order to know enough to do the primary research you need in order to earn the PhD. Secondary research traditionally involves a lot of time in libraries, though now it's increasingly likely to involve a lot of time on the internet. Secondary research is important when you're doing the preparatory work before some primary research, since it vastly reduces the risk that you will simply reinvent the wheel through not knowing what has been done before.

---

[1] Lovecraft, H.P. (1943) The Case of Charles Dexter Ward, in *Omnibus 1: At the Mountains of Madness* (1989). London: Grafton Books, p. 236.

Again, the importance of the secondary research is pretty specific to the one doing the preparatory work, and the secondary research doesn't take on wider importance until the primary research is realized.

Although secondary research is very useful for numerous purposes, it doesn't usually lead to breakthroughs in human knowledge (for instance, discovering the cause of diabetes or finding a better way of teaching people with dyslexia). So, although secondary research is useful, it's usually primary research that answers the important questions, the ones that other people also want answered. There are, of course, exceptions, for example meta-studies that reassess the data from a (large) number of studies, often from a number of sources, in order to address research questions across the collection. Sometimes such meta-studies can make breakthroughs, perhaps by identifying an overlooked factor or an unnoticed assumption. For example, in 2001 Ben Oppenheimer and colleagues identified white dwarf stars, the first direct evidence for dark matter, from a collection of data that had been lying around for between 6 and 30 years.

Designing empirical studies: three key steps [2]

1 What's the question?

Probably the most thought-intensive step in study design is deciding what the question is. Questions come from lots of places: theory, observation, prior work, problems in the world, gaps in the literature . . . but formulating the right sorts of questions takes thought. Bad research questions are a common cause of (at best) wasted time and (at worst) failed research, or (occasionally) of tragedy when a mistaken result is used for public policy-making. A good research question reduces the problem space in an area. This means that the answer, whatever it is, eliminates one set of plausible possibilities. The next research question will then further reduce the problem space, and so on, until there is only one sensible explanation for the problem which corresponds with the facts. Good examples of this approach can be found in the history of medicine – for instance, Pasteur successively eliminating possible answers for the cause of decay in foodstuffs. In order to ask the right research question, you need to identify what is important for you to know, out of what might be known. This typically involves remembering whatever motivated you to ask the question in the first place. You also need to assess whether what you want to know is something that you can reasonably – and feasibly – study within your available (or acquirable) resources: time, materials, instruments and so

[2] This section draws on material introduced and rehearsed in a variety of teaching contexts and presented in a different form in Fincher, S. and Petre, M. (eds) (2004) *Computer Science Education Research*. London: RoutledgeFalmer. Used with permission.

on. Resolving the question into something you can address often involves breaking it down into smaller, more tractable questions, and choosing one of those. There are a number of tips on finding questions in Table 8.1 at the end of the chapter.

2 What evidence will answer the question?

The second step is deciding what sort of evidence will satisfy you in addressing the question (if not answering it). It's also important to identify who else you're trying to satisfy. Your supervisor, a reasonable, sympathetic colleague or a sceptical competing researcher might have very different criteria for what evidence would be convincing, so you need to consider evidence from different viewpoints. What would a sufficient answer look like? What evidence would be 'good enough' to underpin that sufficient answer? Answering this requires that you consider how the phenomenon of interest is manifest: how it is observable (directly or indirectly) in the world. This allows you to phrase your question in terms of things you can observe directly – in other words, to 'operationalize' your question. In order to consider what evidence might be 'good enough', you need to assess different types of evidence in terms of which is stronger or weaker in the context of what it is important for you to know. How strong must the evidence be to serve your purpose?

One way to approach this is to consider what kind of evidence made you think the question was worth asking in the first place: both why that evidence (be it introspection, anecdote, a line of discussion in the literature) was enough to make you ask, and what was missing from that evidence in providing an answer. Another approach is to consider what sort of answer would *not* be sufficient – what would a 'non-answer' look like? Thinking about what an answer *isn't* is a way of eliciting requirements for what it should be, thereby clarifying the evidence requirements. Thinking about what sorts of answers would be inadequate can also help in distinguishing between the question you're interested in and related questions. A third approach is to consider the counter-evidence. People tend to seek confirmatory evidence, to prioritize evidence consistent with what they believe to be true. But often insight lies in the 'surprises', the unexpected, the contradictions. Considering the nature of counter-examples, contradictions, exceptions and other forms of counter-evidence can be a way of reflecting on the question (and of exposing inadequacies in the way you've been thinking about the question and formulating it).

3 Choose a technique that will produce the required evidence

Choosing the means comes last, after sorting out what you want to know and what it means to know it. Choosing the methods or techniques follows from the question and from what evidence you need to address the question. This is true whether your research is theory-driven or inductive. The techniques for eliciting beliefs from decision-makers are quite different from the techniques for measuring the physical properties of materials – choosing appropriate techniques requires a clear understanding of what kind of phenomenon is being captured and what the available techniques can and cannot deliver. One handy tip is to look for stories about previous projects which answered the sort of question that you want to answer. They're likely to give you some useful ideas about how to go about answering your question.

What about methodology? Many disciplines (especially long-established ones with an accepted theory base) have widely-accepted methodologies – specific aggregations of methods or techniques that might be termed 'approaches to investigation'. In such disciplines, researchers have consolidated a substantial body of knowledge and evidence, and on this basis they know what sorts of questions they wish to ask. Over time they have associated specific suites of methods with questions of particular sorts. The questions are usually tied closely to existing theory and relate to a substantial body of existing evidence.

Methodologies offer certain advantages – for example, allowing researchers to compare and contrast results. They can also have certain disadvantages in that the methodology can become a sort of lens through which researchers view the world – and not everything will be within focal range. The availability of an accepted methodology does not absolve good researchers from justifying the choice of technique in terms of the evidence required, nor from considering the relationship between question and evidence requirements. Blind adherence to methodology can lead to all sorts of embarrassing slips.

Researchers who choose the means first are starting from the wrong place, because they've chosen an answer before they've really considered what the question is. Sometimes starting from the wrong place reveals a weak understanding of the process of research. For example, starting by asking 'How can I design an experiment in order to prove X?' suggests that the researcher doesn't understand the role of experiments; they're seeking proof, when experiments can only disprove. Even well-established methods are of little utility if they address the wrong question – for example, it's difficult to design an experiment well if the question is not precise and focused, or if the key variables are not understood.

Of course, the 1–2–3 scheme is a simplification (most models are). The three steps are not strictly discrete: working out what the question is usually requires thinking about evidence, which entails thinking about what can be observed, what data might be gathered and how it might be analysed. In practice, the design of empirical studies is a highly iterative process that cycles through question, evidence, techniques and analysis repeatedly.

And, of course, there are times when circumstances shape decisions – for example, when a fixed-term opportunity demands action before adequate planning is possible or when a naturally-occurring set of data is on offer: 'have data set, will analyse'. Of course, we respond to pragmatic constraints and opportunities that are 'too good to miss', but planning a study before the question comes into focus is a dangerous step, even if it is sometimes warranted.

What end is implied?

One way to think about how to begin is to consider where you intend to end. What's the destination? And how will you know when you've arrived? What suitable evidence looks like depends on the type of question that you're trying to answer. Thinking backwards from the goal is a powerful planning tool. For example, what might the results of a given study look like and how might they be reported? What might the data look like and how might it be analysed? Imagine that you've been wrestling with the 'nature-nurture' debate concerning how much of human behaviour is determined by genetics and how much by environment; imagine further that through brilliant research you have found the answer, and that the proportions are 42 per cent and 58 per cent respectively. Once you've finished celebrating, what can you do with that information? Come to that, what exactly does that information mean? Phrased this way, it's not exactly a very helpful answer, and you start realizing that it would be better to have started from a more useful phrasing of the question.

Connected questions are 'What is the end?' and 'What will I do with the answer if I get it?' We call this the 'So what?' step. It's not enough to ask the question you start with, you also need the question that comes next, to consider the implications and utility of the possible outcomes of your question. So what if the results are as I predict? So what if they're not? Asking 'So what?' helps you to consider the question in terms of what an answer might contribute to the discourse, not just in its own terms.

A useful strategy is to draw the question as a box, and draw a line out of it for each of the logically possible answers. Beside each answer, you should be able to write:

- 'This answer is interesting because . . .'
- What you will do as a result of this answer
- Why this answer would usefully reduce the problem space
- What the practical implications would be (very useful if you're looking for funding)

If you can't do this for one or more of the answers, then you're gambling time, effort and reputation. Even if you're lucky, it will be clear from your research design that you've asked a flawed question and made a lucky guess. Examiners view such sins in much the same way as driving inspectors view learners who overtake on blind bends on the hunch that there's nothing coming: you may be lucky on one particular occasion but nobody in their senses is going to give you a driving licence.

Thinking about the destination should help you to establish the following.

- The importance of the question (why is it worth answering?)
- The likely significance of the findings (what you'd know as a result, what the findings would let you do next, what practical implications they have)

- The implications for theory (how the findings relate to available explanations and predictions)
- The limitations to generalization (whether or not your conclusions are likely to apply to other data)

These considerations distinguish questions worth asking. By now you should realize that research quality is often founded not in what the answer is, but in what the question is.

The value of evidence

Doing good research and designing good studies relies on knowing the value of evidence. Theories are supported or contradicted on the basis of evidence. It's not simply a matter of 'more' evidence rather than 'less', or 'good' evidence rather than 'bad'. It's a matter of whether the evidence is sufficiently sound and convincing for its purpose, a matter of understanding enough about evidence to be able to assess whether it is 'strong' or 'weak', and hence to determine how much you're willing to rely on it. Designing research well entails producing evidence that is 'fit for purpose'.

Evidence is not proof. In general, it is whatever empirical data is sufficient to cause us to conclude that one account is probably more true than not, or is probably more true than another.

One thing to keep firmly in mind when doing research is that you're not looking for evidence to support your hunch. A classic error is to set out to prove something rather than to investigate something. What you're doing is looking for evidence which will answer your question one way or the other. The trouble with reality is that it tends to make much better sense with hindsight than with foresight, so nailing your colours to a hunch is a recipe for ending up sooner or later being publicly wrong. Good research is about asking good questions, not about gambling on what the answers might be.

'Fitness for purpose' and the notion of sufficiency are clearly different from a 'one size fits all' notion of evidence. They suggest that different standards of evidence apply for different purposes. Some purposes need strong evidence. For example, deciding whether light therapy reverses Alzheimer's symptoms would demand compelling evidence of efficacy. Some purposes need only weak evidence. For example, a 'demonstration of concept' might only need evidence that something can be done, leaving clarification about how well the goal is accomplished to further research. An evaluation study whose goal is to identify deficiencies in a design may only require responses from a handful of participants. Some purposes need only counter-examples. For example, when one is trying to dispute an assumption or a universal claim, one only needs a single counter-example. The historic example is the one 'black swan' discovered in the eighteenth century that contradicted the until-then-universal claim that 'All swans are white'.

We need to assess the nature and quality of the evidence: how reliable the evidence is likely to be (will repetition by different researchers, at different times, with a different sample of the same population, produce consistent results?), and how robust (will repetition across different related tasks, or across different environments or contexts, produce comparable results?). We need to understand not just the value of different forms of evidence, but also how different forms compare and how they might fit together. In the same way that we report the standard deviation associated with a mean, we must report the uncertainty and error associated with evidence – hence enabling assessment of its fitness for purpose.

Pilot studies

Pilot studies are the first defence against oversight (or stupidity) and the bias it may invite. A good pilot study is practical; it lets you work out the bugs. It provides a chance to test the feasibility of the protocol, to practise the procedures and actually use the equipment, to check the timing, to expose disparities in interpretation (particularly those between the researcher and the participants), and importantly to try out the analysis on genuine data. It can expose design flaws, hidden assumptions and unexpected problems – and generally spare you pain and embarrassment downstream.

If a pilot study is really going to do all that, then it has to try out every aspect of the main study. It must be a genuine 'dress rehearsal'. It must use the full protocol, the actual instruments and materials, and participants who are representative of the target population (not students standing in for experts, or car mechanics standing in for rocket scientists). The protocol (the specification of procedures, instruments and materials of data collection and analysis) must be tried out, debugged and tried out again until it is clear that the protocol will work as intended and that it will generate data which will be pertinent and can be analysed usefully.

It is also crucial to pilot the analysis; what goes wrong with an analysis can reveal fundamental shortcomings in the study design. For example, the data collection may fail to meet the prerequisites of the proposed statistical tests. It's better to spot problems early than to collect inadequate or irrelevant data.

It's true that pilot studies are expensive of time and resources, but the consequences of omitting them are likely to be even more expensive. Many students don't see the point – until it's too late and their study has gone hideously wrong. In that sense, conducting pilot studies is like investing in a smoke detector: an annoying expense, but one that can avert catastrophe.

Types of research and research focus: machetes and magnifying glasses [3]

So, research is about exploration in the pursuit of knowledge. In the Old Days, the first stage of exploration would often involve explorers with machetes hacking their way through dense undergrowth, notebook and pencil in pocket. The result of this would typically be a set of sketch maps drawn from whatever vantage points were available. Some of the information would be quantitative, involving measurement – 'about five leagues wide' or 'too deep to wade across'. Some would be qualitative, involving the types of thing present: 'dense jungle' or 'range of hills' or 'here be dragons'. The maps would be imperfect and incomplete, but at least they'd give you some idea of what was over the horizon, and of whether you'd found a modest island or a mighty continent. Subsequent explorers would fill in the gaps with some basic surveying tools and produce moderately accurate maps; if someone decided to build a town or stake mining claims, then they would bring in theodolites and measuring chains, producing extremely precise maps.

It's similar in research. Someone discovers a new area of research, and hacks around in its undergrowth for a while, armed with the equivalent of a machete, a notebook and a sweaty shirt. This might translate into participant observation or unstructured interviews in some disciplines, or digging a trial trench in others. The purpose of this machete stage is understanding the basic layout and geography: assessing the lie of the land. The questions at this stage tend to concern what's there.

If the area looks interesting enough, then a fresh batch of researchers arrive, with tools that will give more accurate results, perhaps via field experiments. The purpose of this chains and compass stage is beginning to map the land more precisely, to capture it in a regular model or map, with specified dimensions and relations. The questions at this stage are concerned with what exactly is observable, but also how the land is configured and why that structure results in swamps in the south.

If it's really interesting, then the equivalent of theodolites will appear, in the form of controlled experiments. The purpose of the theodolite stage is to address very precise questions that arise from the model, and to use precise observation to eliminate any sloppiness or misconception arising from earlier, less precise assays. The questions at this stage are concerned with working out which bits of the map are wrong.

This recalls a quotation from Sir Eric Ashby, to the effect that, although we like to think about research in terms of great cartographic expeditions hacking our way through the jungle with machetes, more often 'research is crawling

---

[3] This section is quoted from Rugg, G. and Petre, M. (2007) *A Gentle Guide to Research Methods*. Maidenhead: Open University Press, pp. 33–6. Used with permission.

along the frontiers of knowledge with a hand lens. The vast majority of research activity concerns questions of minute precision, the sort of detail that hones theory and drives controlled experimentation. Measured precision is what characterizes the Ordnance Survey map and distinguishes it from the swiftly hand-rendered sketch in the field notebook. Each map has its time, its purpose and its place in the process.

Why, you might wonder, don't people start with controlled experiments and cut out the preliminaries? For the same reason that you don't begin exploration with theodolites and measuring chains: these are comparatively slow, and you need to decide whether it's worth investing time and effort in getting so much detail about a small part of the terrain when you don't even know what's over the next hill. The machete and notebook may be imprecise, but they give you a pretty good overall idea of the big picture fairly fast, which then allows you to decide which places merit more detailed investigation.

Within primary research, there are various types of research, such as case studies, field experiments and formal experiments. Most students get lost in the big picture of this, which is why we're having a go at it here. The next sections look at types of research ranging from the equivalent of machete-and-notebook exploration through to millimetrically-accurate surveys with theodolites and measuring chains.

Describing things: what are the entities?

When you're Out There with your machete in your hand and your note-book in your bag, trying to make sense of the surroundings, one of the first things you need to decide is what categories to lump things into in your sketch maps. Some are pretty easy – rivers and mountains are pretty much the same wherever you are, for instance. Others are more difficult. 'Forest' might at first sight appear an easy one, but it isn't: European forests are very different from tropical rain forests and from cloud forests, for example, and within tropical rain forests there's a big difference between high canopy forest and secondary growth in terms of how easy it is for you to move around. As a result, you'll need to work out which categories to use in your sketches and notes. This will probably be completely qualitative – you're saying what kind of things you're seeing, but you're not trying to quantify and measure them.

It's much the same in research – you can do useful work just by describing something that hasn't been described before. The splendid Anna, a PhD student of our acquaintance, for instance, investigated which criteria people actually used to prioritize tasks, as opposed to the criteria advocated in the textbooks, and found some fascinating things. That didn't require numbers, just categorization and description.

Readers with archaic tastes will probably already have guessed that this maps quite neatly onto mediaeval scholastic questions such as *'quae sunt entitiae?'* but we'll refrain from venturing down that particular route . . .

Counting things: the utility of rough measures

Although you can do useful work just by categorizing, describing and sketching, there's a limit to the usefulness of this approach. Imagine that you have returned, sweaty and mud-stained, from the hinterland, notebook and machete in hand, and you're sitting in the captain's cabin, describing the types of forest and swamp to the captain. Sooner or later you're likely to be asked questions such as approximately how broad and deep a particular swamp is. You could, if you felt so inclined, treat this as a sordidly plebian question, and expostulate at length about the socially constrained nature of measurement, or about the simplisticism inherent in the assumption that one can draw a clear limit to the edge of something like a swamp, but this is unlikely to gain you much respect. A captain of the old school might respond by having you keelhauled for being a smart alec; a captain of the new school might coldly suggest that a rough set or fuzzy set formulation might resolve those particular problems, and then ask whether, for instance, the swamp appeared to have any parts too deep to be waded through. Categorization can be complex, but fortunately there are some sophisticated literatures relevant to this, so if you have any lingering anxieties you might be reassured by reading up on them.

In field cartography, you can do a lot of useful work with some basic arithmetic; it's much the same in field research, where you can do a lot of useful work by putting some approximate numbers onto things. In the case of Anna's work on criteria for prioritizing, for example, an obvious step was to count how many people used each of the criteria.

There are various statistical tests which can be used on results of this sort – simple counts of how many things fit into which categories – and a statistically knowledgeable colleague should be able to advise you on which test will be best suited to your needs.

Planting coffee bushes: systematic change

Both the approaches above (describing things and doing some basic counting) are good, solid approaches. They have their limits, though. They just describe things as they are; they don't tell you anything about possibilities for change. Suppose, for instance, that your expedition discovers a new variety of coffee bush growing in the highlands, whose beans produce coffee tasty enough to render a regiment of fusiliers speechless. You realize that this might make your fortune and you decide to try setting up some plantations in a more geographically convenient location. At three of the locations, the seedlings die ignominiously; at the fourth, they flourish and prosper, and soon provide you with enough income to endow a chair in comparative osteology at a leading university.

What you have done in this example is to try changing something and to see what happens. In three cases you got one result, and in the fourth you got a different result. This shows you that it's possible to grow the new variety of coffee somewhere away from its native valley, and also gives you some rough numbers about how often the move will be successful. A lot of applied research is done in just this way: you try something out in a natural setting and see what happens. The something may be a new method of training staff, or of scheduling tasks, or educating people; for each of these, you'll need to identify different things to tell you what effect, if any, has occurred. If you do this in just one setting it's usually called a case study; if you do it with a sample of more than one, it's usually called a field experiment.

If the things that you measure consist of discrete categories, as in the previous approach which we described above, then you can probably apply the same sort of statistics based on how many things fell into which categories. If the things that you measure consist of scales (for instance, the height of the seedlings or the weight of beans per bush) then you can use a different set of statistics, but that's another story, described in the next section.

Moving earth around: systematic manipulation of factors

Sticking with the coffee plantation example for a moment, the field experiment of raising seedlings in different settings was able to tell you that the bushes could be grown away from their native valley, but it couldn't tell you what made one location suitable and the others unsuitable. This is an obvious problem – for example, what would you do if your one and only plantation was menaced by coffee blight? You might be tempted to list the factors which the suitable location and the native valley had in common, with a view to identifying a suitable location for a second plantation, but that would probably be a long list; most of those factors would probably turn out to be irrelevant, and how could you tell which the relevant ones were? This is where controlled experiments come in.

What you could do is to change the factors in a systematic way and see which of them made a difference. You might wonder, for instance, whether it was something about the soil that made a difference, or something about the climate. What you could then do is ship some samples of soil to several places with different climates, and then plant seedlings at all of these. If all the seedlings planted in the same soil flourish regardless of climate, then that's a pretty strong hint that soil is a relevant factor. This in turn raises more questions, such as what it is about the soil that makes a difference, and you can tackle these questions in just the same way (e.g. if you wonder whether it's something to do with bugs in the soil, you could try growing some seedlings in sterilized soil and others in unsterilized soil).

The key thing about this approach is that you're identifying a factor which might make a difference, and systematically varying it in some way, while keeping everything else the same. This allows you to exclude possibilities in succession and thereby narrow down the set of possible answers. If you do this correctly, then the answer is pretty obvious. You might, for example, give your respondents either a scenario where someone is described as female, or a scenario which is identical except that the person is described as male, and see what differences (if any) you get in the responses. If there are systematic differences between results from the male and the female scenarios, then the only plausible source of these differences is the wording of the scenarios, since everything else in the study is consistent – if you randomized whether each respondent received a male or a female scenario, then there's no other systematic difference between the two conditions which could explain differences in the findings.

For some research of this kind, you measure the results by counting how many things fall into each category (for instance, how many seedlings fall into the 'died ignominiously' category versus the 'grew and prospered' category). More often, though, you'll be measuring something on a scale (for instance, the height of the seedlings at various ages, or the weight of beans on each bush, or the temperature at which you're growing the seedlings). If what you're doing to the seedlings consists simply of increasing values for one factor systematically and seeing what happens on another factor (for instance, increasing the temperature at which you raise the seedlings and seeing what that does to the height at various ages), then you can probably analyse the results using statistical tests of correlation. If what you're doing to them consists of putting them into separate batches and measuring something about each batch (for instance, the batch grown in peat and the batch grown in loam, and measuring the height of the seedlings every week) then you can use a third family of statistical tests, which deals with measures of variance.

Identifying the things to measure, and the appropriate scale or equivalent on which to measure them, is technically known as 'operationalizing your metrics', and is a Good Thing. If you can get the hang of identifying metrics which bear some relation to reality, and ways of measuring them which allow you to ask and answer powerful questions, then the research world lies at your feet.

That concludes this set of extended analogies and metaphors. Research is about answering questions (hence Table 8.1, later); before you get too far into asking questions, it's a good idea to know what types of answer are possible, and for which types of question. The next sections discuss ethics and pitfalls in research design.

Ethics

Ethics are pretty damned important. The trouble is, everybody has a different idea about what is ethical. What we can do is give you a focal concept, introduce an enlightened approach based on principles, say something about background context and discuss the implications of things that people do in research, so you can think about it for yourself.

Duty of care

The focal concept in research ethics is 'duty of care'. As a principled researcher, you owe a duty of care to a variety of parties, including your predecessors, your research community, your colleagues, your subjects and, interestingly enough, yourself. For example, if you're gathering confidential information from respondents about their most embarrassing experiences, then you have a duty of care to these respondents, which includes making sure that their names remain out of the public domain. If you remember nothing else, remember to ask yourself: to whom do I owe a duty of care, and what is it?

Principles for studies involving human participants

A wise man named Professor John Oates has argued compellingly that 'Ethics review is, in essence, the application of informed moral reasoning, resting on sets of moral principles'. This translates into taking an approach to research ethics based on principles (and therefore putting responsibility firmly on researchers). Different articulations of principles have been offered, all of them small sets and all with strong commonalities. Here's a set paraphrased from Professor Oates.[4]

- **Principle 1, compliance with protocol:** research with humans should comply with an explicit protocol (set of procedures) defining how informed consent to participate is sought, gained and recorded, how data is collected, stored and accessed, and how participants are informed of their rights within the study.
- **Principle 2, informed consent:** potential participants should always be informed in advance and in understandable terms of any potential benefits, risks, inconvenience or obligations associated with the research that might reasonably be expected to influence their willingness to participate.
- **Principle 3, openness and integrity:** researchers should be open and honest about the purpose and content of their research and behave in a professional manner at all times.
- **Principle 4, protection from harm:** researchers must make every effort to minimize the risks of any harm, either physical or psychological, arising for any participant, researcher, institution, funding body or other person.
- **Principle 5, confidentiality:** except where explicit written consent is given, researchers should respect and preserve the confidentiality of participants' identities and data at all times, as specified in the protocol.
- **Principle 6, professional codes of practice and ethics:** where the subject of a research project falls within the domain of a professional body with a published code of practice and ethical guidelines, researchers should

[4] Open University Human Participants and Materials Ethics Committee (2006) Ethical principles for research involving human participants, internal document, used with permission. Milton Keynes: The Open University.

explicitly state their intention to comply with the code and guidelines in the project protocol.

You need to find out about your university's ethics review procedures early and ensure that you comply with them. Early, (a) because some institutions (especially those with medical schools) have elaborate procedures and intermittent ethics committee meetings and (b) because ethics review is another useful sanity check on your research design – normally conducted by highly experienced and competent people.

Human participants

There's a line attributed to a German researcher from about a century ago, who allegedly said: 'We must not be anthropomorphic about human beings'. It's a line with more depth than first appears, and bears thinking about.

However, when you are dealing with human subjects, you have to take into account the effect that your research will have on them. Milgram's experiments into obedience to authority would almost certainly not get past an ethical panel today, because of the psychological effect they would have on subjects who discovered that they were capable of giving someone what they believed to be a fatal electric shock, just because an authority figure told them to do it. That's an extreme example, but useful for making the point clearly.

It's tempting to think that your own research couldn't have that effect on anyone. The trouble is, Milgram didn't think that his research would have that effect. He asked his colleagues, professional psychologists, what his subjects were likely to do. The consensus opinion was that the subjects would refuse to give shocks at quite an early stage of the experiment. Research into humans involves finding out about how they work. People don't often have a very accurate image of themselves, for various reasons. It can be profoundly disturbing to become aware of aspects of oneself which had previously been unsuspected. That's what happened to Milgram's subjects.

There isn't a clear answer to all of this. You need to think it through for yourself. It will make you a better person, especially if you can resist the temptation to fool yourself.

Tales of horror and how to avoid them

Every research student hears about some tale of hideous PhD carnage, and some collect them avidly. There are many ways of getting things wrong in research, but in the case of PhD research the predominant way is to ignore, avoid or evade your supervisor. A typical example is the student who sent out a long, badly designed questionnaire to numerous organizations without taking advice (or gaining approval) from their supervisor first. The questionnaire failed to produce anything useful and made the student, the supervisor and the institution look silly in the eyes of a large number of organizations (with attendant impact on job prospects for the student and collaboration prospects for the supervisor). The worst research is usually carried out by students who vanish from sight for months on end, and then hand in something which their supervisor has never seen.

But students rarely do research so damaging or dreadful that it is spoken about as a tale of nameless horror. The more common form of academic suicide is doing something so boring or pointless – and so badly constructed – that the examiners can find no merit in it.

Boring, pointless research

It's very tempting, when the time comes to choose your research topic, to go for something easy, on the grounds that you're risk-averse when it comes to your degree and you want to do something that looks safe. So, you cobble together a safe-looking little questionnaire with predictable questions about a trendy topic, send it out uninvited to a large number of people, a small number of whom reply, and write up the safe-looking results. No surprises, no challenges – no novelty, no originality; no evidence that you've learned anything in the course of your long, expensive education. A colleague of ours calls this 'stamp collecting'. The collection makes no contribution beyond its mere existence.

'Stamp collecting' tends to have two key ingredients: a conventional approach and an overworked topic. Some questions have already attracted considerable time and attention from other researchers and just doing a similar thing again is unlikely to result in a breakthrough (e.g. 'Can learning styles be used predict outcomes in problem-solving tasks?'). Either the conventional approach or the overworked topic has to change. Shifting to a different topic that shares some of the same issues, asking the same question in a new context or importing a radically different approach from another discipline can provide an alternative – in effect, stepping from the trodden path into a pleasantly muddy field.

A useful principle is to think about the 'So what?' question. Say you've discovered that the majority of participants in your gadget design study like blue mouse buttons better than pink mouse buttons: so what? Does this finding contribute to a coherent theory of aesthetics, or is it just a gee-whiz finding without any further significance? Who is it useful to, besides the gadget manufacturer buying plastic dyes? If you can't answer 'So what?' or the companion question 'Who cares?', then you need to avoid asking that research question in the first place.

So, the effective strategy for a risk-averse student is not to do something obvious or conventional, but to ask their research question in such a way that, *whatever they find*, the results will be interesting and useful.

A neat example is Carmel, who was interested in people's perceptions of internet banking. It would have been obvious for her to (you guessed it) cobble together a questionnaire to ask people what they thought about internet banking. Inevitably, that had already been tried commercially by large specialist companies, so the likelihood that she would discover something new (instead of collecting the familiar stamps) was slight. Instead, Carmel used the findings from those surveys already described in the literature as her baseline. She took a scenario-based approach, so that she could compare her scenario-based findings to those survey-based results and assess whether scenarios had any advantages. Scenarios were unexplored in this context, so whatever she found would be useful. She also added a twist. The scenario introduced Chris, who had some money and wanted to decide where to invest or save it. Half the scenarios asked the question: 'What advice would you give him?' The other half asked: 'What advice would you give her?' That one word of difference opened a window onto differences of response that a conventional questionnaire would be unlikely to reveal. Female Chris received advice about nice, safe places to save the money to earn predictable returns and avoid losses should the market take a dive; male Chris received advice about making a lot of money (if all went well) by taking a few risks with investments.

Seeking supporting evidence for a preconceived idea

It is surprisingly easy to find large amounts of evidence for even the most silly ideas. One exercise we use to demonstrate this to students involves dividing them into groups, then giving each group the name of a living thing which may or may not be a human (for instance, it may be a kangaroo or an ant). Each group then has to list as many arguments as possible for their living thing being a human being (for instance, that it has two legs, or that it constructs homes), with the other groups trying to guess whether or not they are describing a human.

A frequent version of this problem involves setting out to measure an effect without thinking about (a) whether that effect exists or (b) what the wider context is. For instance, a lot of research by computer science students involves setting out to measure how much better their software is than the previous industry standard; if their software doesn't perform better, they end up with several years' worth of embarrassment and wasted effort staring them in the face.

Asking an unanswerable question

There are questions that, although compelling, are too abstract, too elusive to operationalize or simply far too costly to address effectively. A question may be an important one, but unanswerable. For instance, do different Palaeolithic tool assemblages reflect (a) different activities within the same group or (b) different groups of people, such as different tribes or cultures? Both explanations fitted the facts equally neatly for a long time, until techniques were invented for identifying how tools were used.

Asking a useless question

Just because a question can be answered, that does not mean that it's of any use. For instance, discovering that a particular group of people (e.g. those with low scores on the Smith & Wesson dance test) have particular difficulty in learning foreign languages is unlikely to help anyone who is trying to teach them a foreign language – the teacher will be much more interested in finding out about better ways of teaching them. Trivial studies, addressing questions whose scope is too small to make them generalizeable, relevant or interesting to others (e.g. 'Do coloured mice improve student productivity?') are a form of stamp collecting, as are 'one shots' – studies which at best provide 'gee whiz' facts for dinner parties but don't aggregate or contribute to an accumulation of evidence. A well-formed research question will usually have very clear practical implications for someone.

An improbable-sounding instance involves research into flamingo breeding. Captive flamingos are often reluctant to breed. Research indicated that this was because flamingos would only breed when they believed that the flock size was large enough. The practical implication of this was that putting mirrors beside the flamingo enclosure would make the flock appear twice the size, which did in fact encourage the flamingos to breed.

Useful questions about your research

There are some simple useful questions you can ask yourself about your research. If the questions (or the answers) make you angry or nervous, then you should rethink your research design. (Hint: the answer to each question should be 'yes'.)

- Are you trying to find something out, rather than prove something?
- Do you ever find yourself being surprised by what you find in your data?
- Do you ever decide, on the basis of your data, that your previous ideas about an area were wrong?

The three ignoble truths (with apologies to the three noble truths)

It's also possible to produce no findings at all, usually through ignoring the Three Ignoble Truths:

- **First ignoble truth:** hardware will break and software will crash
- **Second ignoble truth:** resources won't be there when you need them
- **Third ignoble truth:** people will get sick, die and fail to deliver

Table 8.1 Finding the right question

Do first things first	There's a reason why experts spend more time planning than novices. Good planning and preparation save time blundering around in the jungle. First, work out what you want to know (refine your question), then work out how you'll know it (the evidence requirements), and *only then* choose techniques.
Work backwards from where you want to end up	If you know where you want to end up and work backwards from that, then you're likely to get to your goal efficiently. If you blunder off in a random direction, hoping to find a goal, then you're likely to end up lost.
Ask a smaller question	How does one eat an elephant? One bite at a time. If your question is too big, ask a smaller question. A life's work takes a lifetime, but it's achieved one step at a time.
When planning research, aim to reduce the problem space, not to find The True Answer	If you gamble on finding a result, then you're probably doing things wrong. You should phrase your research question in such a way that, whatever you find, it tells you something useful. You should work on the metaphor of the ship's captain making maps of an unknown sea, rather than the metaphor of the ship's captain gambling on finding El Dorado. Knowing that a stretch of sea is empty is just as useful as knowing that there is an island in it. Don't set out to collect data in support of your belief. Ask yourself: 'How could I tell if my belief was wrong?' If you can't answer that question, then you're doing politics, not research.
If bright people have been looking at a problem for more than three years and still don't have a solution, then the solution is probably somewhere unlikely	Two to three years is about the time span for several bright professionals to try the obvious approaches, write up their findings and present them at a conference. If no solutions are being reported after three years, this is probably a significant absence. In this situation, don't rush in trying the obvious approach, especially if the area is a hot topic: do some lateral thinking about different approaches.
Question received wisdom	What 'everyone knows' is often wrong (let anecdote help shape your questions, but then seek independent evidence in order to find answers).
Respect failure	Nils Bohr said, 'Science is not "that's interesting" but "that's odd" '. Great research often comes from surprise. The only bad study is one that doesn't inform you; what information does your 'failure' provide?
Know what can and cannot be shown with different sorts of evidence	Rigour comes from understanding the nature of the endeavour and being vigilant for bias and limitations. Know the value of evidence: not 'good' or 'bad', but stronger or weaker. Know the value and limitations of your tools – for example, sometimes your question will be precise enough for a definitive experiment; sometimes you'll need a different research method. Avoid confusing statistics with rigour: find out what statistics can and cannot do, then go and find a good experimental statistician to consult. Be vigilant about bias; be honest; go and read a good book on the subject.

9

Critical thinking

> *But Jack Aubrey's mind, though logical in mathematics and celestial navigation (he had read several papers to the Royal Society, with great applause on the part of those Fellows who understood them: gloomy fortitude on the part of the rest) was less so where laws were concerned . . .*[1]

Everyone is entitled to their opinions (although legal systems in most countries have strong views about whether or not you are allowed to express some of those opinions in public). This isn't the same as saying that all opinions are right, or that all ideas are 'only' opinions, or that all opinions and ideas are equally worthy. As you might imagine, this whole topic is far from simple, and it has far-reaching implications for research, both in terms of theory and practice.

For example, it's tempting to assume that the more evidence there is for an idea, the more likely it is that the idea is correct. By this reasoning, there's an infinite amount of evidence supporting the claim that all numbers are even numbers, since there's an infinite number of even numbers. However, there's also an infinite number of odd numbers, and an infinite number of prime numbers, and so on. Viewed in this context, the claim that all numbers are even is clearly not one which holds up well; the existence of just one odd number would be enough to show that it was wrong, let alone an infinite number of non-even numbers. So, some claims can be shown to be inconsistent with what

---

[1] O'Brian, P. (1997) *The Nutmeg of Consolation*. London: HarperCollins, p. 172.

actually happens in the world (and therefore untrue), even if there is an enormous amount of evidence which happens to be consistent with those claims.

In some cases, it's possible to demonstrate pretty clearly that a particular idea is wrong, either because it conflicts with reality or because of internal contradictions in its logic and evidence. In some disciplines, such as medicine and engineering, testing an idea against reality is straightforward in principle (though often difficult in practice) and is the usual benchmark against which ideas are measured – for instance, testing whether a particular treatment improves patient recovery rates at a higher level than a placebo, or testing whether a particular model of superconductivity makes better predictions about which materials will be superconductive at room temperature.

In other disciplines, this emphasis on checking ideas against what happens in the world is viewed with reserve, or even hostility. This isn't because of researchers being unable to think clearly, or not wanting to offend anyone's beliefs; there are more substantial reasons, such as ugly lessons from history, where researchers collaborated with social agenda ranging from the sordid to the downright criminal, without stepping back and questioning those agenda. It's a difficult area, without clear answers. It's made even more difficult because it's one of those topics where the decision not to do something is as active a decision as choosing to do something. It's easy to come up with emotive arguments in both directions.

So, where does that leave you? It leaves you doing a PhD in a world where different disciplines favour different approaches, and where simple weight of evidence in favour of your pet idea is not enough; a world where you need to sift among the contradictory evidence and ideas to decide which are fatally flawed and which are not. How do you do this? That's what critical thinking is about.

Reprise on a theme: research is a discourse

The word 'discourse' keeps cropping up: 'research is a discourse', a dialogue involving examination of and reasoning about a particular topic or field. The research dialogue involves an exchange of ideas and often contention and persuasion (it usually, although not always, stops short of bloodshed). It is the negotiation of knowledge or understanding (cf. Foucault). What is a thesis? A premise maintained or promoted in argument. In brief, an argument.

That's why (after all these centuries) a PhD culminates in the submission and defence of a dissertation: they are the active demonstration of competent engagement with the discourse. By publishing, discussing and defending, we are:

• Engaging in the discourse – 'negotiating new knowledge'

- Presenting a thesis which is founded in evidence (new or existing) and argued soundly
- Not just generating results, but defending them robustly so that they have an impact on the discourse – and change the state of knowledge
- Not just having ideas, but communicating and defending them
- Most importantly, exposing our research to the scrutiny of our peers – and so exposing it to challenge and falsification

This 'negotiation of knowledge' is why passing a PhD requires both rigour and rhetoric. As one colleague phrased it: do good work, tell a good story.

Rigour

Rigour is vigilance against bias, manifest as disciplined practice and reasoning. It involves:

- Systematic investigation, purposeful, focused activity and gathering evidence in order to produce helpful/useful output to answer a question, or to solve a problem
- Conforming to standards of practice in the discipline
- Founding research in and relating it to existing knowledge
- Providing insight/understanding into a particular subject by offering new analysis (identifying and addressing gaps, identifying key factors, patterns and relationships) or new synthesis (gathering knowledge and reasoning over it to produce new knowledge)
- Offering only well-founded conclusions, based in evidence
- Appropriate, self-critical analysis
- Generating 'reliable' knowledge

Rhetoric

Rhetoric is the art of communication and persuasion. It involves:

- Using language effectively to convey ideas, to influence, to persuade
- Honest reportage: clear descriptions of what has been done
- Clear communication of processes, results and ideas
- Systematic argument – with a clear and explicit chain of reference
- Anticipating and addressing alternative perspectives and alternative accounts

There is no point in producing great results if they're not communicated well. Swiss physicist Ernst Stueckelberg missed out on at least one Nobel Prize because he published his theory about how light interacts with atoms in an obscure Swiss journal, with the result that his work was overlooked when the panel was handing out prizes.

Critical thinking and how it is manifest

Science is not a cut-and-dried body of knowledge which someone has collected once and for all: it is an attitude of mind, a way of finding out. Unless these facts are appreciated, science degenerates into mere scholarship and its study has a narrowing instead of broadening effect on the mind. [2]

So what is critical thinking? Critical thinking is about curiosity, about continual questioning. It is also about developing a healthy, deliberate, 'mindful' scepticism and applying it even-handedly to all aspects of your research.

Critical thinking is the basis for rigour. Some interpret rigour as strict observance of procedures or strict enforcement of rules – but adherence isn't enough without understanding, and researchers march readily into pitfalls via unthinking application of procedures. Naïve researchers who put techniques before questions are in danger of conducting what Richard Feynman identified as 'Cargo Cult Science'[3] (referring to the behaviour of certain Pacific island peoples, who built runways in order to tempt aeroplanes to land and deliver cargo) – mistaking scientific method or statistics for rigour *per se*, without understanding the roles of observation, reflection, scrutiny and critique in maintaining the scientific 'attitude of mind' and working mindfully with theory. Taking procedures and rules for granted is just as dangerous as taking assertions for granted.

Critical thinking is why 'the only stupid question is the one you didn't ask', because nothing is exempt from scrutiny. It's like combining the intellectual licence of a 2-year-old with the intellectual power of a forensic accountant. It involves:

- Being curious
- Wondering why
- Taking nothing for granted
- Comparing claims and evidence
- Following the audit trail

Critical thinking is about 'digging deeper' and is manifest as critical depth in a paper or dissertation. Digging deeper means asking the question that comes *after* your research question, and the question after that. It means not stopping at the first predicted outcome or first set of data, but asking 'So what?'. What does this result mean? What are its consequences? What are its limitations – what more do we need to know?

[2] Holmstrom, J.E. (1947) *Records and Research in Engineering and Industrial Science: A Guide to the Sources, Processing and Storekeeping of Technical Knowledge with a Chapter on Translating*, 2nd edn. London: Chapman & Hall.
[3] Feynman, R.P. and Leighton, R. (1985) *Surely You're Joking, Mr. Feyman!* New York: W.W. Norton & Co.

What's theory got to do with it?

So, research is a discourse, the 'substance of research' isn't just data and variables and the business of research isn't just hypothesis and observation – more than that, research is based in ideas and reasoning, in reflection and critique and in dialogue among researchers with a common aim of explaining the world. Theory is a vehicle for that dialogue. It is our attempt to provide usable, general explanations for phenomena in a way that accounts for both the visible and the hidden factors, that generalizes across situations or events and that ultimately accounts for causality and allows us to make predictions about the phenomena. Theory tries to answer 'Why?' as well as 'What?'.

It's useful to think broadly, in terms of a 'method of science',[4] an approach to inquiry based on systematic reasoning and empirically-based evidence. 'Method of science' is a process of theoretical and empirical reasoning, rather than a specified empirical strategy. It is characterized by principles such as articulation, validation, exposure to falsification and generalization. 'Method of science' views 'scientific method' as just one way among many of gaining knowledge. It respects the roles of both inductive reasoning and deductive reasoning in the give-and-take between empirical investigation and theory. Inductive reasoning (arguing from the particular to the general) emphasizes the identification of regularities. It is a way of generating theory and of asking better (more informed, more focused) questions. Deductive reasoning (arguing from given theories, models or axioms to make statements about the behaviour of particular cases) emphasizes hypothesis-testing. It is what drives scientific method, making and testing predictions and considering the adequacy of proposed 'answers'.

This broader view values description – witnessing the world – as well as prediction and hypothesis-testing. It sees the relationship between theory and evidence as a dynamic, two-way give-and-take. It embraces both theory-driven (deductive) and data-driven (inductive) investigations. Deduction tests the predictions or hypotheses derived from a theory in ways that allow them to be disproved; it draws inferences from observations in order to make generalizations (in order to generate empirically-grounded theory which may or may not subsequently be subject to deductive approaches).

Scientific method revolves around theory: scientific inquiry produces predictive theory which generates hypotheses that can be falsified. But where does theory come from? With 'method of science' we recognize that the process of articulation – making phenomena explicit in sufficient explanatory detail – is a crucial part of research and of theory generation. We need to articulate assumptions, meanings, constructs and their relationships in order

---

[4] This argument was first presented in Fincher, S. and Petre, M. (2004) A preface to pragmatics, in S. Fincher and M. Petre (eds) *Computer Science Education Research*. London: RoutledgeFalmer, pp. 9–17. Used with permission.

to help clarify what we think we know and how we think we know it. We're offering different accounts of 'what' and 'why' – and we're offering evidence to justify choosing among the competing accounts. We're making best estimates and reasoning about the probability of error.

Theory is a way of focusing our thinking about why things are as they are. Falsification allows us to eliminate some theories, but we can't be sure that what survives is a 'true' theory – just that it's theory that hasn't been disproven yet. We work with 'best approximations', in which we have more or less confidence, depending on what evidence supports them.

Style, epistemology and rigour

There is a traditional divide in most areas between 'neats' and 'scruffies'. The 'neats' concentrate on formalisms to provide clean, abstract descriptions of the area; the 'scruffies' concentrate on understanding what is actually going on, even if they can't express it very neatly. Relations between the two groups usually vary between cool disdain and bitter feuding. 'Neats' typically have more academic street credibility, because they typically use intimidating mathematical representations. 'Scruffies' typically have more credibility with industry, because they typically have a wonderful collection of 'war stories' and know just what sort of things go on when the Health and Safety Executive isn't watching. Some people straddle the divide and have both a wonderful fund of stories and the ability to use intimidating representations. These people frequently end up as the 'gurus' in a field, and apparently get quite a few free meals and invitations to nice conferences as a result.

Anyway, returning to planning research, there is a spectrum of research types ranging from formal to informal. At the formal end of the scale are abstractions – for instance, mathematical modelling of an area, or trying different representations of the same topic.

Next along the scale is the formal controlled experiment, straight out of the textbook – for instance, comparing the responses from two groups which you have treated in different ways. For this, you will know which variables you are manipulating and which you are measuring; you will have thought carefully about sample size.

Around the middle of the scale is the field experiment, where you are not able to control all the variables that you would like to and are trading that off against the realism of experimentation in the outside world. For instance, when redecoration time comes round, you might manage to persuade your establishment to paint the walls of one computer room a tasteful shade of green to see whether this calms down the users and reduces the number of complaints they make about the computers, compared to the users in the standard-issue hideous orange rooms. For this, you will know which variables you are manipulating and which you are measuring, but you will be horribly aware that other variables may be scurrying around looking for somewhere to cause you trouble.

At the scruffy end of the scale is the collection of squishy observational data with a very small sample size. A good example of this is the eminent sociology professor who allegedly studied tramps via participant observation (i.e. passing himself off as a tramp and socializing with them). The result can be extremely interesting insights into an area, plus data that nobody else has, plus clothing that smells of methylated spirits.

Epistemology and rigour

Fundamentally, the divide between 'neats' and 'scruffies' has to do with what their goals are, what sorts of evidence they prefer, what their criteria are for rigour and what level of error they're willing to tolerate. In other words, it's epistemological. Epistemology is to do with what we believe constitutes 'knowledge', how we can know something is 'true' and how we share that knowledge. By defining the grounds for knowledge, epistemology sets out which knowledge claims are legitimate. By implication, it also sets out what *questions* are legitimate (or even allowable): what kinds of questions can be – or should be – asked, and how we go about answering them.

Different disciplines have different systems of creating, understanding and communicating knowledge, which are not necessarily transferable to other disciplines. For example, we can't apply the way astrophysicists theorize about and investigate the creation of the universe to the way educators develop and deploy pedagogies in primary schools. The questions are different, the 'burden of proof' is different and the way evidence is discussed is different.

One thing to remember about evidence is that some aspects of it are social constructs and others aren't. The proportions vary. In the physical sciences, for instance, heat is clearly something which exists independently of human belief systems – there were hot things in the universe long before the first hominids wandered across the world, and there will probably be hot things long after the last hominid is dead. The systems which we use to measure heat, though, are social constructs: the instruments are based on what humans can perceive or can imagine perceiving. At the other end of the spectrum, concepts such as 'bravery' or 'good taste' are found in most human societies, but are pretty much entirely human creations which are mapped onto different behaviours and different abstract concepts by different societies. Even when there's reasonable consensus about an area, it's normally necessary for human beings to adopt a simplified version of it, since the human brain couldn't cope with the information load of trying to handle every specific instance and bit of evidence relevant to an issue.

Each discipline has its own standards of rigour, its own conventions of evidence and argument which members of that discipline – and of that discourse – must understand. Learning the tools of the trade involves learning not just the methods but also the disciplinary context, the knowledge concerns the methods were designed to address, and the associated assumptions and limitations on use.

There can be multiple ways of studying a phenomenon, but that doesn't mean 'anything goes'. Each study must be rigorous in its own terms.

Truth

Validity (or 'truth') in research involves a combination of factors, including the accuracy of our observation, the quality of our reasoning and the completeness of our explanation. Rigour is the systematic pursuit of validity through disciplined practice and reasoning. Truth, according to Vance, is a precious jewel, the more precious for being rare. It is not a researcher's job to keep the price up by keeping the supply down.

We have various ways of trying to establish validity, all bound to critical thinking and the research discourse. Two of these are replication and repetition, which both address the reliability and robustness of the findings and also expose the study design and conduct to the scrutiny of more minds. Replication is the reproduction of a study by another researcher, using the same protocol under the same conditions. Replication tests how 'reliable' the findings are – that is, how consistent outcomes are when the study is repeated 'verbatim'. Replication is the standard for laboratory experiments, but is not necessarily feasible in human studies research because social environments are by their complex and changing nature difficult to control and reproduce. As a result, repetition is the standard for human studies: reproduction of a study by another researcher, using a closely comparable protocol under comparable conditions. Repetition tests 'robustness', how consistent the outcomes are across different related tasks, different related environments or different related contexts.

However, as any social scientist knows, truth is a tricky and relativistic thing to pin down. There are good grounds for arguing that truth in the strictest sense is a meaningless concept. A neat way out of this is to argue that there is an asymmetry, derived from the mathematics of infinity. There is an infinite set of propositions which correspond with a given slice of reality and can therefore be described as 'true'. However, this is not the same as saying that all propositions are equally true and valid. There is a different and also infinite set of propositions which do not correspond with a given slice of reality and can therefore be described as 'not true'. So, how can you decide whether or not a particular explanation is demonstrably untrue, and how can you choose between those explanations which are consistent with the facts?

If we look at the explanations consistent with the facts, we will usually find that they vary in their neatness of fit. The normal convention in research is to adopt the simplest explanation which maps onto the most facts most neatly; as you might expect, this leads to debate about which explanation fits this description most accurately from among the candidates. This approach is also the basis of falsification: you propose an idea, test it out as hard as you can and see whether any of the tests show it to be false. If not, then it's a candidate for an adequate explanation, at least until a better one comes along.

More about evidence

Critical thinking accounts for the difference between 'data' and 'evidence'. Data is not necessarily evidence – it becomes evidence when its relevance to the question is established. Therefore, the quality of evidence lies not just in the quality of the data but also in the quality of reasoning about the data.[5]

Operationalization (or, getting useful data)

In order to design empirical research, we must map from the question to the evidence needed to answer it, from what we want to know to what we can observe in the world. This mapping is called 'operationalizing'. The validity of a study depends on the link between idea and observation: between a construct (your concept or notion of the thing of interest) and what can be observed, recorded and ultimately measured in some way. Usually, this is a simplification; the process of operationalization selects one or more observable aspects of the phenomenon to focus on and capture. The observation or measure is a sort of proxy which stands for the construct. But the things we capture – recordings, descriptions, categorizations, measures – are not the phenomenon. If the reasoning that links the question to the evidence, or the proxy to the construct, or the measure to the phenomenon, is faulty, then the data may be irrelevant or misleading.

Researchers are often distracted from what *should* be observed by what *can* readily be observed. The dangers of errors in operationalization are summarized neatly in a process called the 'McNamara fallacy', after the US Secretary of Defence who quantified the Vietnam War:[6]

The first step is to measure whatever can be easily measured. This is OK as far as it goes.

The second step is to disregard that which can't be easily measured or to give it an arbitrary quantitative value. This is artificial and misleading.

---

[5] Paraphrased from Mislevy, R.J. (2001) Basic concepts of evidentiary reasoning, www.education.umd.edu/EDMS/EDMS738.

[6] The expression of the fallacy is attributed to Daniel Yankelovich in 'Adam Smith' (George G. W. Goodman) (1981) *Paper Money*. New York: Summit Books, p. 37. The McNamara Fallacy is also quoted in Charles Handy (1994) *The Empty Raincoat*. London: Hutchinson, p. 219.

The third step is to presume that what can't be measured easily really isn't important. This is blindness.

The fourth step is to say that what can't be easily measured really doesn't exist. This is suicide.

Representativeness and generalization

Empirical study involves selection. We select a sample to represent a population. We select a task (or a small number of them) to represent a repertoire of activities. We select a setting (or a small number of them) to represent an environment. We select observations and measures to represent a phenomenon. And so on. Selection entails an obligation: to consider whether whatever you selected represents accurately what it was selected from – the population, repertoire, environment, etc. it was meant to typify. A considerable amount hinges on the answer. If the selection is too particular, too idiosyncratic or in some way not representative, then the findings are limited to that selection. The legitimacy of any general claims you make is based in the representativeness of your selection. Representativeness (the ability of a specific instance to stand for the larger group of which it is a member) is the key to generalization. If the selection, and hence the study, is representative, then the study's outcomes can be generalized to the greater population, to other related tasks, to the greater environment and so on.

Models

All models are wrong, but some are useful. [7]

Accounts of phenomena (whether informal analogies or mathematical models) are generalized explanations. Good accounts are 'parsimonious' – as simple as possible while still describing the important features of the phenomenon and being consistent with the data. As such, accounts are selections (choosing which are the important features), abstractions (addressing the essence while omitting detail) and simplifications (focusing on selected features of a complex problem). Good accounts describe the available evidence adequately and allow predictions and other inferences to be made.

A model is one form of account: a schematic (hypothetical) description of a phenomenon (typically of something that cannot readily be observed directly) that accounts for its properties or behaviour. Models are a mechanism for critical thinking, a device for providing insight into the issues or the nature of the phenomenon. Often models are based on analogy. Sometimes they are mathematical representations of a situation that support formal inference.

---

[7] Box, G.E.P. (1979) Robustness in the strategy of scientific model building, in R.L. Launer and G.N. Wilkinson (eds) *Robustness in Statistics*. New York: Academic Press, p. 202.

Sometimes they are conceptual – sets of concepts or ideas in relationship. Sometimes they are structural depictions of a physical system. Sometimes they are procedural descriptions of a process or interaction. Their role is to simplify the complex and make it manageable, to make a generalization concrete by representing it graphically or symbolically, to reveal possible relationships between important variables.

Comparison and analogy

Very often, models are based on an analogy – for example, an atom is like a solar system, with the electrons orbiting the nucleus. In every analogy some things are the same – but some things are different. That the true power of analogy in critical thinking lies not so much in the similarities but in the differences. Understanding the ways in which an atom is *not* like a solar system provides crucial insight into defining and distinguishing characteristics.

Statistics and uncertainty

Statistics is a scientific tool for reasoning about numerical data and for modelling uncertainty. It is a problem-solving tool – not a panacea. Using statistical methods well requires understanding, attention to context and critical thinking, not just formulaic application of techniques.

Roughly speaking, statistics is about working out the signal-to-noise ratio: establishing whether variations in data are meaningful (signal) or just chance fluctuations (noise). And it is about working out if the 'noise' results from natural random variability or from error. Statistical tests model uncertainty. They provide a probability that a set of results is due to random variability – and arguments are made on the basis that the less probable it is that differences are due to random variability, then the more probable it is that there is a significant effect (signal rather than noise).

That's why good application of statistics requires an initial, critical examination of the data: for assessing the structure and quality of the data, for summarizing the data and picking out interesting features and for helping to identify an appropriate further analysis strategy. What's the quality of the data: are there errors, oddities, missing observations? What's the nature of the data: how large is the sample; how many variables are there and of what type (e.g. continuous or categorical); what's the distribution of the data; what's the spread; what's the precision?

Often, that's enough – the initial exploration provides all the evidence required to provide concise descriptions of general trends and patterns. Enough to compare new results to previous results. Enough to identify interesting differences and enough to make clear that the data is too 'dirty' to sustain further analysis.

Bias

Bias is when beasties creep in unnoticed to corrupt the evidence, when results are distorted due to factors that have not been taken into consideration. There are lots of 'beasties' lurking (e.g. extraneous or latent influences, unrecognized conflated variables, selectivity in a sample which renders it unrepresentative). The very act of experimenting introduces the potential for bias. This is referred to as the Heisenberg, or uncertainty, principle: you can't observe without influencing what you're observing. Observing phenomena changes them.

Rigour demands that researchers be ever-vigilant against bias, which can creep in at any point in research: posing of questions, interpretation of theory, planning, each reasoning step, implementation choices, use of equipment, execution of the study, data collection, analysis, interpretation of evidence and even reporting. Bias can take many forms: experimenter interference (in the data); projection (in the analysis); limitations of human reasoning (e.g. confirmatory bias); theory (theoretical ideas influence the selection and interpretation of evidence); the sample (improperly selected, too small to permit any reliable conclusion, not representative); participants (who may deliberately or unwittingly alter their behaviour or responses); design; conditions; apparatus; reporting . . . dangers lurk: beware.

Giving structure to thinking [8]

One of the keys to critical thinking is not just to think things, but to make the thinking explicit. Externalizing and representing thought makes it available to scrutiny, both by the thinker and by others who might engage with the ideas.

The brain dump

One of the interesting challenges of 'rhetoric' is to force complex thought into a single line of narrative. It's a problematic constraint, and one that defeats many. Writing coherent academic prose demands order, prioritization, clarity and specificity. Thoughts don't often start that way. They are born and nurtured in a complex, multi-dimensional, multi-modal 'space'. There's a reason why backs of envelopes and whiteboards persist as the tools of choice for many creative endeavours – a transitional, non-linear, less constrained representation can often help to capture thoughts and process them for articulation as argument. Visual tools like sketches, mind maps, structured diagrams (such as flow charts, time lines, decision trees, etc.), tables and so on can all help to

---

[8] This section is informed by and draws from the Open University's Learning Space study skills site on 'Extending and developing your thinking skills': http://openlearn.open.ac.uk/course/view.php?id=1644.

externalize thoughts and then begin to organize them into a form suitable for communication. The process of representation is part of thinking; it helps to focus and specify ideas, and externalizing thoughts allows the thinker to examine and interrogate them differently, creating a sort of dialogue between thinker and represented thought. Sometimes the process is more important than the product, revealing questions or assumptions that require further investigation; sometimes the product has value and is worth communicating to others.

Assumptions

Assumptions are things (facts, axioms, constraints, conditions, etc.) we overlook or take for granted. Critical thinking demands that we look again. Assumptions can have the advantage of making a problem more manageable by simplifying that problem and reducing the problem space. Sometimes we make assumptions explicitly, but more often assumptions are hidden or unnoticed until we make a deliberate effort to identify them – and of course it's usually the hidden assumptions that impede progress. Exploration of assumptions plays a crucial role in critical thinking, exposing constraints (inherent or imposed) and beliefs (including what constitutes a 'good' solution).

Assumptions also condition our expectations, sometimes in ways that create unnecessary obstacles. For example, a student learning to write computer programs was given an assignment to read an existing program, about a page or two long. She began, and then stopped: 'It can't be this hard,' she thought. She consulted a friend, an expert programmer: 'Can you show me how to read this program?' 'Sure,' he said, and proceeded to read the code line by line over a substantial period. She sat aghast: 'If I'd known it was just hard, I could have done it myself.' Many tasks are easier, if they're begun with accurate expectations.

Write down your assumptions. Prioritize them: which have the greatest impact? Which do you consider immutable? Group them into types: which are defining assumptions? Which lead to constraints? Which are make-or-break? Which are about values? Examine them critically. Is each necessary, or not? What if one of the crucial assumptions could be removed? (Experts innovators think this way, posing questions like: what happens if we remove gravity?) Examination of assumptions can (a) save you from embarrassing and time-consuming oversights and occasionally (b) transform your thinking about your research question or research design.

Applying structure

Generating lists and messes of ideas is one thing. Putting them in order, identifying structure, seeing the overall message as well as the individual items, is quite another. That's where disciplines of thinking come in, to help you consider ideas systematically, from different perspectives (including the

Big Picture), and from that to assess relative importance and identify relationships and patterns. The next step is to apply structure, whether by identifying and drawing out relationships in the ideas, by building a framework of emerging concepts, by mapping the ideas onto a model or by imposing a structure from the literature.

In any case, what's needed is an 'organizing principle' (or a series of them), a basis and a focus for bringing order. Hierarchical structures can be useful – stratified tree structures based on priorities, contingencies, or dependencies. Distinguishing between the general and the particular can help draw out structure. Information or resource flows can be an organizing principle – for example by analogy to the inland waterways system, with canals and rivers interconnecting into a transportation system across a landscape, and locks and elevators overcoming disparities of level and helping to manage the water flow. Other organizing principles might include: organizational structure, geography or other spatial organization, conceptual location (e.g. position in an argument), chronology, complexity, pros and cons, 'known-ness' – the degree to which ideas are understood and substantiated – methodology, sources or social structure (grouping ideas by who or which community originated them and hence structuring in terms of 'schools of thought') and so on.

Try different organizing principles, different groupings and different representations. Writing ideas on Post-it notes or index cards can help, allowing you to shuffle them and deal them out or regroup them physically.

Problem-solving techniques

A number of systematic step-by-step processes for thinking about problems and solving them have been articulated. (DeBono, Polya and TRIZ leap to mind as examples.) One typical (and brief) example is DANCE:[9]

> D – Define and clarify what the problem really is. What are your goals?
> A – Think of alternative ways of solving the problem
> N – Narrow down the range of possible solutions
> C – Choose the ideal solution and check what the consequences might be
> E – Effect action using the best solution

Different perspectives

There are lots of places to look for ways to extend your repertoire of thinking tools: literatures on problem-solving, rhetoric, design and innovation, creativity, soft systems, etc. Here's a selection of techniques for considering different perspectives and thereby seeking critical balance in your formulation of arguments.

---

[9] Rose, C. and Nicholl, M. (1997) *Accelerated Learning for the 21st Century*. London: Piatkus.

- Devil's advocate: adopt alternate points of view, one supportive and one hyper-critical, and argue the case
- PMI: identify plus (advantages), minus (shortcomings) and interesting points.[10]
- Force field analysis: list forces acting for and against a change.
- Inverting propositions: don't just consider your proposition or hypothesis; consider its inverse and its converse (e.g. if you're thinking 'does feminist discourse reduce smoking?', then consider: 'does smoking inhibit feminist discourse?').
- General and particular: consider your proposition or argument at different levels of granularity, from the general case to particular, concrete examples.
- Rival perspectives: have more than one account, perspective or hypothesis and test each systematically against the available evidence (tables can help here): what does each account give you that another doesn't and which accounts for the evidence better? Which offers better insights?

Critical thinking is not just about making a particular argument. It's about considering issues from all perspectives, in order to produce a balanced argument, and draw robust and defensible conclusions. It's about seeking truth.

---

[10] de Bono, E. (1992) *Serious Creativity: Using the Power of Lateral Thinking to Create New Ideas*. New York: Harper Business.

10

Writing

*What will you need to write? • The dissertation: core concepts •
Dissertation FAQs • Journal papers • The process of publication • Papers
from theses • Paper checklist*

> *He wrote in a complicated style, overloaded and lacking in charm. Not that he
> was indifferent to language and its nuances; on the contrary, correct use of
> language was for him a moral question, its debasement a symptom of moral
> breakdown.* [1]

If you're an experienced academic and someone is trying to persuade you to
take on a person you've never heard of as a PhD student, then one of the first
things you ask is whether they can write. This is shorthand for 'write good
academic English, preferably in various styles to suit different needs, ranging
from journal articles to plausible opening letters to potential funders'. If the
answer is 'no' then you are in a strong bargaining position if the other person
really wants you to take this student on, since nobody in their senses is keen to
take on a student who can't write. A point worth noting is that this refers to
good academic English, which is *not* the same as formal grammar – there are
plenty of cases of students who write very good academic English, even
though they are not native speakers of English and their formal grammar is
wobbly in places. Conversely, there are many native speakers of English whose
understanding of academic writing is woeful.

So, what do we mean by 'good academic English' and why is it not the same
as formal English grammar? What types of writing do you need to know, and

---

[1] Thucydides (1972) *History of the Peloponnesian War*, ed. R. Warner and M.I. Finley. Harmondsworth:
Penguin, p. 9.

why? How can you send out the right signals with your writing, and avoid sending out unintended wrong signals? This chapter and the following chapters deal with these issues, with the process of writing (e.g. writer's block) and the structure and style of academic writing.

What will you need to write?

The core of your PhD is your written dissertation; you need to know the appropriate structure, format, style and content for this. Your university will have published guidelines about structure and format, which you should follow scrupulously: departing from these sends out a signal that you are clueless. You should know the appropriate writing style for your discipline, and use that; the content overlaps with writing style, and this is a subject to which we return later.

If you intend to continue as an academic after your PhD, you will also need to publish in the appropriate academic venues for your discipline (usually journals and conferences). These also have strict conventions about structure, format, style and content, and if you ignore these, then you probably won't get published.

If you intend to continue as an academic after your PhD, you will also need to learn how to write funding proposals, which also have strict conventions. Although this is an important topic, it goes beyond the scope of this book; we'll simply observe that some time spent picking the brains of skilled writers of funding proposals will be time very well spent.

You may also, depending on your career path, need to write some or all of the following: press releases, articles for trade magazines in your discipline, promotional material for your department and/or website, policy documents, technical reports, technical manuals and patent applications. These, as you might guess, all have their own conventions, and their own ways of reading and writing between the lines, and these can vary considerably between disciplines.

In this book, we focus on the written PhD dissertation and on writing journal articles, which are the two most important topics for most PhD students. Once you've grasped the concepts behind these, you should be able to learn the rules for other types of writing fairly swiftly – the key points to remember are that there are different rules for different types of writing, and that if you can find out the reasons for those rules, then you'll probably find it much easier to write well in those styles. A lot of the reasons are very mundane practical ones, to do with the process of publication and printing; it's well worth finding them out.

The dissertation: core concepts

The dissertation is the piece of written work which shows that you have the skills and knowledge required to make you worthy of a PhD, such as being able to design, conduct and publish an original piece of research. A key word is 'shows'. You need to know what the relevant skills and knowledge are for your field, and then make sure they are very visible in what you write.

Getting the form and voice of the dissertation right is just as important as getting the content right – indeed, they're essential to conveying the content. If you doubt this, remember the ground rules: a dissertation should stand on its own – if the examiner misunderstands it, then that's the candidate's problem, not the examiner's. The chapter on the structure and style of writing contains more information about the structure and style of a typical PhD, and the reasons for them.

Dissertation FAQs

Q: *Do I need to include everything I've done?*
A: No. If you decide that a subset of data, or an entire study, does not contribute to the overall composition of the thesis, you don't need to include it. Note, however, that this does not apply to the situation where one study shows that your initial hunch was clearly wrong: in this case you have to include the study. If you do research sensibly, then you will be phrasing your questions as a series of reductions of the problem space, rather than a search for confirmatory evidence, so this issue should not be a problem for you.

Q: *Do I need to include the raw data?*
A: That depends on the conventions of your discipline; check with your supervisor and your institutional regulations about PhDs. The usual principle is that the appendices should include examples of what you used at each stage, starting with instructions to respondents, continuing with examples of any data collection instruments that you used, and also showing one or two examples of completed response sheets or whatever it was that you used. This allows the examiners to check what you did at each step, and to satisfy themselves that you did it right.

Q: *How long does the thesis have to be?*
A: The real answer is that it is as long as it needs to be to do its job, and no longer. The full significance of this answer won't make much sense to you

until you've supervised undergraduate projects and taught research methods for a while, so the more immediately helpful answer is to check the regulations and ask your supervisor. The lesser answer is: within the maximum page or word limit set by your institution.

Q: *I've just discovered a mistake in my analysis of the data, two days before I'm due to hand in. What do I do?*

A: Good question. Whatever you do, *don't lie.* Get in touch with your supervisor immediately and ask for advice about how to handle the corrections. If it's a major mistake, you'll need to redo the analysis, for all sorts of practical and ethical reasons. If the mistake is comparatively trivial and you're about to run out of time on your thesis, your supervisor may be able to suggest ways of buying time within The System so that the deadline is not an issue. Another possibility might be a rewrite which simply cuts out that part of the analysis from your write-up completely, if the mistake only applies to a manageably small subset of the write-up.

Q: *I'm writing up, and I've just discovered that someone else has published something almost identical. What do I do?*

A: Don't panic. It's usually possible to present the same material from at least two different viewpoints, if you know what you're doing. Talk to your supervisor about this. You should be able to rephrase your work to take the other person's work into account, and to differentiate yourself clearly from it. For instance, they might have studied a different social group from the one you studied; if so, you can put more emphasis on the social group aspect of your work and less on the methodological novelty. You might well be able to get some benefit from comparing and contrasting your results and the other person's.

Q: *I've developed writer's block. What can I do about it?*

A: The standard-issue books have plenty of ideas, and there are some in Chapter 12 in this book. Examples include deliberately doing something completely unrelated to writing up; writing something deliberately inaccurate, so that your subconscious rebels and makes you start writing the truth; rewarding yourself with treats; setting yourself small, manageable goals; and getting a friend to help motivate you.

Q: *Can I write-up in the same style that you use in this book?*

A: You must be joking. This is the style we use over a cup of coffee; the style we use in our academic articles is very, very different (and a lot less fun, both to read and to write).

Journal papers

This section focuses on journal papers, but much the same principles apply to conference papers and other forms of publication such as book chapters. We have gone for journal papers rather than the other types on the grounds that publishing a journal paper is usually viewed as a sign that you are a fully-fledged academic – there is a general assumption that the other publication venues are variable in their selectivity and quality control, but that journals are exclusive and discerning. This is far from invariably true, but it's a useful rule of thumb, especially if you're aiming for an academic career and want to get some useful things on your CV.

Supervisors differ in their opinions of students writing journal papers. Some think it is a Good Thing, and encourage it; some think it is a Bad Thing, and discourage it; others again think that it is a Good Thing in some circumstances, but not in others (e.g. if it is likely to be used as a displacement activity by a student who ought to be spending every last second finishing their write-up because the deadline is next Tuesday).

So, the first thing to do regarding writing a journal paper is to check with your supervisor about the wisdom of this scheme in relation to your particular situation. If they say no, with good reason, then take their advice; if they give you their blessing and send you off to get started, then you need to think about what to do next.

Where to publish

The first question is venue (i.e. where to publish). This involves consideration of the prestige of the journal, the readership of the journal, the degree of match between your chosen topic and the focus of the journal and the acceptance rates of the journal. The usual strategy is to go for the most prestigious journal that you have a reasonable chance of being published in, which then raises questions of how to assess your chances. A cup of coffee with someone knowledgeable is a good idea at this point.

These things having been done, you need to do some basic homework, which is neglected by a surprising proportion of aspiring researchers. The first thing is to read the guidelines for contributors to your chosen journal. These are usually printed in the journal, or available on its website, or (as a last resort) from its editor. The guidelines will tell you the word limits for articles, the procedures for handling tables and figures, the number of copies to submit, etc. All these guidelines are there for a good reason. If you follow them, then the editor will be more likely to think positively about you. It is inadvisable to antagonize editors needlessly. The following sections say a bit about each of the main topics in the guidelines, to explain their purpose and to suggest ways of improving your chances of success.

The focus of the journal is important. Journals have to focus, because of the sheer volume of research being published – even very specialist journals have to reject a high proportion of good papers because of space limitations. (Journal editors work to a page budget each year, which limits how much they can publish.) You therefore need to make sure that your article is relevant to the journal you are submitting to. If in doubt, contact the editor (politely) and ask. Journal editors are normally serious players in their research field, unlike commercial editors, so the editor will be the person who makes the decision about how relevant your paper is. If you are skilful and/or lucky, the editor may like the idea behind your paper and may give you some suggestions on how to present it (e.g. which themes to stress and which to play down). This advice is important and should be treated seriously (though remember that following it does not guarantee acceptance).

What your submission should look like

Your submission should contain a covering letter, the relevant number of hard copies of your article, a soft copy if required and anything else specified in the guidelines to contributors. The letter should be polite and brief; it should make it clear which author is handling the correspondence (if there is more than one) and should give full contact details for that author. The article itself should follow the guidelines for contributors. The next few paragraphs describe the guidelines and explain why they matter.

The word length issue is important because of the page budget. The editor may have to choose between publishing one longish article and squeezing in two short articles, and will certainly be keeping an eye on the page budget. Tricks like using a small font or wide margins will not be well received. The page budget in the journal will be calculated from the number of words in your article (including tables and figures), not from the number of pages in your manuscript, so small fonts or wide margins won't deceive the editor for long.

Once your article has got through this initial check, the editor will send out copies to reviewers, who will give their opinion on it. Procedures vary between journals. Most prefer to send hard copies to the reviewers, since reviewers like to scribble on hard copies and don't like having to print off papers from soft copy which may be in an inscrutable format or font. Editors will therefore ask contributors to send enough hard copies for each reviewer, plus one for the editor's files. If there are two reviewers, you will be asked to send three hard copies; one journal we know of used to ask for eight hard copies. If you send too few hard copies then the editorial team will have to make some copies themselves. Editorial teams have better things to do with their time than photocopying your manuscript, so it is a good idea to send the right number of copies.

Some journals ask for electronic submission. The editorial team of these journals are unlikely to take kindly to your submitting a soft copy written in Grunt2004 or some other format which their system has never heard of, and will probably not be interested in your assertion that this is a technically superior format to what everyone else uses. Similarly, if you submit soft copy to a journal which asks for hard copy submissions, then the editorial team are unlikely to add you to their Christmas card list – soft copy submissions are a wonderful idea in principle, but reality is rather different.

Some journals use double-blind reviewing; others don't. In double-blind reviewing, the reviewers don't know who you are and you don't know who the reviewers are. For this purpose, the submission guidelines may ask you to put your name and contact details on a separate sheet from the rest of the paper, so they can be detached before the papers are sent to the reviewers. Editors of such journals will not want to spend part of their morning applying correction fluid over extraneous authors' names.

Reviewers may or may not scribble on your manuscript; copy-editors certainly will. A small proportion of contributors submit copy so clean (i.e. manuscripts so free of errors) that they are remembered by the editorial team for this fact alone. Most, however, require a noticeable amount of copy-editing, often involving mistakes with references (e.g. a paper described in the main text as having been published in one year, and described in the references as having been published in a different year). For this purpose, copy-editors and reviewers need double-spaced text so they can note what needs doing. Submitting a single-spaced manuscript is a sign that you are an amateur and probably clueless.

The guidelines will specify that the article has not been submitted for publication elsewhere. If you submit the same article to two or more journals simultaneously and are caught doing it (you probably will be, because the number of available reviewers for a given area is usually small), then you will be blacklisted from the relevant journals (i.e. banned from publishing in them). This is because multiple submissions waste the time of everyone involved, and because there are legal implications involving copyright if two editors publish the same article. Editors are no keener on legal hassles than anyone else. Submitting different papers describing different aspects of the same topic is usually admissible, but you need to be careful about the degree of similarity – if the two papers are very similar, the relevant editors are likely to take a dim view.

What happens next

After you have submitted the article, you will receive a letter of acknowledgement from the editor at some point. Editors are busy people, and the acknowledgement may take a few weeks. The paper will then go out to review and be reviewed/sat on/lost by reviewers for weeks or months. At some point after this, the editor will make a decision about what to do with your paper. If you're lucky, the editor will accept it subject to neatly specified changes. If you're unlucky, it will be accepted subject to satisfying the requirements of the reviewers, which will be enclosed with the editor's letter, and will contain confused, vague, verbose and mutually contradictory requirements. If you're moderately unlucky, your paper will be rejected. You should aim to have a reasonable proportion of your papers rejected; if they are all accepted, you're probably aiming too low and should go for a more prestigious venue. (Increasing your rejection rate by writing worse papers is not a good strategy . . .)

The wise thing to do with corrections is to take the initiative. Draw up a list of the required changes, work through them systematically and write a covering letter listing the changes and saying clearly and specifically how you have made them and where. This makes life much easier for the editor, who may well give you the benefit of the doubt and accept the revisions without passing them back to the reviewers. If you're unlucky, you may need to go through another round of slugging it out with the reviewers. Taking advice from experienced and wise colleagues is a good idea at this point.

The process of publication

Acceptance

When and if you get through to this stage, you will receive a letter or email from the editor informing you that your paper has been accepted for publication in the *Journal of Nude Mice Studies*, or whatever the venue is called. You may be asked to send some more hard copies and/or soft copies of the accepted version of your paper.

Copy-editing

At some point after this, you will hear from the copy-editor, who is sublimely unconcerned with the academic content of your work but who is very interested indeed in its presentation. The copy-editor's job is to ensure that your article is presented with proper spelling, grammar, punctuation, etc. and also to ensure that things like dates and figures are internally consistent. The copy-editor will find inconsistent references, missing references, inconsistent numbers between text and tables and so forth, and will send you a list of questions to answer. A typical question will be along the lines of: 'Page 8, line 7 refers to Smith 1999, but the references show Smith 1998. Which is correct?' You then have the rewarding task of trying to track down the original article again, so you can find out what the answer is. Skilled and experienced researchers will generally reply with a complete list of answers on the same working day, and be much appreciated by the copy-editor; novices will generally not manage this, and will realize why their supervisors have placed so much emphasis on getting references exactly right. If the corrections require an excessive amount of copy-editor's time, then you may be required to pay for that time (and copy-editors are not cheap), so there are also financial implications in getting it right.

Tables and figures

One frequent source of annoyance to all parties is tables and figures, lumped together here because the implications are pretty similar for both of them. Many printers, for obscure technical reasons, handle tables and figures separately from text, and insert them into the text after it has been sorted out. Others don't. The guidelines to authors will specify what you need to do with tables and figures. For many journals, you have to put each table and figure on a separate page at the end of your manuscript, and indicate in the text where each one should go (usually via a blank line, and then a line saying 'TABLE 1 ABOUT HERE' at the appropriate point in the text). If you include your tables and figures in the text when you have been told not to, then the usual outcomes are either that you are asked to rewrite the article in the right form, or that the printers produce beautiful text, accompanied by figures and tables which look as if they have been dragged through mud, and which stand in hideous contrast to the crisp, professional-looking tables and figures in the other articles of that issue. You can, if you wish to make a few enemies, tell the editorial team that in an age of electronic publishing the most technically excellent solution is to work from the soft copy with embedded tables and figures; it might, however, be a good idea to ask yourself whether the editorial team are using their current procedure out of uninformed stupidity, or whether there might possibly be other factors involved which they know about and you don't.

Proofs

The next main stage involves the proofs. These are the printer's pre-final version of what your article will look like when it appears in the journal. For technical and logistical reasons, proofs appear at the last moment and are usually sent to authors with instructions to check them for accuracy, and to reply within a specified and extremely short period, normally between 24 hours and three days. You might want to think about the implications of that, such as what happens if you are on holiday when the proofs arrive, and the proofs contain a disastrous misprint which makes you look like an idiot or a charlatan. You might also want to think about how much you know about copy-editing, and how you would indicate a misprint in a way which didn't end in tears (for instance, with your helpful comment of 'this should read "24" you idiot!' reproduced in full in the published version). The proofs arrive with helpful guidelines on how to correct them, but it's useful to practise proof-correcting in a safe environment before this stage (as usual, a cup of coffee with an experienced colleague is useful here – they will probably be able to tell you which secretaries have been concealing their expertise in copy-editing and proof-reading from you). It's also a good idea to line up a colleague to keep an eye open for proofs if you are away at the critical time.

Miscellaneous points

A couple of miscellaneous points: first, make sure that the soft copy you send with the final version of the manuscript is the version from which the manuscript was prepared. It is incredibly irritating to the editorial team to discover that you have helpfully changed the text, so that the soft copy does not correspond to the hard copy. Second, don't try to change the content of the manuscript at proof stage – only correct errors introduced by the printers. Adding a couple of words can have a knock-on effect that extends to later pages and adds considerably to printing costs. Editors have a correction budget as well as a page budget, and will not love you if you do bad things to either of these.

It's worth mentioning at this point that copy-editors are usually more human than they appear from their lists of questions, so if you're lost and confused, try phoning or emailing them and discussing the situation constructively with them. (They are usually working to tight deadlines, so contacting them quickly via phone is more helpful to them than belated letters in the post.) Faxes can be a very useful way of handling some parts of the corrections – you can annotate the relevant page and fax it through to the copy-editor.

Once you've got through this stage, you can add the article to your CV and wait for (a) the copies of the journal to arrive in the post and (b) the journal to appear on the library shelves. Some journals send you offprints (i.e. copies of your article in splendid isolation); others send you a smaller number of copies of the entire issue of the journal where your article appears. Be miserly with these; it's tempting to give them proudly to everyone in sight, but they'll need to last you a long time. Most departments will want a copy of the article for their records, to be used when the next research metrics or assessment exercise comes along; it's a good idea to give them an offprint rather than a hard copy of your own accepted draft, because when the time of the Great Annual Departmental Report comes along they will need to include things like the ISBN and page number details for your article, which will not appear on your own draft but which will definitely appear in the journal, and probably appear in the offprint.

A closing point: most journals ask you to sign a copyright waiver as a condition of publication. The Society of Authors is conducting one of its quiet, polite and very efficient campaigns over this issue, and some journals are already changing their policy as a result. In the meantime, there's no need to be paranoid if you receive a copyright waiver form, but you might want to contact the Society of Authors as well as the usual experienced colleague if you have questions about this. The Society is helpful about all sorts of things and offers a fascinating range of services to members (including free legal advice on publishers' contracts); anyone who has had a book published, or a serious offer of publication for a book, is eligible for membership, and the Society's rates are very reasonable. It is also an affiliated trade union, which led at one point to the situation where Prince Charles (a long-standing member) had Terry Pratchett as his union boss.

Anyway, back to the closing paragraph. The main things to remember about journal articles are:

- Most articles are rejected
- Leading researchers have developed thick skins, failed researchers haven't
- Reviewers are only human, so don't take it personally if they're rude and contradict each other
- Leading researchers are leading researchers because they learn from their experiences
- Even leading researchers had to start somewhere

That's the end of this bit, apart from wishing you good luck.

Papers from theses

These guidelines are the ones that we use. We don't claim that they are perfect, or that they are the only truth. You might, however, find them useful as a starting point. The guidelines are intended for use with undergraduate and taught MSc dissertations as well as for PhD students; institutions vary about policy in this area, so don't be surprised if the system in your institution is different.

Before starting

- If you or your supervisor think that the work might possibly be publishable, then agree ground rules for publication as early as possible – preferably before you have committed to a particular project. If you can't agree at this stage, then you won't agree later. If it looks too acrimonious, then think about doing a different project, maybe with someone else. This is also particularly important in relation to intellectual property rights if the concept might bring in money.
- Agree venue – where you will submit the paper.
- Agree what you will do if the paper is rejected. You do not want to have all the team independently submitting revamped versions of the paper to other journals without your name on them. One sensible option is to agree who will take on the lead role if the paper is to be submitted to another journal; that person will normally then become the first author. This can be repeated until success or exhaustion.

Authorship

- Authorship should be agreed at the outset with all parties – normally the student and supervisor(s), with the student as first author. If you can't agree, then forget about writing the paper.
- If the work is a compilation of several projects, then the compilation writer should be first author.
- Authors should have made a substantial contribution to the work. A single advisory session (e.g. from another member of staff) will not normally constitute a sufficiently substantial contribution. If you want to take advice from other members of staff about some part of your work, then check first with your supervisor to avoid inadvertently causing bad feeling.

Submission and revisions

- All authors and co-authors should agree to the final version before the paper is submitted.
- Don't submit to more than one journal at a time. Journals blacklist people who do it (i.e. they never publish anything by that author again). There are sound reasons for this – multiple submissions of this sort can lead to an editor inadvertently breaking the law via breach of copyright. It also wastes the time of the editors and referees, who are usually overworked and who do not like having their time wasted.
- If the paper is accepted subject to revision, then all authors and co-authors should have a reasonable opportunity to comment on the revised draft before it is submitted (e.g. by being sent a copy, with a request for any comments within two weeks).
- All authors and co-authors should be kept informed of any developments within a reasonable time of their occurrence (e.g. a verdict from the venue).

After publication

- Each author and co-author should receive at least one offprint of the paper.
- All authors and co-authors should receive at least one copy of any publicity about the work.

In case of disputes

- Seek advice from relevant people in the first instance, before matters become too unpleasant.
- Where possible, keep a written record of agreements at each stage – for instance, agree authorship via email.

Paper checklist

Content

- Do you have a clear question?
- Have you demonstrated why the question is interesting?
- Have you demonstrated why the question is non-trivial?
- Have you demonstrated why the answer is non-obvious?
- Is your 'red thread' evident; do you have a clear and coherent argument?

Setting your paper in context

- Have you located your work with respect to the existing literature?
- Is it clear what theory informs your work and how your work contributes to theory?
- Have you discussed the assumptions, antecedents and limitations of your work?
- Have you discussed how your work leads forward to future work?

Evidence

- Is your evidence clearly presented, according to the standards of your discipline?
- Is your interpretation distinguished from your data?
- Do your conclusions follow from your evidence?
- Can someone repeat or replicate your work based on the description given in the paper?

Due credit

- Have you agreed on authorship and on the order in which authors are listed?
- Have you acknowledged the people who should be acknowledged?
- Are the citations accurate and complete?

Use of literature

- Have you cited the seminal text(s)?
- Have you cited the classic texts?
- Have you cited the foundational text(s)?
- Do you have at least five references on the first page?
- Do your references span the period from the seminal paper to last year?
- Have you included a reference which shows you know the literature which goes beyond the standard references for a particular topic?

Venue

- Have you decided on the venue?
- Have you checked for deadlines (if applicable)?
- Have you read and followed the guidelines for authors?

Presentation

- Have you followed the guidelines for authors?
- Are figures and references in house style?
- Have you spell-checked the paper?
- Have you used appropriate national spellings and punctuation (British or American)?
- Do the headings provide useful and sufficient signposting?
- Does your presentation conform to the conventions in your discipline?

11

Writing structure and style

Writing style • Academic style: an example • Academic style: sending signals • Writing structure • Academic style: summary

> *Still, it gave the facts – some of them – and apart from being dated 'off Barcelona' in the customary way, whereas it was really being written in Port Mahon the day after his arrival, it contained no falsehood . . .* [1]

One sobering thought for most PhD students is the sheer size of the written thesis they will have to produce. It will probably be the largest single piece of written work that they produce in their life. Most students are understandably intimidated by this. The reality is not so bad, once you understand how to break down the problem into manageably small chunks, which is what this chapter is about. The written thesis consists of a series of chunks, in the form of chapters; each chapter in turn consists of chunks, in the form of standard chapter sections. By the time you're down to that level, you're dealing with a few pages at a time, which is far more manageable. This chapter looks at structure and style in writing, both generally and specifically for the written thesis. Structure, style and content are inextricably intertwined, so this chapter also contains a fair amount about content.

In your thesis, you are showing that you have the skills that make you worthy of a PhD, and that you have done a piece of work which is worthy of a PhD. At the heart of the thesis is a clearly stated research question. It doesn't

---

[1] O'Brian, P. (1990) *Master and Commander.* London: W.W. Norton & Company, p. 335.

need to be hugely original, or huge: just original enough and big enough. Answering this question often involves answering a series of sub-questions; each of these sub-questions will usually correspond to a chapter in the thesis. Many students find it useful to draw this as a series of boxes, with one box per chapter, and then draw smaller boxes within each chapter box, representing the various sub-components of each chapter.

We'll return to structure in a moment. First, though, we will look at style, and why writing style is more than just social convention: academic writing style in particular has good reasons for being the way it is, which overlap considerably with writing structure and with content.

Writing style

Different types of writing use language for different purposes. In commercial writing, for instance, the purpose is frequently to persuade the reader. This is very different from informing the reader. For instance, an advertisement will typically focus on the strong points of a product, with little or no information about its weak points or about the strong points of competitors.

In most of academia, this sort of blatant sales pitch is viewed as somewhere between tacky and downright unethical. To take an extreme example, if you only describe the successes of your new cure for cancer, and don't mention that it has a 90 per cent fatality rate among the other patients, then you're doing something criminally unethical. So, the convention in academia is that you give a full account of what you found. How do you do that? As you might expect, this is something which has received a lot of attention over the years, resulting in conventions about what is best practice in the structure for writing up your findings. At a sordidly practical level, when you write up your results in a journal article, the publishers are keen to keep your word count down, so they can squeeze more articles into each volume, so there are conventions about writing style which allow you to say what you found in an efficient way that involves as few words as possible, even if it's not very readable.

A key principle at this point is that if you show that you know the specialist conventions about structure and style, then that strongly implies that you know what you're doing in other related areas as well; conversely, if you don't show that you know the normal conventions for structure and style in your field, then the examiners will assume that this is because you simply don't know them, and don't deserve a PhD. So, how do you show this knowledge?

Making examiners happy

Work backwards from where you want to end up. You want to end up with the examiners looking pleased and relieved as they finish reading your thesis and settle down to watch the latest re-run of *Buffy the Vampire Slayer* or whatever examiners do in the evening. You do not want to end up with the examiners looking worried or angry. How do you do this?

A good way to start is to look at things from the examiners' point of view, particularly the external examiner's. If you're eminent enough to be an external examiner, you'll be chronically overloaded with work, and be torn between a desire to see standards maintained and a desire to get the whole business over with as soon as possible. The result of this is that you will want to see a thesis which is a clear, unequivocal pass. The thing you will least want to see is something which might just about scrape through with major revisions: this will entail weeks of further hassle for you if the wretched candidate ends up sending allegedly improved revisions to you for approval. So, what makes you as an external decide that something is a clear pass rather than a thing of horror?

The basic issue is whether the thesis is an original contribution to knowledge at an appropriate level for a doctorate. If the relevant boxes can be unhesitatingly ticked, then everyone is happy and can get on with their lives. You as a candidate can tackle the first couple of boxes ('original' and 'contribution to knowledge') by some judicious phrasing. If you use phrases such as 'this extends the classic work in this area by Smith and Jones (2002) by applying rough set theory' then the 'originality' bit is pretty clear: your original bit is the extension of Smith and Jones' work. If you use phrasing such as 'these findings have significant implications for research in this field, which has typically viewed this topic as of comparatively minor importance' then the 'contribution to knowledge' bit is also pretty clear. Judicious phrasing by itself is not enough; you need to have done good research as well. However, good research needs to be clearly presented or there is the risk that the examiners will miss the needle of your original contribution in the haystack of your rambling prose. A good structure is useful for supporting the judicious phrasing; there should be clearly demarcated subsections which deal specifically with the originality and the contribution to knowledge of the topic you're investigating and/or of the method you're using. (These will have suitably tactful titles: entitling them 'original contribution to knowledge' is generally viewed as a bit tacky.)

The third box ('appropriate level for a doctorate') is not so easy to point to at a specific place in the text; like the lettering in a stick of rock, it runs all the way through. The tip about getting a couple of journal articles published to show you're working at the right level is quite a useful one, but if you have to resort to that as an argument in the viva, then you're in trouble – it's best viewed as a nice extra and/or as a last resort, not as a main component of your case. The examiners will be reading between the lines of your thesis, and if you have written the right things between the lines then everyone will be happy. Most of this will consist of numerous small things, minor by themselves, but major when taken together. For instance, if you've been developing a taxonomy of social inclusion problems in secondary education, then showing that you have read some of the literature on taxonomic theory is likely to send out the right signals to the examiners, but will not by itself be enough to demonstrate doctoral-level research – you'll also need to use the right language and technical terms throughout, to refer to the right literature, to discuss the findings at the right level of abstraction and so forth. If you get into the habit early on of reading and writing between the lines, then you will do this automatically when you write up, and significantly improve your chances of a straight pass.

Blood in the water

Swimming in shark-infested waters is a bad idea if there is blood in the water. It is an especially bad idea if the blood is yours. Much the same principle applies to writing. Critical readers can detect blood in the water a long way off, and will come cruising in at speed looking for a kill. Sometimes they go for a quick kill, but on other occasions they decide to play with their victim for a while first. It's not a pretty sight.

Another analogy for the same problem, which is less eye-catching but more directly applicable, is the wolf-pack. Wolf-packs will run near potential prey, sizing it up for signs of weakness. If an animal looks healthy and capable of looking after itself, they ignore it instantly. If an animal looks ill or weak, they go for the kill. If your writing (or presentation, if you're giving a seminar or conference presentation) looks healthy and professional, then you will probably be left alone. If there are signs of weakness, then the wolves start closing in fast. Begging a metaphorical wolf-pack for mercy has about the same chance of success as begging a real wolf-pack for mercy if you're a plump caribou in the middle of a long, cold, hungry winter.

So, what do you do about it?

Step 1: stay indoors until you're ready

The first and most simple step is not to go into predator territory if you have open wounds. If your work isn't good enough, then don't present it; go back and get it right, instead of presenting inadequate work and making apologies for it. Here is a good example (from a seminar by a colleague): 'We found the following results . . . however, feedback from the subjects afterwards indicated that our initial instructions had been ambiguous. When we replicated the initial experiment with revised instructions and a new set of subjects, the results were as follows . . .'

The subtext here is: 'I take it utterly for granted that you redo an experiment without hesitation if you have to, regardless of the time and trouble – trying to plead for mercy and present inadequate data isn't even on the agenda for me.' The key aspect of the presentation here is that the second sentence follows immediately from the first one, without hesitation, and plunges straight into the results without making a big thing out of the fact that the researchers took the trouble to redo the experiment. Somebody who treats this level of professionalism as taken for granted will probably have been meticulous about everything else in their study too, so the predators know there's not much point in trying their luck.

One thing which novices usually get wrong involves sample sizes and amount of data. Here is another good example, from an MSc thesis: 'There were three groups of respondents, each with four subjects . . .' (followed by description of subject groups). That works out as 12 subjects. Twelve. Not a couple of thousand, or even a couple of hundred. The average novice would at this point start making apologies for the small sample size, with blood gushing into the water at a rate which would have every shark in the neighbourhood abandoning its previous plans and heading inwards for an unscheduled easy meal. This thesis simply described the subject groups and moved on to the next section.

The subtext in this example is: 'This thesis is about a test of concept. For what I'm doing, I don't need a large sample size, and I know it. Now, let's move on to the next thing, which also shows that I know what I'm doing.'

Sample size and amount of data are important; however, the figures required will vary dramatically depending on whether you're doing data-driven work, test of concept or method-mongering. Not many novices know this. Even fewer know that excessively large sample sizes are often an indication of poor experimental design and inadequate knowledge of inferential statistics, both rich sources of blood in the water. If the previous paragraphs have left you with an uneasy feeling, then you might want to consider reading about types of paper, experimental design and inferential statistics.

Step 2: send out the right signals once you are ready

Show you're a professional: use the language and conventions of professionals in the discipline. If you don't know what these are, then you need to learn them. Reading this book, and other texts on this topic, is a good start. Make your language and non-verbal signals as different as possible from those of the clueless beginner.

Know your enemies

Remember your enemies at this stage. The real enemies are the people you could be confused with. Differentiate yourself from them tacitly, not explicitly. If you mention them explicitly, then you have added an unwelcome item to the audience's agenda, namely deciding whether you really are different from your enemies, as you claim. If you do it tacitly, then that item shouldn't be an issue.

The keen beginner

One enemy is the keen beginner who hasn't read the literature in depth and who makes classic novice mistakes. You need to send out a strong signal that you don't fit into that category. The good old cup of coffee will help you to find out about classic novice mistakes. The good old reading through the classic literature back to the year dot will help you with the literature in depth. It's surprising what you find if you go back more than about 20 years – a lot of researchers are too hungry for fortune and glory to bother doing their homework properly, and to discover that they are reinventing the wheel. There's no long-term substitute for reading the literature. The short-cuts in this book are about identifying the best ways to do things efficiently and well, not about ways of avoiding the literature. The literature, like research methods, is your friend; the more you have in your repertoire, the more situations you can tackle confidently.

The intelligent layperson

Another enemy is the intelligent layperson. If general knowledge is enough to tackle the problem, then you shouldn't be bothering to tackle that problem. This is where counter-intuitive results from the literature are useful.

The snake-oil merchant and the self-proclaimed genius

Other potential enemies are the snake-oil merchant and the self-proclaimed genius, both of whom peddle their own patent panaceas. Claiming that you have solved a problem which has baffled the best minds in the field (including, by implication, the audience) is not something which will endear you to your audience and is about as advisable as marching into a mediaeval Mongol war camp and shouting, 'Genghis is a sissy!' at the top of your voice.

Don't show weakness and doubt

You should never show weakness, apologize or ask for mercy. If you've done the work right, then there's no need to do this. If you haven't done the work right, then don't present it – go back, do it again and get it right. (Note, though, that this applies to fatal errors, such as a crucial flaw in the data collection: all research includes unanswered questions and things that could, with the benefit of hindsight, have been done differently, which are a normal part of research, and can be honestly presented in a positive way, indicating fruitful areas for future research.)

There are lots of words and phrases which indicate weakness. Some of these are 'weasel words', whose purpose is to help you wriggle out of committing yourself to an assertion and substantiating it. Weasel words usually have no place in academic writing, and certainly not in a dissertation. It is not normally good enough to say that something 'seems' to be something else: is it or is it not? Similarly, 'probably' isn't good enough. Weasel words suggest that the author has not looked hard enough or is making speculations which cannot be substantiated.

Whenever you justify something, you raise the question of why it needed justifying in the first place, and whether your justification of it was good enough. Anything which involves assumptions is also leaking blood (e.g. 'presumably the respondents believed that . . .'). Words such as 'probably', 'presumably' and 'must have' are another way of saying, 'I have no firm evidence for this, and am guessing.' If you have evidence, present it; if you don't have evidence, and the issue is important, then get evidence and find out whether you are actually right in your guess. Speculation is something which should either be explicitly labelled as speculation (and therefore of only tangential relevance) or saved for the closing stages of the discussion section where you are discussing future work, or preferably both.

Vagueness is not acceptable. From an actual examiner's report:

> In an academic argument the details should all be nailed down, as far as this is possible. Often it is best to omit things of which one is unsure. If this is possible they should not be present anyway. If it is not possible, they must be established definitively. Otherwise the conclusion will inherit the lack of precision. Then the whole work may simply become a piece of unproven speculation, which is unacceptable for a doctoral thesis.

One thing worth watching out for in this context is the temptation to use public-domain principles as explanations. The reason for this advice is that these principles are often untrue or seriously misleading. This is one case where the internet is positively useful – the sci.skeptic and alt.folklore.urban newsgroups are rich sources of widespread beliefs which have no basis in truth. Make sure you have a proper academic source for any explanatory principles you want to use. If you can't find one, then it might be because the principle just isn't true . . .

Don't bluff

If you don't understand something, make time and work on it until you understand it. If you try to use technical concepts without understanding them properly, the critical reader will spot it instantly.

One apparent exception to this is when you are using advice about specialist tests (generally in the context of choice of statistical test). The normal convention in many disciplines is that in such cases, where the expertise is outside what a researcher in the domain could be fairly expected to know in detail, it is acceptable to take advice from two or more independent authorities in the relevant area and follow that advice. If they get it wrong, then that isn't your problem, because you've taken reasonable steps. You'll still need to understand what the statistical results mean, though.

Academic style: an example

The example below is from a paper by one of the authors and a colleague. It has been chosen specifically because its topic will be unfamiliar to most readers, making it easier to demonstrate the way in which language is being used at both the explicit and the 'between the lines' levels.

> Direct evidence for hemispheric asymmetry in human and proto-hominid brains is in principle obtainable via endocranial fossil remains. Unfortunately, the number of suitable skulls is limited, particularly for older species. Much the same problem applies to attempts to infer handedness from the weight and size of hand bones, on the principle that a more extensively used hand will be more robust (and therefore have larger bones) than the non-preferred one (Roy, Ruff and Plato 1994). There is evidence of such asymmetry in the long bones of the upper limb and shoulder girdle of Neanderthal specimens (Trinkhaus, Churchill and Ruff 1994; Vandermeersch and Trinkhaus 1995) but the paucity of suitable pre-Neanderthal material limits the scope for this approach.

There are several specific types of coded language in use here. These include the following.

Technical terms

Technical terms signal membership of the relevant research community: 'hemispheric asymmetry, protohominid, endocranial, robust, non-preferred, long bones, upper limb, shoulder girdle'. 'Robust' is a technical term, the converse of 'gracile'. 'Long bones' is also a technical term, contrasting with 'short bones'.

References

References signal familiarity with relevant literature: (Roy, Ruff and Plato 1994); (Trinkhaus, Churchill and Ruff 1994); (Vandermeersch and Trinkhaus 1995). All three are from within six years of the submission date of the article, and all are specialist journal articles.

General academic language

General academic language signals membership of the general academic community: 'in principle, via, much the same, infer, there is evidence of such, paucity'. Note how specific claims about inferring handedness via specific methods are supported by references, while a broad statement about lack of suitable fossil material is not supported by a reference. Within this research community, the lack of suitable fossil materials is a generally agreed truth which does not require a supporting reference; the authors have already demonstrated their membership of this research community via their familiarity with its literature and technical terms, so can make the broad statement without a supporting reference. Writing for a different research community, a supporting statement might well be needed (for instance, if the different research community had not reached a consensus about the lack of suitable fossil remains, or was completely unaware of the issue).

Note also how an entire approach is described and rejected in two sentences. The authors throughout assume that their readers will be familiar with a range of technical terms relating to physiology, such as 'endocranial' – this assumption is made because the paper is for publication in a journal catering for a well-defined research community (laterality researchers). This assumption reduces the need to unpack and explain terms; this in turn means that the writing can be terse and efficient. If the authors deal with terms unlikely to be known to the readers, then it is necessary to explain each term on the first occasion when it is used (as happens later in this paper when the authors describe flint artefact manufacture).

Academic style: sending signals

Everything you write sends out some sort of signal between the lines, either through what is there, or what is not there.

Good signals to send include:

- I'm a professional with the right attitude
- I know what I'm doing

Bad signals to send include:

- I am ignorant, clueless and in despair
- I am lazy, dishonest and rude, and I deserve to be hanged and flogged

How do you communicate these things? They vary in easiness.

I'm a professional with the right attitude (easy concepts, but hard work)

- I pay attention to detail in things like spelling and the layout of the references
- I've done all the work I should have done, and demonstrated this in the write-up
- I've done a meticulous job of work and demonstrated this in the write-up
- I've presented this work neatly and exhaustively, following the conventions of this area

I know what I'm doing (requires knowledge of your chosen field and hard work)

- I know all the key texts, have read them and have cited them correctly
- I have read other relevant things as well and have cited them correctly
- I know and understand the technical concepts in this area and have been careful to use all the relevant ones somewhere in my write-up

I am ignorant, clueless and in despair (all too easy to communicate, especially in the second year of a PhD)

- I have not read the key texts
- I have made classic mistakes without even realizing it, and have not had the wit to show my draft to a reliable mentor who would have spotted them ages ago
- My work contains apologies and pleas for mercy

I am lazy, dishonest and rude, and I deserve to be hanged and flogged (effortless, if you're a sinner)

- My work contains hardly any references
- My references are all from the internet, popular magazines or textbooks
- My spelling, grammar and presentation are dreadful
- I have attempted to conceal the dreadfulness of my spelling, grammar and presentation with jokes, clip art, a fancy binder, coloured pie charts and a grovelling acknowledgement to my supervisor
- I have misspelled my supervisor's name and got their title wrong in the grovelling acknowledgement to them
- There is no evidence in what I have written that I have done any work
- Some paragraphs of my text are much better written than others, and bear a strong resemblance to articles on the internet
- I have done things which my supervisor specifically told me not to do
- My text compares theory and academia unfavourably with the 'real world' but I have not put my money where my mouth is and gone away into the 'real world'

If these things apply to you, then you will probably not even be allowed to start a PhD – the initial selection process will almost certainly detect you and hurl you into the outer darkness (though you might manage to bluff your way onto an MSc, only to be failed when your dissertation erupts onto an unwilling world). It is unlikely that anyone fitting this description will be conscientious enough to bother reading this book anyway; we have included this section largely as a reassurance to virtuous but insecure students, so that they know they aren't as bad as they sometimes fear.

One useful tip is to go through your text with a highlighter, highlighting any words or phrases which would not be familiar to the average person on the street. This is particularly useful for your first page, and especially for the first paragraph, where first impressions count. If there's hardly any highlighter on the page, it might suggest a lack of engagement with the academic literature – or worse, a lack of academic content. On the other hand, if there's hardly anything *not* highlighted, it might suggest an indiscriminate jargon binge (and a very tedious read). Balance matters: judicious use of technical language shows authority and provides explicit connection to the academic literature; setting that usage within a readable narrative demonstrates clarity of thought and communication. So, consider each bit of highlighting: is this instrumental (e.g. purposeful use of technical precision), or is it obfuscation (i.e. using impressive words just to show off or, worse, to mask an underlying weakness)?

A tip so obvious that it's easy to forget: get your spelling and punctuation right. If necessary, buy a dictionary and/or go on a training course. They will probably be the best investments you will ever make. If you're claiming to be a highly educated professional and you can't spell or use punctuation correctly, then you're off to a bad start.

The phrasing and style you use can send out both intended and unintended signals; Table 11.1 gives some examples. Although it's couched humorously, the underlying points are serious – learning to send out the right signals between the lines is an important skill.

Table 11.1 Reading between the lines: some classic examples

You say	Others read this as meaning
Smith says	I haven't read many journal articles
explains Dr Smith	I read too many magazines
enthuses Dr John Smith	I read too much Barbara Cartland
there is general consensus that (a)	there is some agreement that
there is general consensus that (b)	I don't have any specific references but this sounds like a plausible claim
it is clear that	I think
it is arguable that	I hope

a larger sample might prove	I don't understand anything about inferential statistics or survey methods
a recent study found that	I don't have a reference for this, but I'm fairly sure it's true
there is some anecdotal evidence that exciting	some people told me in a bar that I haven't grasped the point of academic writing yet
achieve it's potential	I want to look as if I've wasted years of education
excede it's potential. A serendipitous instance of such hegemony is	Here's where I start plagiarizing stuff from real researchers who can use big words correctly
objective	I don't understand research methods properly
bias free	I don't understand research methods properly
I think	I am clueless, and also haven't heard about the third person passive
(though cf. Green *et al.* (in press) for an interesting re-evaluation of this literature)	I've read the advanced literature, so sod off
e.g. Green and Brown 1998; Smith and Wesson 1999; Jekyll and Hyde 1999; Young, Gifted and Black 1999	I've read lots of stuff, but I can't distinguish among the papers
Smith (in press)	I'm on such good terms with Nobel Prize winners like Smith that they send me preprints of their papers
Smith (*pers. comm.*)	Smith mentioned this when we met in the toilets at Schiphol Airport on our way to the conference last year
a strong similarity to the debate in the 1950s over X	I'm thoroughly familiar with the literature back to before most people in this area were born, so sod off
per se	I had a proper classical education, and can use sophisticated Latin terms correctly, so . . .

Writing structure

The core of your PhD is your thesis: the argument that you're proposing, together with its reasoning and evidence. If you've got this clear in your head, then everything else should follow. Your institution will have written guidelines for some parts of the dissertation (word count, page margins, etc.) and your discipline will have conventions about structure and style for the actual content (e.g. whether you have a 'method' section within each study or not). These will provide you with a fair amount of the structure you need; it's then a case of matching what you have done with that structure.

The following sections describe areas that you may find it useful to consider when planning the structure and content of your dissertation.

Chapter titles, section headings, etc.

A good test is to look over the table of contents of your thesis to see how much a reader can anticipate about the research just by scanning the headings. Some useful questions to ask yourself about the table of contents are:

- Where is the research problem stated? Can you tell what the problem is?
- Where is the methodology described? Can you tell what was actually done in the research?
- Where is the evidence presented? Can you tell what kind of evidence it is?
- What is the approach or stance adopted for the work?
- Is a new model or theory presented?
- What is important about this research?
- What are the conclusions?

The research question

This is the central part of your thesis; it is horribly easy to forget to state the research question explicitly, precisely because you are so familiar with it that you cannot imagine anyone else not knowing it. Some things to ask yourself are:

- Where does the statement of the specific research question occur in the introductory chapter (i.e. how long does the reader have to wait to discover what the particular focus of the dissertation will be)? Is there a one-sentence or a one-paragraph statement of the thesis?
- Is the statement of the research question clear and concise?
- Is the statement of the research question phrased as aims, objectives, questions, goal, problems to be solved, challenges to be addressed – or in some other form?

Theory and evidence

Theoretical context provides the rationale for your work; evidence underpins your claim to have made an original contribution to knowledge. You might want to ask yourself the following questions:

- How is theory presented in the dissertation?

- How is theory used in the argument?
- Is it clear what theory the research relates to?
- How well is the design of the research related to theoretical underpinnings?
- Is it clear how the research contributes to theory in the domain?
- What are the proportions of theory and evidence?
- Is the evidence presented objectively?
- Are the premises stated?
- Are the methods described in a way that allows replication/repetition?
- Is the interpretation distinguished from the data?
- Does the interpretation-as-evidence follow from the data?
- Do the conclusions follow from the evidence?

Introduction

This is where you should (a) create a good first impression and (b) show your reader that there is a good reason for your spending several years of your life researching this topic. Typical ingredients of an introduction are:

- Statement of problem/question
- Broad rationale for problem/question
- Description of relevant literature (including schools of thought which disagree with your own)
- Explanation of language and terminology (if needed)
- Aims, goals, objectives
- General statement of contribution
- Description of, and rationale for, research approach
- Plan for the remainder of the dissertation; overview of argument

Literature review

This reviews the literature, as opposed to simply reporting it. Its aims are:

- To frame your research (setting it in the context of existing theory and prior research, showing how it is motivated and showing why it is needed and significant)
- To distinguish your research from other work
- To show clearly to the reader that you know your subject thoroughly

Given that the literature review should frame the research, it makes sense that it should be presented at the *beginning* of the dissertation. Many dissertations add additional, specific references throughout the work – for example, elaborating a technique or providing corroboration or contrast within a discussion section. Some distribute the literature review throughout the dissertation on an 'as needed' basis, in effect providing an introduction and literature review for each major part of the research – this can be effective, but is also risky. It is unusual and inadvisable to leave the literature review to the end (such a dissertation would not normally be considered to be well written).

The review should contain:

- An arguably comprehensive/representative collection of literature
- Seminal papers
- Selective papers relating strictly to the focus of the thesis

The range of literature needed is discussed throughout this book, as is the desirable number of citations. The key to the literature review is establishing a well-founded base of 50–150 papers on which you can draw reliably. The required range of publication dates is also discussed throughout this book.

Citations should take the following forms:

- A methodical, 'objective' summary of a given paper
- Single-sentence statements
- Direct quotations
- Collective paraphrasing – grouping papers as members of a line of thinking
- Editorial paraphrasing – choosing to report what serves the argument (i.e. reporting what the paper has to contribute to the argument, not what the paper is about in its own terms)

The report of the paper should be distinguished from its interpretation. You should ask yourself whether the literature is just reported or whether there is analysis and sense-making.

Tables and their uses

Tables can't just stand in isolation – they must be described in the narrative and *relate to it*. Remember to check that the tables are labelled in the required format, and that they are labelled consistently. Common uses are:

- Summary (e.g. of results, statistical analysis, literature)
- Comparison (e.g. a comparison of research methods and outcomes across a number of studies)
- Providing context and assisting navigation (e.g. through a line of argument, through the dissertation)
- Establishing categories and establishing what those categories include
- Providing a framework (e.g. for ideas and their relationships or for techniques and their applications)

How to Lie with Statistics gives a good overview of sins to avoid in your tables (see 'Some further reading').

Illustrations and their uses

Good uses:

- To provide a conceptual map (a navigation aid through ideas, arguments or processes)
- To emphasize key points
- To illustrate (i.e. show pictures of things described in the text)
- To provide an alternative representation (i.e. alternative to text, tables, etc.)
- To summarize
- To contrast two things
- To clarify

Bad uses:

- As part of a sinful attempt, usually futile, to cover up for bad writing
- As comic relief (usually inadvisable)

Final chapter(s)

Your goals here reflect those in the introduction: you use the final chapter(s) to show the reader that you have achieved something worthwhile over the last few years and to create a good closing impression. Typical ingredients of the final chapter are:

- Summary of results (may be compared explicitly against objectives stated in the introduction)
- Discussion about how the results generalize
- Discussion of limitations (phrased positively)
- Statement of contribution to knowledge
- Future work (phrased strongly and positively)
- Speculation (in moderation)

Appendices

What goes into appendices? Answer: material that needs to be available to the reader, but doesn't need to be in the main text, such as:

- Data
- Detailed statistical analyses
- Instruments (e.g. questionnaires)
- Examples
- Code (if the PhD involved writing software)
- Glossary of terms

Remember: examiners read appendices. Kind examiners read them to find reasons to spare you; unkind examiners read them to find evidence of sin.

Academic style: summary

What you need to remember is to get your cabinet-making skills visibly onto the pages. Your references are an obvious example. Do you have the key references in your bibliography? Do you have the right spread of dates? Do you have references showing independent reading outside the standard stuff? Do you have references showing that you're a nit-picking perfectionist who has done thorough background reading? And so forth. Another obvious example is the types of study you've conducted. If you're working in a discipline where cabinet-making includes doing big surveys with heavy stats, and in-depth case studies without stats, then you need to make sure that your studies are clearly (but subtly) presented in a way which fits neatly into that framework. At this point, style intertwines with content and structure; we'll now move on to other issues involved in writing, in the next chapter, after some tips about style.

Some classic style mistakes, and how to avoid them

- Don't waffle. It's your responsibility to be clear, not the examiners' responsibility to divine your meaning.
- Don't try to evade an issue by vague or ambiguous wording – examiners are very good at spotting this and will grill you mercilessly about it in the viva.
- Don't simplify. Write for fellow professionals or you'll come across as not understanding the full complexities of your area.
- Don't use big words if you aren't absolutely sure of your meaning. A big word, wrongly used, will make you look like an idiot. Examiners will almost certainly know bigger and more esoteric words than you do, and will not be impressed by your ability to misuse a thesaurus.
- Don't follow the conventions of another discipline or country in the style of your write-up. If you don't know the conventions of your discipline, find them out. If you disagree with them, then do so *after* you've got your PhD, not in your write-up.
- Finally, and most important, don't forget the three golden principles: don't lie; don't try to be funny; but above all, don't panic and blurt out the truth . . .

12

The process of writing

Removing distractions • Getting started • Surprising yourself • Finding a focus • Keeping going • Obstacles • Allow time for reflection, review and housekeeping

'Now just listen to this one, will you,' he said, 'and tell me whether it is good grammar and proper language.'[1]

One day, if all goes well, you will have to produce the final written thesis derived from your research. Most people have strong feelings about this point. These feelings include dread, confusion, despair and being utterly sick of the whole topic. If you are in this state, then be reassured: these feelings are completely normal and are fixable. So, what do you do about it?

If this happens to you, the first thing to remember is that it happens to pretty much everyone else too. Successful researchers and writers are not ones who've never encountered these problems; they've encountered the problems, and come through. So can you. This chapter is about the process of writing, with particular reference to common problems, but also with reference to things that will help your writing process when things are going well.

If you're reading this chapter because you're going through one of these problems, and feeling bleak and low, then one thing worth remembering is the bottom line of writing the thesis: it doesn't have to be entertaining or elegant; it just needs to show you have the skills that merit awarding you a PhD. There may some day be researchers who win the Nobel Prize for literature, but it's highly unlikely to be for what they write as researchers.

Anyway, on to process.

---

[1] O'Brian, P. (1990) *Master and Commander*. London: W.W. Norton & Company, p. 225.

One key concept is working backwards: knowing where you want to end up with your writing – for instance, knowing which question you want to have answered by the end. Another key concept is structure: knowing what the chain of reasoning and evidence is in the text that you're writing. These are both discussed in detail throughout this book. If you've got these under control, then at least you shouldn't feel lost. However, academics are human beings, and as such there will be times when you feel dispirited, or unable to face writing, or unable to start. There will also be times when you have trouble mentally organizing the mass of detail that you have to deal with. The rest of this chapter contains lists and tips which you may find useful if you're in this situation.

Removing distractions

The shoebox

Put your out-takes and extra ideas in a safe place, such as a shoebox, for later use. Then stop thinking about them while you write your dissertation.

Don't edit until you have a complete first draft

One exquisite paragraph is not much use out of context – better to flesh out a first draft before diverting yourself into a perfectionistic editing loop.

Sharpen your pencils

Writers, like tennis players, often develop 'rituals' to help them focus on the task at hand. The trick is to put a strict time limit and structure on the ritual, lest it become a distraction in itself. So, for example, sharpen three pencils and sweep the desk clear – then begin.

Getting started

Talk to a friend

Tell an intelligent friend the 'story' of what you're trying to write. Tape-record what you say, including how you answer your friend's questions. If you don't have a friend handy, imagine one, and talk to the tape recorder.

Write it 'wrong'

A number of 'tricks' have to do with moving as quickly as possible away from initial generation and recasting your task as rewriting or editing. Writing something that's definitely not what you want will give you something to react against and correct – which is often easier than starting from scratch.

Question–answer

Either with a friend, or by yourself, conduct a question–answer sequence, starting with, 'What's the message?' with each question following on from a previous answer and 'why' and 'how' featuring regularly.

Amanuensis

Get someone else to play 'amanuensis' (a literary assistant) and to write a narrative based on what you tell them. They may do a good job, or they may write something inaccurate; either way, you'll have something to respond to.

Throw away the first half hour

Promise yourself that you'll throw away whatever you write in the first half hour. That means that you can write garbage, a letter to your mother or a version of what you intend – anything, as long as it's prose. The idea is just to start composing sentences and paragraphs, without regard to quality. (If it's good, you can always keep it, but if it's bad, you promised yourself.)

Just start typing

Sometimes it helps to start up the 'subsystems' separately – for example, to start typing anything just to get seated in the right position with fingers moving, then typing canned text just to get a flow of words from mind to hand, and only then to start composing.

Don't start at the beginning

Skip the introduction and start with the material which is most familiar, or easiest to express. Alternatively, start with the most challenging part.

Extreme writing

Set a target, and then sit with a friend and write collaboratively, intensively, for a fixed period. Short periods – even just five minutes – can be surprisingly effective.

Surprising yourself

Change mode

Sometimes just changing the way the writing looks (e.g. type font, formatting) or the kind of writing (e.g. from academic paper to children's book), or the mode (e.g. visual instead of verbal), or the medium (e.g. paper instead of computer) can make the material look 'fresh' or expose something different.

Write the Ladybird version

Ladybird is a publisher of children's books, including early-reader non-fiction. Distil the most fundamental story and write it in very simple language.

Storyboard, with pictures

Follow film-making practice and sketch out a 'storyboard' of the narrative, with a frame for each of the key statements, using pictures instead of words. You can even talk through the narrative, acting out the frames. Hokey, as Buffy might say, but potentially inspiring.

Finding a focus

The red thread

Remind yourself what your Big Picture is before you dive down into detail. At the heart of good presentation is a good 'plot' – not in the sense of fiction, but in the sense of a connected sequence of elements, each leading to the next. The dissertation must have a clear 'narrative spine'. Swedish academics use the image of a 'red thread' running through the text (like a red thread woven through plain muslin). The red thread involves clarity about what's important and what's peripheral. Another way to think about it is that all the elements of your dissertation must ultimately contribute to the Big Picture – and work that doesn't contribute to it should be left out. If you continually reassess the Big Picture and the red thread that runs through it, then you'll be in a good position to make a coherent account of your work.

Find a model

Find a paper or chapter that does the sort of thing you're trying to achieve (e.g. presents a study). Analyse what makes it exemplary for you: what it contains, how it's organized, what gives it its character. Distil a template from the model, then start filling it in with your own material.

Work backwards

Start by thinking where you want to end up: imagine the finished paper, or the finished chapter (you might use a model to help you, see above). Then work backwards from the product, identifying major components, sorting out critical paths to those components and so on, until you find a place to start.

Headings

Write the headings before trying to write the text. This allows you to fix the overall 'story' or structure in your mind and to work through the sequencing of presentation before you get bogged down in details.

What's it for?

For each section (or paragraph), write a comment on its *role* in the document (e.g. this is where I introduce my thesis; this is where I outline the major competing theories; this is where I give a precedent for the method I've used).

Keeping going

Incentives

Give yourself mini-incentives (e.g. line up treats somewhere nearby and allow yourself one after each section that you draft; give yourself a play day after a solid week's writing).

Progress table

Set out your section headings in a table and fill in the word count and time as you complete each one. Total the word count at the end of the day.

Obstacles

Writing is not a single activity. It is not just 'writing down', not just a simple transcription from mind to page. Rather, it is many activities: analysing, elaborating, remembering, synthesizing, mapping, ordering, articulating, clarifying, editing, criticizing, structuring, sense-making – as well as transcribing. With so many cognitive activities interacting, of course it's complex and demanding. Having the right expectations about it helps to make it less daunting. Having a few disciplines helps to make it manageable.

Perspectives on writing

- Writing is difficult, and it takes time. Do the calculation: how many useful sentences can you write in five minutes? If you extrapolate how long it will take you to write the article, chapter or whatever you're writing, you can then plan your writing schedule more realistically.
- Writing is about getting the ideas straight, where 'straight' is the operative word (see our discussion of narrative spine, or 'red thread').
- Writing imposes certain demands: substance (something meaningful to say); linearity (a clear sequence of reasoning and evidence); and completeness (no gaps in the story).
- Dodgy material (sloppy thinking, poor mapping to theory, dodgy results) makes writing difficult.
- Trouble with writing may indicate problem areas in your research rather than problems in your attitude – if you encounter trouble with writing, then look closely at what you're trying to do and the materials you're using.

For many people, writing is associated with fear. Educators talk about 'fear of failure' (anxiety about the consequences of getting it wrong or 'not being good enough' becomes an obstacle to engagement and progress) and 'fear of success' (anxiety about the consequences – the increased expectations – associated with success becomes an obstacle). It's important to recognize and face your fears. OK, so it's scary. But it's not impossible. The key realization is that *any writing is better than no writing.*

Once you've written something down, you've reduced the number of activities you have to do. Separating the activities is one of the disciplines that can help in writing. Writing can be approached as a series of 'passes': dumping ideas, prioritizing ideas, putting ideas in order, elaborating an initial structure, generating sentences from notes, editing for structure, editing for language, checking for redundancy, editing for 'voice' and so on. One of the most important aspects to isolate is 'dumping ideas'. Once you've got something on paper, you can shift from generating to responding, and turn 'writing' into 'editing' for a while. A good tip to remember is: no editing until everything is written once.

Another discipline is Keep It Simple, Stupid (KISS) – a principle that applies to most design activities. The simplest language that does the job – the simplest vocabulary, sentence structure and rhetorical structure – is often the best. Keeping it simple is different from 'schematic writing'. Whereas schematic writing reduces expression to the barest essentials (leaving out much of the detail and often realism), good 'simple' writing provides all the necessary information and detail in the most direct way possible. Think of the difference between the London Underground map and an Ordnance Survey map. Both represent the key paths, but one does so realistically, maintaining the relationships of the paths to the surrounding context and indicating the nature of the terrain.

General advice

- Writing is a skill, and like most skills it improves and becomes easier with practice
- Make a commitment to write something every day and to produce a finished piece of writing – a couple of pages – every week
- Try to present material in writing at every supervision session
- When someone critiques your writing, take the time to analyse the critique: why did the critic make those comments or suggest those changes?
- If someone copy-edits or redrafts your writing, take the time to analyse the changes: why those changes, what do they change and how do they improve the prose?
- Organize the ideas/concepts/material before you start to write
- Be precise

Writing obstacles raised by students

Problem: starting to write anything; not starting to write because the subject is not 'good enough'

Try just 'dumping ideas' as a first step. Remember: any writing is better than no writing. Don't worry about whether it's 'good enough'. It probably won't be until you finish writing it – writing it is part of the process of making it 'good enough'. (There's a research literature on this subject . . .) Until you put marks on paper and let people scrutinize them, you won't be able to get feedback about how well you've managed to convey your ideas, or on how interesting your ideas are, or on what insights they inspire in others.

If you have trouble writing something, it probably means you haven't got it clear in your mind yet. Write whatever you can, and then consider why it's so uncomfortable or seems incomplete. Gnarled sentences often signal tangled thoughts – so look again at the dense bits.

Consider writing tricks such as:

- Tell it to a friend over coffee. You might also try having the friend tell it back to you.
- Play 'Eliza'. Eliza was a computer program that simulated a therapeutic dialogue. Actually, the program only had a limited number of conversational gambits, none of which added any new information, but those

few could be, to coin a phrase, effectively elicitative. So to play the Eliza game, you simply start with an initial remark and then build on that through some simple-minded questioning. For example: 'I want to write about purple elephants.' 'Why?' 'Because purple elephants are more interesting than grey ones.' 'What makes them more interesting?' 'Because most elephants are grey, and purple ones are unusual.' 'Are all purple ones unusual?' Every so often you can throw in a *non sequitur* (although it doesn't have to be 'What do purple elephants have to do with your mother?' – the type of *non sequitur* Eliza might use). What you're doing is asking yourself repeatedly: what do I think, why do I think it and why should anyone else care?

Problem: structuring the narrative

- I know the main points but I don't know how to present them
- I can't progress from the draft to writing the final version
- lack of clarity
- finding a clear structure

Good writing is typically a process of drafting and redrafting. So don't expect to get from ideas to polished prose in one step. Going from ideas to *notes* is usually reasonably easy. So what's the difference between notes and prose? Usually: structure, order and complete sentences. The key is finding the right structure – first the structure of the ideas and then the linear structure of the argument or story you want to make about the ideas.

Try some of the tricks for structuring ideas:

- Mind maps. Once you've got all the ideas mapped out, then you can try to arrange them into a linear order.
- Put ideas on index cards – one to a card – and then 'sort' or arrange them in different collections or structures. Again, you can do this in a series of 'passes': grouping by relatedness of concepts, grouping in terms of dependency, grouping thematically, prioritizing, ordering . . . trying to sort the index cards in different ways can help reveal ideas that don't fit (so that you consider why they don't and why you want to include them) and also highlight the ideas that are focal.
- Outlining: experienced writers often advise writing a very detailed outline as a first step. Different sorts of outlines can help: content outline (just a detailed hierarchical structure for the content, e.g. headings and subheadings); headings with small abstracts for each, indicating the storyline; headings with 'roles' (what the section is and why it's there, how it serves the overall argument).

Problem: using too many words to write something that my supervisor does laconically

Solving this is a matter of practice, both of writing and of editing. Remember KISS. But also understand that 'simplicity' is not just a matter of word count – sometimes a few more words can make the writing simpler and more accessible. Work at the structure of the argument and review your draft for structure (the 'highlighter test' might help). Chaos and disharmony often result when you're not sure where something fits, and so you distribute bits of it all over the place.

Before you hand a draft to your supervisor, do an editing 'pass', looking specifically for redundancy or wordiness. When your supervisor does the cut, analyse the changes: what was expendable and why? What role had you thought that material played?

Problem: needing to develop an academic writing style

Collect exemplars of papers that have a good writing style and an appropriate voice. Analyse the collection: what do the examples have in common? What makes them appeal to you? How do they handle tough aspects of writing? How do they highlight and present key ideas? How do they introduce vocabulary? When you're writing, consider how one of those authors might have structured or phrased your material. See if there's an analogous passage in one of them that you can use as a model.

Problem: it's easy to grasp my results from a table, but I find it difficult to explain the same thing in words

Tables and graphs should always be introduced in the text. It's not enough to say 'The results are in Table 2'; Table 2 should be discussed in the narrative, and possibly also in the caption. This doesn't mean describing Table 2 exhaustively, item by item. It means leading the reader through the significance of Table 2 and its role in the argument. What does the table show? How do you intend it to be interpreted? The text should describe the key features of the table that lead you to a particular interpretation. It should relate the information presented in the table to the greater argument. What messages do you mean to convey by presenting the table? The narrative should summarize the table and articulate your messages about the table.

Problem: lack of consistency (e.g. reference style)

This is just editing. Style is various and often personal. The keys are to meet the requirements of whatever forum you're addressing (journals often have style guides) and to be consistent with whatever style you're using. You can choose your own reference style for your dissertation, so choose one that makes sense for you and then use it consistently. If you use a tool like the bibliographic software, EndNote, you can easily alter the style for different uses.

Problem: deadlines (always missing them)

Writing is hard, and it takes a long time. Always allow at least twice as much time as you think you might need. Consider how long you think the job will take; double the number, increase the units (be they hours, days, weeks or even years (!)) and add one. So, if I first think a job will take five minutes, I can sensibly allow 11 hours.

Deadlines don't go away. As your career progresses, there will be more deadlines and more responsibilities competing for your time. Cynical readers may wonder whether skill in meeting deadlines will result in The System viewing you as a safe pair of hands and dumping more work on you, until you reach your level of incompetence. Readers versed in realpolitik might answer that this depends on whether you exhibit skill in meeting The System's deadlines as opposed to your own. We couldn't possibly comment on this.

Allow time for reflection, review and housekeeping

You should have already written up a fair amount by the time you reach the end of the active research in your PhD. Some bits, like the references, you should have been conscientiously building up as you went along. Others, like the 'method' section if you're doing an experimental PhD, can be written up as you do each study and are unlikely to change significantly.

What will change most are your introductory and discussion sections for each chapter (including your initial chapter with the main literature review). Over the course of the last few years you will almost certainly have realized that the real issues in the topic you're studying aren't the ones that you expected at the start, so the literature review you write in year three will be very different from the literature review that you wrote in year one. This is completely normal and healthy; it would be worrying if you studied a topic for several years and concluded that your initial hunches were as accurate a set of insights as those obtained by several years of study. It's highly likely that this is what happened to Thucydides, who stopped writing his great work in mid-sentence and then almost certainly returned to rewriting his opening chapters, to identify themes whose importance he had missed originally. By this stage, you will probably feel remarkably little sympathy for a humourless pedant who died centuries before Christ was born, but if a genius of his stature encountered this problem, then there's no shame in your encountering it too.

So, what is the implication for you? The implication is that you will, if you have any sense, seriously consider writing your introductory and discussion sections again, from scratch, at this stage. This will allow you to make sure that your narrative spine is good, with each section leading neatly into the next, rather than looking like a collection of random things strung together more in hope than expectation. You can, for instance, pose a neat set of questions in the introduction, make sure that each set of tables in the results relates clearly to one of these questions, and then discuss the answers to the questions one by one in your discussion section, with all the potential loose ends neatly tied off.

Using the cabinet-making analogy again, you need to polish the final work. Make sure that the first pages the examiners read are all pages which display your skills – good references, evidence of expertise, good presentation, etc. Allow plenty of time for this. Fixing minor punctuation errors in your references is not conceptually taxing, but it takes a lot of time if you have made a lot of minor errors.

13

Presentations

Content • Form • Other handy tips • The three golden rules of public speaking • A brief checklist for presentations

My formerly silent tongue waxed voluble with the easy grace of a Chesterfield or the godless cynicism of a Rochester. I displayed a peculiar erudition utterly unlike the fantastic, monkish lore over which I had pored in my youth . . .[1]

This chapter deals with 'live' presentations such as seminars and conferences. Some of the issues relating to this topic are also relevant to written work – for instance, how to deal constructively with criticism, whether from the audience ('live' presentations) or the reviewers (written work). It would be a good idea to read our chapters on writing as well as this chapter if you're about to do a presentation. The main thing that you need to bear in mind when doing presentations is the distinction between content and form, and is summed up in a variation on some song lyrics: 'It ain't just what you say [content], it's the way that you say it [form].'

Content is substance: ideas and results. If there is no content worth mentioning, then the best that you can hope for is to be viewed as entertaining. That does not help you in an academic research career, where you are assessed by your peers in terms of how much interesting content you have to offer. Speakers who give content-free talks can get pretty rough treatment from academic audiences. One such talk in an old university department was interrupted after ten minutes by one of the audience banging a fist on the table and saying, 'Are you going to say something worth listening to? Because if you're planning to continue with this bullshit then I'm leaving.' This is not

[1] Lovecraft, H.P. (1917) The Tomb, in *Omnibus 2: Dagon and Other Macabre Tales* (1985). London: Grafton Books, p. 25.

the sort of reception that you should be aiming for. We will return to content soon.

Form is presentation: phrasing, pacing and delivery. The form gives a lot of information about what sort of person you are, and what sort of researcher you are. There are plenty of popular books about public speaking which give detailed advice on what to wear, how to speak and so forth during a presentation. Unfortunately, the rules are somewhat different for public speaking, for teaching, for business presentations and for research presentations, so you need to be careful about which rules you follow for which setting.

Content

Most presentations are divided into three parts. The classic advice is: 'First, tell the audience what you're going to say. Then say it. Then tell them what you've just said.' This is usually very good advice. The opening section sets the context, explains why your topic is important to the audience and prepares them for what comes next. The main section contains the main content and is usually the longest. The closing section summarizes what you have just said. Each of these sections may have subsections, depending on the length of the talk.

The key determinants for content choices are: the audience, the time available and of course what you have that's worth saying.

Audience

Giving a highly technical presentation to an audience with only basic knowledge of the area usually results in a very bored audience. Giving a novice-level talk to a highly knowledgeable audience is extremely embarrassing for everyone concerned. The best strategy is to consider the audience well in advance. If you're speaking at a conference, then look at previous proceedings, read the author instructions, talk to colleagues who have attended the conference in the past. If you're giving a seminar at another university, ask whoever invited you about the likely audience. If you're speaking at a workshop, ask the workshop organizer about the attendance list. If you're lecturing a class, then sit in on someone else's lecture to the same or a similar class. Most organizers are only too happy to answer questions about the audience, and will treat such a question as a sign of professionalism on your part.

Things you want to know about your audience include: how much the audience members already know, what the typical level of expertise is (e.g. academic researcher in the same field, PhD student, professional practitioner) and what the typical orientation is (e.g. technical development or pedagogy). This helps you to decide how much general background you need to present and what level to pitch to. If you have a topic which is unfamiliar to the audience, then you need to lay the foundation and sketch out the key concepts. If you have to cover a topic which is already familiar to the audience, you can include just enough detail to show that you understand the topic, but move on fairly rapidly to material which is less familiar to them.

Texts about business presentations and public speaking usually emphasize the need to make the presentation interesting. There is often an implication that this should be done by keeping technical detail to a minimum (not a wise strategy for academic presentations) and by using plain English (always a good idea).

If you're doing a PhD, you're likely to give two main types of presentation. The first is lectures to students on MSc or undergraduate courses, as part of your CV development. The second is talks to other researchers (for instance, seminars, conference papers, internal presentations on your progress). The two have quite different requirements.

Students want to be told what they need to know to pass the course. Your job as a lecturer is to direct their study: to provide a structure, identify the priorities and keep them engaged enough to pay attention. You will need to give a clear, coherent, simple overview of the area, based on established wisdom and with unnecessary detail removed for the sake of clarity. This is laudable; unfortunately, the world is seldom clear, coherent or simple, so for lectures you will have to present a version of reality which is not a lie, but which is also not the complete story. If you are lecturing to students, you will be expected to produce handouts with references to respectable journal articles, textbooks and other sources of information to back up your talk. This too is laudable.

The purpose of presentations to other researchers is to demonstrate that you (a) know what things are like at the sharp end of research, (b) have been at the sharp end yourself and (c) have achieved something at the sharp end which will be of use to at least some other researchers. Unfortunately, these other researchers may not be in your audience. An important feature of research talks is that you will have to present your own results to professionals who will usually know a lot more tricks of the trade than you do, and who may be hostile (for instance, if you have antagonized them by giving a simplified account). Questions at seminars are often viewed as a sort of academic blood sport, and some academics (although fortunately not the majority) enjoy scoring points by 'drawing blood', by finding fault in research presentations. (Finding fault in others' research reassures them about their own status.) Attempting to hide behind established wisdom won't help, because you should be reporting work too recent for any established consensus to have been reached. You therefore need to have your content right.

Time

There is only so much you can fit into the time available. It's probably less than you think. Too many students spend half a talk in introductions and preliminaries, wasting valuable time and demoralizing the audience. Associate time with important points – points essential to convey the character and shape of your research, points important to your line of reasoning, points concerning the implications of your research, and so on.

It is essential to cover enough of the design and structure of your research for the audience to grasp its character. So, your talk should include the five classic key ingredients:

- **Research question:** including what motivates you to address it and why an answer will be important
- **Context:** what is already known, what the issues are, what other approaches have been tried or are being tried
- **Your research design:** what you're doing, what evidence you expect to find
- **Findings:** what evidence you have produced so far
- **Take-away message:** what you want the audience to remember about your research

You'll need balance among these elements: don't sacrifice the evidence, otherwise your take-away message won't be convincing. Don't short-change the context, otherwise the research choices may not make sense. Don't forget to motivate the question, otherwise the audience might wonder why you're bothering. And so on.

Start by distributing half of the available time equally among the five – and then allocating the remaining half to the elements that are most important for you to convey. A handy tip for timing is to have a master sheet in front of you which tells you which topic you should be covering at what time – for instance, '10.15 – slide about software failure rates'. Rehearse the presentation and time yourself, then add or (more often) subtract material and try again until your timing is right. For short presentations this is simple and effective. For longer presentations it is not much fun rehearsing an hour's worth of material for the third time, so a better strategy is to rehearse once, adjust the amount of material if necessary and have a plan about which bits to add or leave out depending on how the time goes.

One of us once had to give an eight-minute presentation as part of a job application, where ability to keep to time was one of the skills being judged. Our strategy was to rehearse the talk several times (including rehearsal to an empty room) and adjust the material until the talk took between seven and nine minutes. When we gave the real presentation, we deliberately did not check the time on a watch; instead, we watched the audience, whose expressions told us how near we were to the finishing time, and finished within seconds of the specified time without apparently needing to check the time. Showing off? Yes, but it made the right impression – most speakers have difficulty keeping to time on an eight-minute slot even with time checks, so keeping to time without looking at a watch or clock was an indicator of professional skills.

The message

What's your 'take-away message'? Think of a talk as an extended abstract, rather than a full journal paper: your aim is to convey the unique character of your research, with enough detail so that the audience can grasp the big picture and understand what distinguishes your research from other related work.

Form

Form – the way in which you present your content – overlaps with content in places, but usually the distinction is fairly clear as well as useful.

Conferences (including student conferences) can be an excellent place to observe different presentation styles. In some areas, such as safety-critical systems research, widely different aspects of academia and industry are represented, and the audience can be treated to a succession of speakers using extremely different approaches to the same topic. One of us once witnessed an eminent academic in a bright pink cocktail dress giving a state of the art PowerPoint presentation, followed by an equally eminent academic in well-worn tweeds using OHP slides which looked as if they had been written on the way to the talk in a taxi with dodgy suspension.

First impressions

The audience will usually have an impression of you before they even see you. This can come in various ways. In a job presentation, they will probably have seen your CV. (Do you have accomplishments in your CV and covering letter which create a good impression?) In an academic setting, they will have seen at least the title of your talk and probably a descriptive paragraph about it. (Are these interesting and sending out the right signals about you and your work?) A little homework and anticipation can make a lot of difference.

The next thing the audience knows about you comes from the way in which you are introduced. An ideal start is an introduction such as, 'It's a pleasure to welcome Linda, whose work is already familiar to most of us here via her collaboration with Chris.' A less good start is when the person introducing you has to keep checking your details on a note card and gets your name wrong. If you take a proactive approach to your career, you can greatly improve your chances of getting the first sort of welcome.

The audience will also be forming impressions about you based on your appearance and behaviour. How formally are you dressed? How neatly? Are these both at an appropriate level for the setting of the talk? For a job interview in academia, appearance will usually be treated as significant; for a visiting seminar, the audience will usually be more or less indifferent to what you wear unless it is totally outrageous, and will be much more concerned with what you say in the seminar. If you aren't sure what the dress code is for your chosen venue, then find out. Observe job applicants in your department; go to departmental seminars and see how people dress. Ask someone about dress code over a cup of coffee. (There is an allegedly true story of a very eminent academic with little concern about fashion who was arrested for vagrancy early one morning on the steps of the British Museum, while waiting for that august institution to open. Not terribly relevant, perhaps, but it would have been a shame to leave the story out, especially since one of us was told it by someone who claimed to have heard it from the eminent academic in person.)

Slides

Audio-visual support can be an asset or a distraction. On the one hand, if the audience has only you to watch for an hour or so, you may find that they begin to catalogue your hand gestures and count your nose hairs. Giving them good visual material encourages them to focus on the content, rather than on you. On the other hand, giving them poor visual material encourages them to focus on your typographical errors instead of your ideas.

Beginners often try to put too much onto each slide. Slides are not meant to stand alone, they are meant to support a spoken narrative. Remember, if the audience is too busy trying to read your slides, then people won't be listening to your words. The purpose of the slides is to focus attention and reinforce key points, not to reiterate fully. Use them to provide visual counterpoint (illustrative photographs of the phenomenon of interest; insightful cartoons to underpin a key point; graphical presentation of essential results, etc.), to indicate structure (e.g. simple concept maps; short bullet lists of key ideas; a list of steps in a process, etc.), or to present results which take time to describe and discuss. It's usually a good idea to keep slides sparse, rather than to read words off the slide. The exception is a crucial definition or exquisite quotation.

You need to use large print so that the slide will be readable at the back of the room, and white space so that the audience isn't overwhelmed by indigestible masses of information. Tables of results are a traditional problem in presentations: usually the figures in the tables are too small to be readable at the back of the room. It's a good idea to check the readability of your slides well in advance. It's also a good idea to prepare a handout which complements the slides – most audiences appreciate a one-page handout of connected text covering your key points and a hard copy of the slides, with the slides reduced to a sensible point size so that they can scribble notes on the hard copy during the presentation.

What sort of script?

Different people use different sorts of scripts or notes to guide their talks. Think about what sort of script will support you best.

- **Overheads:** your overheads should be a distillation of the key ideas in the talk. They can themselves provide the cues for your narrative.
- **Notes:** people keep notes of points they want to make, in the order in which they want to make them. Some annotate a photocopy of the overheads to include fuller information and an indication of the 'story' they want to tell about the overheads. Others keep a separate 'text', with indications of how the overheads relate to the notes.
- **Full script:** some people write a full script for the talk – not necessarily to read it (which is not a good plan), but to have a set of words to fall back on if they 'dry up'.
- **Time line:** it's a good idea to know how your talk fills the available time, so that you know how much material you should have covered by the halfway mark and so on. If you have a script, or a set of notes, or just a running order, you can annotate it with elapsed time. Then you can check your progress during the talk.

Mechanics

You need to speak clearly enough and loudly enough to be understood at the back of the room. It's a good idea to check that you can be heard at the back of the room; it's a bad idea to do this by saying 'Can you hear me at the back?' because of the risk of some comedian replying 'Yes, unfortunately.' Beginners often start in a shout and then revert to a mumble after a few minutes. A simple way to reduce this problem is to write a reminder to yourself on your master sheet (e.g. 'Slide 2: are you mumbling?'). Another is to identify a comfortable face in the back row and pitch your voice for that person. A more difficult strategy, but one which is invaluable for many purposes, is reading your audience.

Most beginners start their talk by smiling nervously and then have problems working out how to use the audio-visual equipment, making them more embarrassed. It is a good idea to become familiar with audio-visual equipment well before your presentation – learn how to use as many varieties as possible. Also, assume that the equipment will cause problems and have a fallback ready – for instance, if you are using a PowerPoint presentation, have a set of overhead projector slides ready as an insurance policy, or whatever other technology is available at the venue as a backup. Technology goes wrong, even PowerPoint; a surprisingly common spectacle at conferences is the presenter staring at an empty screen and saying: 'But I checked it on my laptop five minutes ago and it was working perfectly.' Older technologies can go wrong too. One of us was once examining MSc vivas involving 15-minute presentations by each candidate. During one presentation the overhead projector broke down. The candidate didn't panic and the machine was replaced. The candidate carried on until the replacement machine also broke down. The candidate didn't panic and finished the talk with a third machine. Even by the standards of hardened professionals this was an impressive performance and sent out a lot of very good signals. It is extremely unlikely that you will have two machines fail on you, but it is quite possible that one will, and being ready for it will greatly help your peace of mind.

When you start talking, it is usual to begin by introducing yourself, normally with a slide giving your name and affiliation. This is your chance to check the focus of the audio-visual equipment and to find a good spot to stand. A classic mistake is to stand between the audience and your slide, so that you cast a shadow across the screen and have tables of results showing all over your face. You should get into the habit of standing to one side of the screen. You should also get used to pointing at parts of the slide on the screen using your shadow.

A moment spent in reconnaissance is seldom wasted. If possible, check the room where you will be giving your presentation, once from your point of view and once from the audience's point of view. From your point of view, what equipment is there and do you know how to use it? How much space is there for you, for things like standing to one side of the screen? Are there trip hazards such as tangled cables on the floor? Can you see the audience clearly enough to read expressions at the back of the room? Is there space to put your bag, slides, etc.? Where will you keep the incoming and outgoing slides if using an overhead projector?

From the audience's point of view, how visible is the screen from different parts of the room? If visibility is bad, and you have the chance, then consider distributing hard copies of your slides so the audience won't miss anything, and remember to tell the audience that you are giving them hard copies of the slides (a lot of people won't bother to look at the handouts until the end, or a boring bit). Are there glare problems anywhere?

You also need to master the low-level skills of organizing your materials. If you are using overhead projector slides, then you will need to keep them in order. This is a lot less simple than it sounds. You need to take each slide in turn off your 'incoming' stack. Once you have shown it, you then need to put it somewhere (usually your 'outgoing' stack). A useful habit is to work from left to right: incoming on the left, outgoing on the right, as with washing up and other craft skills. However, slides have a bad habit of sticking to each other, making it difficult to stack them neatly without distracting the flow of your talk, and you will often want to refer back to a slide you showed previously, turning your outgoing stack briefly into an incoming stack. One way of reducing this problem, if you know you will be referring back to a slide, is simply to make two copies of the slide. The same applies to slides in a PowerPoint presentation.

Reading the audience

Reading your audience involves looking at the audience and assessing their response to your presentation.

Classic bad signs are:

- People looking out of the window
- People telling jokes to their neighbours
- People shaking their heads
- People at the back craning forward to hear what you're saying
- People at the back asking their neighbours what your slide says
- People looking at their watches or the clock

Classic good signs are:

- People taking notes
- People nodding when you make a point
- People whispering to their neighbours while looking at your slides or hand-outs in an interested way
- People looking at your slides or handouts in an interested way

You need to send out to your audience the signal that you are a professional with a thorough grasp of the subject matter. You can send out some positive signals about this in the same way as when writing. For instance, when you quote one of the classic texts, you can mention in passing a more recent, more sophisticated critique of that classic text which is not widely known except among academic heavyweights.

Audiences who meet frequently (e.g. at departmental seminars or on a well-established conference circuit) often exhibit behaviour which looks odd to an outsider, as a result of group dynamics and history. For instance, a senior figure may savage an inoffensive presentation by a good and unsuspecting student as part of a long-term vendetta against the colleague who supervised that student. This will usually trigger off a retaliatory strike by the supervisor, and within seconds the scene can resemble the academic equivalent of a spaghetti Western – a sleepy Mexican afternoon one moment and a high body count the next. An interesting aspect of this is that many members of the audience will be quite unaware that this carnage is going on, because it will be couched in academic language inscrutable to outsiders. (For instance: 'I presume that you allowed for the anchor and adjust heuristic in the design of your instrument?' 'There was no need for that, because a frequentist presentation was used, due to the inherent problems associated with single event probabilities.' This section is too short to unpack that one . . .)

Other handy tips

Some types of presentation, such as job presentations, are competitive. In such situations it is a good idea to think about what everyone else will be doing and work out a way of doing something different and better. Which topics will everybody else be emphasizing? What will they have failed to think about which you can take as an element in your talk?

It's also a good idea to get as much experience as possible of presentations by attending other people's – for instance, the departmental seminar series. Even if the topic of this week's seminar is utterly unrelated to your work, it's worth going if only to find out how other people do things. (There's also a good chance that sooner or later you'll encounter something from another area which has major implications for your own area.) If the content of a talk is of no interest to you, you can use the time to make notes on any tricks of the trade which the speaker uses, or any mistakes which they make, so that you can improve your own style. One of us learned a great deal about skilful presentation, with particular regard to scaring off questions before they were even asked, during a seminar on learning in rats.

Attending other people's presentations, especially during the first few weeks of the new academic year, is also a good way of learning about professional etiquette at such events. Watching someone being savaged for asking a naïve question, or for giving a naïve talk, is painful, but it's a lot less painful than being savaged in person. You can learn what your peer group's attitudes are towards things such as falling asleep during a presentation (usually considered bad form, but occasionally used as a studied insult), asking hostile questions (frowned on by some groups, venerated as an art form by others) and knitting (usually viewed with considerable ambivalence).

Dealing with nerves

- **Preparedness:** being really well prepared won't stop you being nervous, but it will give you something to rely on as you overcome your nerves. If you've given a practice talk that was well received and that allowed you to sort out any glitches, then you're likely to be more confident in the conference presentation.
- **Crib sheets:** if there's key information you want to remember (e.g. key papers and who wrote them), then write yourself a 'crib sheet' (i.e. list of the key facts and points) that you can take along for reference in case you need it.
- **Anticipate your fears:** think through the things that worry you most. What's the worst thing that could happen? How might you deal with it? Ask someone else how they'd deal with it.
- **Find a friendly face:** it's easier to make the talk warm and conversational if you can view it as a conversation with someone – especially someone who is interested.
- **Pause for breath:** pauses during a presentation feel to you like they last for years, but the audience hardly notices them. Allow yourself pauses to think, to collect yourself, to catch your breath. Your talk will be better for it.
- **Introduce yourself as a student:** if you're really terrified, you can slip in the information that you're a student in a bid to get the audience to treat you

gently. For example, you can credit your supervisor, and you should credit your funding body, if appropriate.

- **Study the question patterns in preceding talks:** many people ask the same sorts of question of all speakers (e.g. methodology, statistics, application, relationship to particular theories). So, if you have a chance, pay attention to what sort of audience is in attendance and consider how you'd answer similar questions focused on your talk.
- **Dress comfortably:** you'll have enough to think about without being distracted by shoes that pinch or clothes that feel inappropriate. So wear something that makes you feel good.

Handling questions

You don't have to disagree with a critic. You can say: 'That's a really interesting point, and I don't think it's been properly addressed in the literature.' You have shown yourself to be courteous and open-minded, and ready to take on board what they are saying; you are also implying that the omission is common to the literature in the area, rather than a failing on your part.

If your audience points out something which appears to be a genuine flaw, then thank them for it, go away and test out what they've said – they may be right, and if so the sooner you fix the problem the better. In such cases it's a good idea to ask them to work through the implications as a response to their question – it might well be that they are wrong, or bluffing, and if so this will become apparent in their response to your courteous reply.

Hypothetical example: you have just described a methodology for eliciting information about the beliefs and values of socially disadvantaged groups. Someone at the back of the audience says that you might find that the literature on requirements acquisition already covers this in more depth. You ask them politely to give an example. Response 1: 'Oh, I'm sure you'll find lots of examples in the literature.' Response 2: 'Well, for a start, there's the problem of missing various forms of semi-tacit and tacit knowledge, such as preverbal construing, taken for granted knowledge and implicit attitudes.' Response 1 is quite possibly a bluff. Response 2 is either an extremely elaborate bluff or an indication that what you thought was a harmless squirrel in the bushes is actually a large bear.

Here are some general tips on handling questions:

- **Practice:** if you've given the talk before (e.g. to an ad hoc audience of students), you'll already have met some questions and had the experience of being 'on the spot'. This will help.
- **Question patterns:** during seminars and other people's talks, pay attention to the sorts of question that people ask. See if you can discern patterns in what people ask about. This gives you a basis for anticipating questions that might arise after your talk, and you can prepare answers for those.
- **Fending off references to unfamiliar literature:** if you don't know the

paper you're being asked about, you can throw the question back to the asker: 'I'm not familiar with that paper; what point does the author make?' Or you can ask the questioner to relate it to literature you *do* know: 'I'm not familiar with that paper; does it fall into the AI camp or the empirical studies camp?' or, 'Is that anything like the travelling salesman problem?' Don't fake it. Make a note of the questioner and ask for the citation after the session.

- **Technical questions:** divert overly technical questions to private discussion: 'That's an interesting point, but it would take a while to answer. Could we discuss it at the break?'
- **Missed questions:** If you're not sure you've understood the question, then paraphrase it back to the questioner: 'If I've understood you correctly, you're asking me if . . .' and then answer *your* version. If you haven't followed the question at all, ask the questioner to repeat it – he or she may ask a simpler version.
- **Long questions:** have paper and pencil ready. If someone asks a multi-part question, or passes off an essay as a question, then making some quick notes will help you keep track of what you want to say in response.
- **Bizarre questions:** treat similarly to overly technical questions; something along the lines of, 'That's a very interesting point, and one to which I hadn't previously given much attention. I'll look into that once I return to the office.' *Don't* offer to discuss it in the break.

Get someone else to record the questions asked, preferably with the names of the askers. You're unlikely to just remember them and you may not have time to make notes. In general, it's a good idea to be prepared to take notes – of people to catch later, or of particularly good points (theirs or yours), or of things you want to follow up.

Have comfort food and bandages ready

The world is not fair. Sometimes people will be gratuitously and unnecessarily rude to you even when you're in the right. Sometimes you won't think of the brilliant and correct riposte until years afterwards. It happens; life's like that occasionally. Sometimes the comments are justified. On other occasions the fairness of comments is more debatable. Here are some examples which happened to other people:

- Opening line in question from audience at conference (witnessed by one of us): 'That was the most ignorant and ill-informed talk I have ever heard.'
- Alleged opening line in PhD viva from external examiner who was allegedly taken away for psychiatric treatment soon afterwards (possibly urban myth): 'Can you give me one good reason why I shouldn't use this thesis to wipe my backside?'
- Suggestion from audience in conference to someone else in the audience

who complained with gratuitous rudeness that the speaker's recommended approach hadn't worked for them (witnessed by one of us): 'Perhaps you should try doing it right.'

A good strategy (once you're out of the danger zone) is to feel utterly sorry for yourself for the rest of the day and seek solace in comfort foods and your personal equivalent of bandages – a small sherry, chocolate, watching a movie with a high body count, or whatever, thus giving your psyche a chance to sort itself out. Then, the next day, you ask yourself what you're going to do about it and how you're going to move on. Were the comments a fair hit? If so, you need to work out how to fix the problem. If not, what are you going to do to reduce the risk of similar unfair hits in the future?

A closing point about strategy and fairness: although it isn't a fair world, there are quite a lot of fair people in it. If you're perceived as a nice person who does good work, rather than an embittered seeker after petty revenge, then more experienced researchers will be likely to talent-spot you and to put opportunities your way. This is something which doesn't usually happen to people who spend their lives in pointless wrangling. (There's the added comfort that if you learn from the experience you might be able to wipe the floor with your assailant next time you meet . . .)

The three golden rules of public speaking

- First golden rule: don't lie.
- Second golden rule: don't try to be funny.
- Third golden rule: don't panic and blurt out the truth.

A brief checklist for presentations

- Have you checked the level of detail at which to give the talk?
- Have you checked what the audience will already know?
- Have you rehearsed the talk? Have you rehearsed it with an audience?
- Are your slides readable?
- Do you know how to use the audio-visual equipment where you will be presenting?
- Have you looked at the room where you will be presenting?
- Do you have a master sheet showing where you should be at which stage of the talk?
- Do you have a backup plan in case of equipment failure?

14

Conferences

The conference process: a novice's perspective • The organizers' viewpoint • Miscellaneous good advice • Getting the most out of networking at a conference – a checklist

When I drew nigh the nameless city, I knew it was accursed.[1]

Researchers have three main ways of keeping in touch with what is going on in their area of research. A swift and efficient way is the grapevine – if Smith and Jones have solved the most important question in their field, then most of the major players in that field will know about it via phone calls and emails within a few hours of the news going public (and probably much sooner, given the way that gossip works). This is fine if you're a major player with good connections to the grapevine, but not so fine if you're a struggling PhD student who still has an uneasy suspicion that the major texts in your field are produced by superhuman figures who live somewhere on the middle slopes of Mount Olympus.

A more feasible way of keeping up to date for most PhD students is reading the journals, which are, depending on your favoured metaphor, the gold standard, the touchstone, or some such indicator of quality. Unfortunately, the lead time for journal papers is about two years, so the journal freshly appearing on your library shelves will contain accounts of work done about three years ago. This is not an ideal situation. However, help is at hand in the form of conferences. Every year, most research fields witness a batch of annual conferences at which researchers from around the world meet to present their

[1] Lovecraft, H.P. (1921) The Nameless City, in *Omnibus 2: Dagon and Other Macabre Tales* (1985). London: Grafton Books, p. 129.

work and to listen to other people's presentations of their work. They also, more importantly, socialize and build their social networks, usually over a drink in the bar. A conference therefore gives you the chance to find out about research which is no more than a year old, and is probably considerably more recent, as well as a chance to meet colleagues from around the world.

So much for the basic context – how does this translate into specific things that you need to know? We shall start with the process, from the viewpoint of the absolute novice, then move on to the process from the viewpoint of the long-suffering organizers, and conclude with some advice about how this knowledge of the processes can be used to help you make the most of conferences.

The conference process: a novice's perspective

There are two capacities in which you can attend a conference. One is as someone presenting work; the other is as someone who is not presenting work. For simplicity, we will proceed with the assumption that you are presenting work, since this includes what you need to know about being in the audience.

There are several main routes into presenting at a conference. One is that you want to publish something and have a vague idea that a conference might be a good place to aim for; this usually leads to some unsystematic searches on the internet and the high-tech equivalent of sticking a pin into the list. Another, more sophisticated, route starts with a desire to see Hawaii or some other exotic place at someone else's expense; this produces some more focused research into possible venues. The most sophisticated route starts with a desire to get a paper into a particular conference because that is the main conference for this field; by a fascinating coincidence, the main conferences are surprisingly often held in places like Hawaii, and are in consequence able to be very selective about which papers they accept.

Whatever the route, it will end up at the same place, namely the call for papers for that conference. The call for papers will specify which types of paper will be accepted, will state the guidelines for each type of paper and will also give the deadlines for each. The main types usually include some or all of the following:

- Full papers (what they sound like: full-sized papers)
- Short papers (also what they sound like: short papers)
- Abstracts for papers (which may be full or short)
- Posters (where you stand in the lobby at coffee and lunch breaks next to posters which you have previously prepared, describing your work)

The main thing to remember about abstracts is that if your abstract is accepted you will need to write the paper at some point. It is horribly easy to forget this and to realize with a chill dread that you will have to write the paper during the fortnight when you have to mark several hundred exam scripts. The other main risk about being accepted is that you will have to live up to the wild claims that you made in the abstract, in the hope of being accepted. The main thing to bear in mind about posters is that most of the people at the conference will walk right past you and your poster; this is nothing personal, but it can feel pretty grim. The other main thing to bear in mind about posters is that most of the people who do ask questions will leave you with a faintly uneasy feeling, either because they've asked questions to demonstrate their own greater knowledge of the field, or because they are strange individuals. Again, this is nothing personal.

So, having written your paper or whatever, you stick it in the post, think about it for a few days and then get submerged in routine tasks. At some point you will receive a verdict on your submission and decisions need to be made. If the verdict is unfavourable, then the decisions involve what to do with the paper (perhaps submit it somewhere else, or throw it away) and whether to go to the conference anyway purely as a spectator, if you have the money. If the verdict is favourable, then you need to do assorted logistical things. If you are a complete novice, or have a taste for the grey side of ethics, then you will face some interesting decisions about how to persuade The System to pay for your travel, conference fees and accommodation for a week in the Hawaii Hilton. If you have not previously checked with The System whether this is OK, then you will be asked to explain just why The System should fork out a couple of thousand pounds for you to have a nice holiday, when the state of the departmental budget means that better researchers than you are only being funded to go to a two-day workshop in Skegness. A wise supervisor will have made sure that the funding for your PhD includes allowance for a conference per year; a realistic supervisor will be aware that this allowance will usually not stretch to a major conference in somewhere exotic.

Assuming that the funding has been approved, you still need to arrange travel, accommodation and the like, which can be pretty stressful if the conference is in (say) Spain, and your Spanish is minimal. If you have acquired a reputation as a pleasant and reasonable person, you may discover at this point that one of the secretaries or research assistants speaks fluent Spanish and is willing to help; if you haven't acquired this reputation, you probably won't make this discovery, and may end up staying somewhere more characterful than you might like.

Moving briskly on past this stage and that stage of finding your hotel and booking in, probably at 2 a.m. local time, we proceed to the point where you step off the bus at the conference venue, stressed out from the journey, trying to carry a briefcase and a coat simultaneously while opening doors with your third hand. What happens next? You follow the signs for your conference; if your conference has more than one set of signs, then you follow the ones marked 'registration'. At the place of registration, you will usually be issued with a badge, a programme of events and a pack of information; from this point on, you can follow the crowd, and not have to make any decisions for the immediate future. There is a non-trivial possibility that the registration people will claim never to have heard of you, especially if you left booking until the last moment, which is a good reason for (a) not leaving everything until the last moment and (b) going with someone who is familiar with conferences. Problems of this sort usually get resolved somehow, but they're something you can do without.

Working a conference

Once you've committed to attending the conference, it's time to do your homework. Most conferences publish preliminary programmes on their websites as an inducement to get more people to attend (if not, you'll have to do this homework in a quiet corner when you reach the conference and receive your conference pack). You need to pay attention to the following.

- Have a look at the attendees list. Who's on the list that you'd especially like to meet? Are they giving a paper?
- Have a look at the sessions and at the paper titles, and plan your attendance. Which sessions are not to be missed? When are there openings for conversations? Who is the first contact you want to target?

If there are key people attending the conference that you want to meet, you might want to start laying the groundwork early. Is there someone attending the conference that you know and who could introduce you? Is there a particular question you'd like to ask that researcher which you could address in an email? (They may not answer, but if the question is interesting they might be more prone to give you a bit of time when you meet them at the conference.)

Once you have your conference pack, really use it. First, find yourself a suitable quiet corner and continue your planning about which sessions to attend. It's usually a good idea to attend the plenary sessions. Many conferences use two or more lecture halls so that two or more talks can be in progress simultaneously ('parallel streams'), in which case you'll need to decide which stream to attend. You don't have to go to every talk every day (and sometimes a strategic conversation over coffee with the right researcher is more valuable than a paper session), but you won't learn anything from talks you don't attend. Each night:

- Skim or read the papers for the sessions you plan to attend the next day
- Have a look at the papers for the other sessions (you may meet their authors at coffee)
- Check your plan for the next day

Each day, take your proceedings to the sessions and:

- Refer to papers for clarification
- Annotate the papers: for instance, if the authors add information during the presentation (there are often extra website addresses that are handy to file with the papers), or if there is something specifically resonant with your own work
- Work out questions to ask
- Have something to do (i.e. read other papers) if the session turns out to be a dud
- Pay attention to what makes good speakers good (and bad speakers bad)

What you get out is related to what you put in – if you 'work' the conference, working at staying engaged, at seeking conversations and at keeping track of information, then you're more likely to make good connections. Remember, much of the 'real' value of a conference isn't derived from the sessions – it comes from conversations in the bar. If you don't drink alcohol, then remember that bars also serve non-alcoholic drinks . . .

We now move for a little while to the organizers' viewpoint, which should help you to understand the niceties of conference procedure more clearly.

The organizers' viewpoint

Why do people organize conferences? There are three main reasons, namely fortune, glory and (in quite a few praiseworthy instances) the good of the discipline. A good conference can bring in a substantial profit to the institution involved, and can bring fame and power (within research circles at least) to the academics organizing it. A well-planned conference can also be an excellent way of revitalizing an area of research which has gone stale, or of starting a new area of research.

So, if you want to start a new area of research, or revitalize an existing one, you might organize a conference. One of the first problems to tackle involves how to attract enough people to make the conference viable. A standard solution is to invite some key speakers, whose talks will be a significant attraction. This is particularly effective if one or more of the keynote speakers gives a talk which either summarizes the current state of the field or (preferably) suggests some really interesting new ideas. A nice venue is another attraction worth trying. The third classic attraction is to publish the conference proceedings; an added enticement is to strike a deal with a journal editor to publish the best papers in a special issue of the journal. The reason that this is a significant inducement involves the way that departments fund conference-going. If several researchers ask for the same amount of money to go to a conference and there's not enough money for all of them, then the pecking order is as follows: published proceedings plus special issue, as first choice; published proceedings only, as second choice; no proceedings as third choice.

We will draw a tactful veil over most of the logistical processes and concentrate on the ones involving papers and posters. If you're organizing a conference with published proceedings, then you will need to liaise with printers, and this can rapidly lead to all sorts of interesting and potentially stressful constraints about word lengths, deadlines and the like. Printers usually work on a basis of having slots set aside for each client, rather than doing each client sequentially, so if you miss your agreed slot because your copy isn't ready you need to book another one. It might not surprise you to know that this will cost you more money. You are therefore likely to be twitchy about whether your speakers will provide copy on time and in the correct format, including correct word lengths. For many conferences, the proceedings are printed before the conference, so that delegates have the proceedings with them when they listen to talks. This is a very visible deadline, so as an organizer you might be less than sympathetic to authors whose copy is not submitted on time, or is submitted electronically in a format which nobody outside Nebraska can read.

Even if all the copy arrives on time and in the right format, the presentations themselves leave considerable scope for interesting things going wrong in strange ways. Talks are normally grouped into batches – the early morning batch between the start of day and the morning coffee; the coffee till lunch batch; the lunch till afternoon tea batch; and the afternoon tea till end of day batch. Each batch will usually be coordinated by one of the organizers, and may be introduced with an overview talk as well as, or instead of, a keynote talk from an invited speaker. Each batch will usually overrun, partly due to starting late because delegates trickled in at the last possible moment, partly due to equipment malfunctioning and mainly because of speakers overrunning by two or three minutes – not a big deal individually, but multiply that by the number of speakers and you soon start running seriously late. Each batch will also usually include at least one speaker who is inaudible, incomprehensible, boring or has unreadable slides.

The implications for you as a presenter are clear:

- Submit your copy in plenty of time
- Follow instructions for authors
- Practise your talk so that you can keep well within your time slot
- Be considerate and try to see things from the organizers' viewpoint
- If you encounter problems, let the organizers know as soon as possible, so that something can be arranged

Miscellaneous good advice

Your very first conference is a glittering opportunity to make a complete idiot of yourself in front of the main players from your research community before you've even finished your PhD. There is, unfortunately, an asymmetry: there is not much scope for making yourself look amazingly wonderful to the same audience, for the simple reason that at this stage in your career you will probably not have anything remarkably novel and interesting to say. (Interesting, yes; novel, yes; both interesting and novel is a possible combination; *remarkably* interesting and novel is much rarer.) Some classic ways of making an idiot of yourself include the following:

- Getting drunk in public
- Being sick in public as a result of a hangover from getting drunk in private
- Having wild sex with someone in the fond belief that (a) nobody else will know or (b) that it won't matter – in reality, everyone will know by coffee break the next morning and your bedmate will probably turn out to be a dreadful mistake
- Asking the same inane question that gets asked every year by a new PhD student who thinks they're being original

Your first conference is a good opportunity to practise your listening skills, even if you're sure that you have a brilliant solution to the problem that's bugging everyone. If you're right, then you'll still be right tomorrow, and learning to be patient is an invaluable research skill. (So is getting your idea into print, rather than blurting it out in a conference and then seeing it appear under someone else's name a few months later . . .)

Your first conference is a good chance to meet people and strike up friendships which might well last for the rest of your professional life. The best way to do this is over moderately sober conversations in the bar, with people who are willing to talk to you (the keynote speakers and other major players may be willing to talk to you, but are understandably wary of being buttonholed by every loon at the conference, especially if the major player in question has come to the conference for a long-awaited chat with a close friend from several thousand miles away that they haven't seen since 1992).

If your first conference is also the first conference at which you are presenting a paper, then you might be excused for feeling a bit stressed. One good way of reducing the stress is to get some experience at public speaking before you go – for instance, departmental seminars, which should be treated as a useful opportunity rather than as an unwelcome obligation to be avoided till the last moment. You can also try running unofficial postgraduate seminars at which you present your work to each other in a constructive, supportive atmosphere (persuading a wise and supportive member of staff to come along and give constructive criticism can be very helpful). Another strategy is to co-author with your supervisor and persuade your supervisor to give the talk, with a promise that you will do the talking next time. You can then learn from your supervisor's experience. If you are talking, then it's a good idea to read the chapters elsewhere in this book on writing and presentations. At this point in your career it's wisest to go for an unpretentious, solid talk which reports what you did in a level tone, neither claiming too much nor too little. Your mission is not to entertain or dazzle the audience – that's the job of the guest speakers. Your mission in your first conference is reconnaissance, so that you'll know what you're doing at your second conference.

Getting the most out of networking at a conference – a checklist

Strategies for covering conferences of different sizes

- Small: aim for comprehensive coverage (i.e. talk to everyone there)
- Medium: aim to talk to as many people as possible, but target those doing related work
- Large: make advance arrangements to ensure contact with key people, and focused targeting during the event

Making contacts at the conference

- Use activities (workshops, working groups, tutorials, 'birds of a feather' sessions, first-timers' events)
- Present a paper (which introduces you to everyone in your audience)
- Ask a good question (others who find your question interesting may introduce themselves to you, and the author will be more likely to remember you)
- Attend demonstrations
- If you hear a conversation that's really interesting, stand visibly on the periphery until you get a chance to make a contribution (a short question or a joke is good) or ask if you may join the group
- Get your supervisor or an existing contact to suggest people and make introductions
- Make early contact with a key person (e.g. someone on the committee, someone well established in the area) and be around when they make contact with others; ask them to make introductions
- Talk to the person sitting next to you in a session – ask a question about the last presentation
- Make it a habit to have lunch with different people every day

- Make connections for other people – refer to other conversations and work and be ready to make appropriate introductions
- When you're in a conversation, avoid 'sounding off' or entertaining people with your opinions – it's much more effective to phrase ideas as questions rather than statements

Have your 'cocktail party introductions' (i.e. brief description of who you are and what you're researching) worked out and ready to mind. Take your business cards and write some specific information on the back that will help your contact recall your conversation. When you take someone else's card, write down where you met them and some characterizing idea or expertise that will help you remember them in six months.

Following up

- Conference contacts tend to have a high attrition rate – but making contacts is still worth it if you make one good, lasting connection
- Always keep the promises you make: do send that paper, or email that information
- Follow up great conversations with a thank-you email
- Suggest visits or specific further interaction to good contacts
- Invite good contacts to your institution – perhaps to give a talk
- If you didn't get a chance to speak to an author during the conference, do it via email afterwards

15

The viva

Stories of nasty surprises • Behind the scenes • The day of the viva •
Preparing yourself • Handling revisions • The viva: hints, lists and things
to remember • Generic viva questions

Once I sought out a celebrated ethnologist and amused him with peculiar ques-
tions regarding the ancient Philistine legend of Dagon, the Fish-God; but soon
perceiving that he was hopelessly conventional, I did not press my inquiries.[1]

The viva (short for *viva voce* or 'living voice' examination) occupies a place in
PhD student myth and legend which offers immense scope to writers with a
taste for scary metaphor, but tact and common humanity prevent us from
exploring that area as fully as we might. In one sense the folklore is right. The
viva is one of the two essential outputs from your PhD. If your written thesis
and your viva are both good enough, then you get a doctorate. If they're not,
you don't. Nothing else comes into play – not how hard you've worked, or
how bright you are, or how much you care about your topic, or how important
it is to the world, or how much you've suffered, or how much you want that
PhD. It's perfectly possible to write a decent dissertation and then make a
disastrous mess of the viva. So, what do you do about it?

Remember what you're doing in the viva:

- Showing respect for the academic system and discipline
- Showing general mastery of the domain and its intellectual tools
- Demonstrating intellectual independence

---

[1] Lovecraft, H.P. (1917) Dagon, in *Omnibus 2: Dagon and Other Macabre Tales* (1985). London: Grafton
Books, p. 17.

- Joining the academic discourse
- Undergoing a rite of passage

The first thing is to understand the purpose of the viva from the examiners' point of view. The PhD is a rite of passage, showing that you are worthy to be admitted to the clan. In terms of the cabinet-making metaphor, it's the point where you leave apprenticeship behind and become a fully-fledged cabinet-maker, if you're good enough. The key point in both metaphors is that neither of them contains any mention of perfection. PhDs don't have to be perfect. They only have to be good enough, where 'good enough' means that you have demonstrated a satisfactory command of the skills required for a professional researcher in your discipline. The level of 'good enough' will be high, but that's different from perfection. Nobody will be expecting your thesis to be perfect – in this context, the whole idea of perfection is only meaningful as a convenient shorthand term. By definition, when your work involves new discovery, there is uncertainty and no absolute right answer. Your work will build on previous work and on established techniques; all of these are ultimately derived from approximations, assumptions and consensus in the field, rather than from God-given absolute truths. Part of becoming a mature professional researcher is being able to accept uncertainty, and to deal with it in a way which is appropriate for the situation in hand. Sometimes an uncertainty is the whole point of the research (for instance, 'Why is this mould growing on my petri dishes?'), but on other occasions you have to accept that you have to live with an uncertainty which is not likely to be clarified in the foreseeable future (for instance, 'Why do things so often form Poisson distributions?').

The obverse of this cheering thought is the implication that your thesis will contain *questionable things*. These provide a starting place for the examiners to do some poking around, to check the extent of your skills. They don't want nasty surprises. They want to be reassured that your mastery of your field holds up adequately under scrutiny. They do not want to discover that your thesis is brilliant because your supervisor wrote all of it for you under the influence of desperate, unrequited love. They do not want to discover that you didn't mention an obvious point because you'd never thought of it, rather than because you didn't think it was worth mentioning because it was so obvious. Two stories illustrate this. (We have chosen stories which are probably apocryphal, so as to spare the feelings of those involved in definitely true stories.)

Stories of nasty surprises

The mushroom story

The mushroom story concerns an agriculture student whose undergraduate dissertation involved looking at growth in farmed mushrooms, a topic of little interest to most of the world, but of considerable importance to mushroom farmers. Much to his surprise, he found that the mushrooms did not grow either continually or in diurnal cycles; instead they grew in cycles of a few hours. This finding was so unexpected that he went on to do a PhD on the topic, producing large amounts of data and analysis. The day of the viva arrived, and went beautifully up to the point where the external examiner asked a gentle, ground-clearing question, namely: 'I take it that you allowed for the central heating going on and off in the mushroom sheds?' After some seconds of horrible silence, it was agreed that the viva would be postponed until after the student had done a post-pilot study to check that the effect was not due to the central heating going on and off. The results of the post-pilot were sickeningly predictable: the student had just spent several years of his life measuring, in effect, how often the central heating went on and off in mushroom sheds.

The woodpecker story

The woodpecker story is similar. We include it partly on the grounds that it's wise to be wary of principles which are always illustrated by the same example – this raises the nasty suspicion that there is only one example – and partly on the grounds that one of us used to wear a safety helmet in the course of a previous day job and can personally testify that they come in very handy when someone drops a bucket on your head. The woodpecker story is also useful because it demonstrates a more subtle and far-reaching effect than the mushroom story.

According to the story, the developers of safety helmets decided to look to nature to find inspiration for a new approach to design. One of them wondered whether there were any animals which experienced powerful blows to the head without suffering brain damage. Inspiration struck, in the form of the woodpecker, which spends much of its waking life banging its head against trees with considerable force. The team accordingly read up on the anatomy of the woodpecker and discovered that it has a spongy base to its beak which absorbs the force of the impact. The team used this inspiration to come up with a design for a helmet which was not designed to stop objects from penetrating the helmet (as with First World War military helmets, for instance), but instead was designed to absorb the blow by deforming harmlessly, preventing most of the energy of impact from reaching the wearer's head (unlike helmets designed to prevent penetration). The designers were proudly demonstrating their concept when, according to the story, a member of the audience asked: 'How do you know woodpeckers don't suffer brain damage?' Painful silence ensued . . .

In the mushroom story, the student failed to identify a relevant variable (the central heating). In the woodpecker story, the design team had not checked a key assumption (that woodpeckers don't get brain damage). The woodpecker story in fact had a happy ending; the current design is demonstrably good and the designers were proved right (even though, as far as we know, nobody ever did check on brain damage rates in woodpeckers). In other cases, however, unchecked assumptions have led to years wasted in pointless research, which could have been spent instead in a useful area. This is quite a different proposition from reducing the problem space by eliminating one set of plausible possibilities.

For this reason, external examiners are likely to poke around in the foundations of your research, checking that you have neither missed anything which you should have thought of, nor made an unwarranted assumption. An example from popular culture might provide a more cheering return to the plot, namely the comic-book character The Incredible Hulk. According to the story, The Hulk was created when a mild-mannered scientist was trying to find the source of people's astonishing strength in emergencies, such as the woman who lifted a car off her child after a crash. That story is fiction and obviously silly, because – dramatic pause – people *don't* have astonishing strength in emergencies; the story of the woman lifting a car off her child is an urban myth. (Try checking the website www.urbanlegends.com if you're thinking of applying for a research grant of your own in this area, before you start budgeting for high-stretch shirts and non-rip trousers . . .)

Most students collect horror stories about vivas, using them to nurture their nightmares. In our experience, failure at viva is rare and is almost always attributable to one of two things:

1 The student didn't listen to their supervisors, or any other advisers for that matter
2 The supervisory relationship had broken down and the student hadn't compensated for it

Therefore, failure at viva is in principle avoidable, given two protective behaviours:

1 Listen to your supervisor
2 Build up an effective personal network and expose your work through seminars and publications in advance of your viva, so that you'll be alerted to oversights early

Behind the scenes

Back to the main story. External examiners are there to check that you know how to make cabinets; how do they set about doing it?

The story normally starts before you see them. At some point in your PhD, you and your supervisor need to choose an external. For some PhDs this is done before you even register for the PhD; for others it happens after you've written up. For most it's somewhere in the last year or so. There are various factors in choosing the external. They should not have a conflict of interest – if they're co-applying with you for a Nobel Prize, for instance, then they will have a substantial incentive to pass your thesis, whether you deserve it or not. Similarly, if your last conversation with them started with you saying: 'Wake up, darling, or we'll be late for my viva,' then questions might be asked . . .

Once the external has been chosen, they will get on with their life until your thesis arrives in the post, accompanied by the appropriate forms and other paperwork. What do they do with it? That depends. Most externals will read the thesis in detail, at least once. Many will read it line by line, making notes page by page. They will look in detail at the references and appendices (the equivalent of hauling the drawers out of a cabinet and checking the joints that were never intended to be seen in normal use). They will check references or assertions which don't look right. They will probably spot the reference to a fictitious paper by Young, Gifted and Black (1972) which felt so amusing at the time. And so forth. At the other end of the spectrum, there are persistent stories about externals who read theses on the train, on the way to the viva. Either way, you want their initial reaction to be the same: you want them to feel the nice warm glow that accompanies the thought: 'Well, this doesn't look like a fail.' So, make sure that the pages which they will look at first are all reassuring – all the pages up to and including the second page of the introduction; the references; and the concluding couple of pages.

The examiners will usually read the thesis independently and then contact each other to discuss it. They have a limited set of options about marks, since you either get a PhD or you don't: you don't get a percentage mark like you do with a final-year project. However, this apparent simplicity derives from a more complex assessment process. The examiners can pass your thesis without changes (unusual, but far from unknown); they can fail it completely (far from unknown); they can recommend that it be considered for an MPhil instead; or, more commonly, they can accept it subject to specified changes of varying degrees of severity. If they all agree that it looks like a straight pass, a straight fail or an MPhil, then their life is simple; more often, however, there are changes required, which means that the examiners have to discuss what needs to be changed. This can be time-consuming and irritating, especially if the changes are needed because your thesis is vague or otherwise badly written. After this, they will need to agree on the game plan for the viva itself – who will handle which bits, and how? Note that they don't simply put together a list of changes ready to give to you. The provisional list will be modified in the light of the viva. If it turns out, for instance, that an apparent problem is simply a matter of your using an unusual name for something instead of a more famil-iar one, then the change might only involve putting in a parenthesis to explain that your term is the same as the more familiar one. Conversely, if the viva reveals major and inexcusable ignorance on your part, then what initially looked like a minor change can turn into a major one, or even a fail. This shouldn't normally happen, but it may happen in cases where a student vanishes into the wilderness, does some research, then writes up and insists on submitting against the advice of their supervisor (rare, but unfortunately not unknown).

The day of the viva

The examiners normally rendezvous in or around the department some time before the viva, and have a pre-viva meeting to confirm their plan of action. They will usually not show much interest in meeting you at this stage. This is nothing personal: they have a job to do, and they need to concentrate on that. Many vivas are held in the afternoon, to give the examiners time to get to the venue; in these cases, the examiners are normally taken off to lunch by your supervisor before the viva. You probably won't be invited: this is etiquette, not a snub. (You may be invited to lunch if you had a successful viva with them in the morning, but that's different.) There are persistent rumours about relationships where the supervisor treats the examiners to a few drinks at lunchtime to get them in a good mood; if true, this is the exception, not the norm.

When they are ready, you will be summoned, and will go into the room, looking and feeling distinctly nervous if you are anything like most other PhD candidates.

Opening gambits

Since you are likely to be nervous, most examiners will make an effort to put you at your ease. Since the viva usually takes place in your department, with the external as the visitor, there isn't much scope for the traditional opening gambit in meetings, namely asking whether you had a good journey. Similarly, the bit where they introduce themselves will usually go past you in a nameless blur, like the following bit where they say how they are going to conduct the session. There are various other gambits which are more likely to get through to you, most of which are open to being misconstrued by nervous candidates.

An example of this is the external who offers you a couple of sheets of A4 listing the typos they've found. This is easily misconstrued as trivial, petty nitpicking which misses the great philosophical points behind your thesis. Not so. It's actually a graceful courtesy. For one thing, it shows that the examiner has paid you the compliment of bothering to read every page in such detail that they've found the typo on page 174 which your spell-checker missed. For another thing, it is much preferable to have that list by you when you fix the typos, rather than being told that there are numerous typos which need to be fixed, but not being told where they are. A third thing is that in some cases the examiners only ask a few token questions and use the list of typos as an indirect way of saying that you've done such a good job on the thesis that it only needs very minor alterations (in such cases, the list of typos is an indirect way of saying that they're not simply going for the minor alterations option because they're too lazy to do anything else).

Another opening gambit which is widely used is to say something about your thesis along the lines of how interesting or readable it was. This gambit can actually mean several very different things. For some academics, 'readable' is a low-grade insult, referring to the sort of thing written by scientists who popularize science (an activity viewed with condescension by many academic researchers). For others, 'readable' is a compliment, meaning that it's possible for a human being to work out what you're on about, unlike most of the turgid grot perpetrated by people writing in your area. How can you tell which meaning you are encountering? One indicator is the reputation of the examiner. If they're notoriously sadistic, then you're probably about to encounter trouble, so don't let that opening sentence lull you off your guard. If the examiner is known as a considerate soul, then you're probably being given a gentle start to the session. However, it's worth remembering that even the most considerate examiner is also a professional academic and likely to take the viva pretty seriously, so don't presume too much. If you encounter this gambit, a fairly safe response is a dry smile and a 'thank you' in a polite tone which implies that you're no idiot.

A third opening gambit which can be misconstrued is asking you to give a brief overview of your thesis. One perfectly understandable response to this is anger: surely if the examiners have read your thesis properly they shouldn't need a brief overview of it? Again, not so. The brief overview is a pretty good way of getting a nervous candidate to open up: they usually become so absorbed in the topic that they forget their nerves. It's also a good way of finding out which aspects of the thesis they find most important, which reveals a lot about their professionalism. In some cases, it's also useful for finding out just what the thesis is supposed to be about, if it's been written up in a particularly vague or unreadable style. Quite often, a thesis will contain stuff which looks promising but which is poorly structured and badly described. If the content is good, then a few skilful changes can make a surprising difference to the thesis; if the content is as bad as the style, then the whole thing needs to be consigned to a nameless pit and erased from human memory. Either way, this opening gambit helps the examiners towards a decision.

It's tempting at this stage to break the third golden rule, by panicking and blurting out the truth about things you did wrong. Don't give in to temptation. Instead, give a clear, previously prepared overview, listing the main findings and the main ways in which this work is a contribution to knowledge. You might want to use a few gambits of your own to show that you know the rules of the game – for instance, a discreet reference to your latest paper in a major journal, or a mention of ongoing work with a major figure in the field. Don't overdo it, though – remember that you're a candidate, not an examiner.

The mid-game

After the opening exchanges the real business begins, and vivas begin to differ. As noted above, examiners have four main options available to them in terms of outcomes: straight pass, pass subject to minor changes, pass subject to major changes and fail. (They can also award an MPhil, instead of a PhD.) They have many more options available to them in terms of how they conduct the viva itself, and it's important to remember that a viva can feel like a grim interrogation to you, but end up with a straight pass.

The straight pass

At one end of the cosiness scale is the situation where the examiners make it clear from the outset that there's little doubt this will be a straight pass, and then ask a few questions for courtesy's sake before heading off with you and your supervisor to lunch/coffee/the pub. You may be asked to fix three or four typos, for form's sake. This outcome typically occurs when you have a good supervisor, when you and your supervisor both know how the game is played, and when you've done a thoroughly good job on your dissertation.

Minor changes

Next down the scale is the viva where you are asked a few technical questions to check on specific points. You probably won't be able to answer all the questions either to your satisfaction or to theirs. Don't let that shake you: nobody can answer all the possible sensible questions, or have done all the relevant reading. An example of this is as follows. You have done a PhD which involves a new taxonomy of human error types. You have done the essential reading (Reason, Hollnagel, Rasmussen and so on). You have also done some good further reading by looking at the literature on formal taxonomic classification in biology. The external examiner asks you whether you have read the literature on use of multidimensional statistics for classification. You haven't. What do you do? Well, for a start, you don't panic. Although the question is a valid one, you have already gone beyond standard best practice in your area by bothering to read up on formal taxonomy. The leading literature on human error isn't based on multidimensional stats and cluster algorithms. Although you could in principle have investigated that route, it's only one of many routes which you could have taken, and it's physically impossible to take all of them. Saying that you could have taken it is very different from saying that you should have taken it. So, you can bounce the question back at the external by making some of the points above, and politely asking what they think the multidimensional approach would offer to this area. You can then get into a debate with them which allows you to demonstrate your ability, which is the main point. To conclude this example, if you make a good case in the debate, you may be asked to add a sentence saying that you chose not to use multi-dimensional stats, and giving the reason for not using them: a pretty minor change.

Major changes

A more serious situation would be where the examiner's question identifies a serious area of ignorance on your part. A good example of this comes from statistics. Suppose you have looked at different groups' perceptions of how car crashes are shown in the popular media, and have gathered some numeric data on the respondents' perceptions. You write this up in neat tables and mention in your discussion that the difference between two groups is significant, and that another finding is highly significant. The examiners reach this point in your thesis and the external examiner says that you have described results as significant and as highly significant, but haven't mentioned the tests you used or the p values involved.

None of the options at this point are good. The least bad is that you tell them which tests you used and what the p values were; the examiners will wonder silently what sort of idiot you were to omit this information and will be on the lookout for further signs of idiocy, but you may well get away with simply adding the missing information. The two other main options are about as bad as each other. One is that you tell them that you use only qualitative methods and don't agree with quantitative methods on principle; you then look like an idiot for choosing a non-qualitative external examiner, and for having gathered quantitative data but not analysed it quantitatively. This issue relates to some serious debates about which skills in a discipline are essential rather than optional, which go beyond the scope of this book: to use an extreme (and genuine) example, should someone be allowed to graduate in French if they refuse on ideological grounds to use standard French spelling and punctuation? If you don't approve of cabinets, that's fair enough, but to undertake an apprenticeship in cabinet-making when you feel that way is a decision that falls somewhat short of being sensible.

The last main option involves your admitting that you have never heard of statistical tests or p values, and asking what p values have to do with significance anyway. This approach might be perfectly acceptable in some disciplines, but in others where statistics form a core skill (e.g. experimental psychology) it would be disastrous. If you've ended up in a situation where your external is asking this sort of question and where your answer is an admission of total ignorance, then you've made a serious mistake in your choice of external, in your choice of discipline or in your approach to your subject. The best that you can hope for with either of the two latter options is some serious revisions. Even if you wriggle out of this particular question, the session will have shifted from a fairly routine check to a serious investigation of whether or not you deserve to pass, and there's a strong likelihood that one of the next questions will sink you fair and square.

The fail

At the bottom of the cosiness scale is the viva where the examiners think that you've made a serious mess of things, and where you exacerbate matters by being gratuitously offensive, ignorant and/or stupid. Usually, but not invariably, these cases occur when the student submits their thesis against the advice of the supervisor. A typical example might be a part-time PhD student who has a fairly influential day job as a manager, and who cobbles together a dissertation topic on job satisfaction based on reading textbooks and professional magazines, then goes on to conduct a badly designed questionnaire and/or some badly designed interviews, and who talks about 'getting all this airy-fairy academic stuff out of the way'. (Yes, this sort of thing has really happened, and more than once.) There isn't much that can be salvaged from such cases. The literature review is too simplistic to lead to an interesting research question; the methods are too boring to form the basis of a decent rewrite; the data will probably be untrustworthy or uninformative because of the flaws in the methods. Work of this sort will fail, and deservedly so. Again, if you think that cabinet-making is overrated and that flatpack furniture is just as good, then you're entitled to that opinion but you would be pretty silly to apply for an examination as a would-be master cabinet-maker and bring along a poorly assembled flatpack as your alleged master piece.

The end game

By the end of the session, the examiners will probably have reached a conclusion about what to do with you. 'Probably' because they will need to check with each other and reach an agreed verdict. They will politely ask you to leave, and will do whatever examiners do while you're pacing around in the corridor, feeling nervous.

What examiners do is to check with each other, reach an agreed verdict and have some breathing space. If your thesis is a clear pass or a clear fail, then they will check explicitly that they all agree. If it's a clear pass, they won't necessarily summon you back 30 seconds after you've gone out; quite a lot of examiners believe in keeping the candidate waiting for a few minutes, on the grounds that it's good for the candidate's soul.

If there's consensus that you'll have to make changes, then nice examiners will draw up a clear list. This might be a longhand list written there and then, or it might be emailed to you a day or two later.

If there's not consensus, then the examiners have to slug it out among themselves. At this point you can reap what you have sown much earlier. For example, if you have produced a couple of decent journal papers out of your work, then that demonstrates that your work is of adequate professional quality, which strengthens the case for anyone wishing to argue that your thesis contains good stuff, even if it's been badly written up. Similarly, if you have done a solid literature review, then that shows that you have a proper professional knowledge of your area, even if your data collection was a bit tatty. Both these examples involve starting early; they're not something you can cobble together in the last week. It's a good idea, a year or so into your PhD, to read your institution's regulations and then get someone knowledge-able to translate them into English for you, so that you can find out about things like indications of acceptable quality in the thesis. If there's something about 'publishable in a peer-reviewed journal', for instance, then getting a couple of publications in a peer-reviewed journal will help your case in the event of a debatable verdict after the viva.

When all of this has been done, the examiners will reach an agreement with your supervisor about the next stages, and summon you back. Some will say the magic words: 'Congratulations, Dr Smith'; others won't. Strictly speaking, you aren't Dr Smith until you've formally graduated, so don't read anything too much into it if they don't use those words; externals are the sort of people who will probably know about the distinction between 'doctor' and 'doctor-andus' and who may phrase their greeting accordingly. The rest of the session will quite probably be a bit hazy. If you and/or your friends have been efficient, there may be champagne ready. The examiners may or may not participate in the festivities; the day will end and in the fullness of time the first day of the rest of your life will dawn.

So, that's what happens from the examiners' point of view. What happens from your point of view? This section is briefer, partly because much of it is covered above and partly because it's also covered in depth in all the other books on this topic.

Preparing yourself

Obviously, the best preparation for a viva is an excellent dissertation. Early in your PhD, discuss with your supervisor whether or not to go for a journal publication or two. Supervisors, and disciplines, vary in this regard. When you write up, allow plenty of time to do a decent job, and pay particular attention to displaying your cabinet-making skills in the thesis. Choose an appropriate external in a sensible way: by this stage in your career you should have a rea-sonable idea of the relevant rules of the game and of the main relevant players.

The week before

In the week before the viva, re-read your thesis and your data, plus some of the key literature. You'll probably be utterly sick of all of them long before this stage, so reward yourself with chocolate, or whatever currency works for you. Organize a mock viva, including a presentation at the start, with at least one mock examiner who knows the craft skills of doing a good viva and presentation. If they're good, they won't be gentle with you in the mock viva, and they will give you constructive feedback about what to change for the real event. A lot of this is likely to involve blood in the water – you'll probably panic gently in the mock session and blurt out needless admissions of weakness such as: 'I know now that I should have used a larger sample size,' rather than something like 'My next study will extend this and will use a larger sample.'

- Go through the 'generic viva questions' (at the end of this chapter) and think up answers.
- Make a list of the questions that frighten you most and compose answers to them.
- Get experienced people to do a mock viva and to debrief you afterwards about what they liked and what they thought could be improved. (Understand that mock vivas are often much tougher than real vivas; mock examiners often play extreme roles so that you'll know you can withstand the worst.)
- Skim through a couple of papers by your examiners, noting their topic area, approach and style.
- Prepare a publication plan for the material in your dissertation (which material, parcelled how, for which venue).

The day before

The day before the viva, check that you are sure where and when the session will take place (there may have been a last-minute change which you missed). Line up a trusted friend to be available for you during the viva day. They will probably organize a tactful bottle of champagne and glasses in a way which doesn't look too much as if it is tempting fate, and whisk you away if it all gets too much – even a pass with minor changes can leave some candidates feeling like a thoroughly wrung dishcloth. Do not go out for some serious drinking the night before: you'll need to be fresh on the day. Check that you know the examiners' names, titles and main publications. This is not to help you grovel; it is to show professional courtesy and to improve your chances of anticipating the direction of their questions. Make sure that you have appropriate clean clothing for the next day and a hard copy of your thesis. Ask your supervisor politely if they will make sure they have a copy of any required changes, in case you forget in the excitement of the moment. (They will probably be planning to do this anyway, but it doesn't hurt to make doubly sure.)

- Mark up your dissertation. Put tabs (Post-it notes or similar) on the pages you're most likely to want to refer to.
- Decide if there's any supporting documentation (e.g. key papers, design

notes, data examples) not included in your dissertation that you want to have along. You'll almost certainly never refer to any of it, but it might make you feel safer.

- Skim through your five key references. If you don't already have adequate notes in your annotated bibliography, then make notes on the key papers: what they did, why they are important, how your work relates to them, implications they have for your work. Be able to refer to the papers by the names of their authors.
- Having done your preparation in good time, do something utterly relaxing and diverting the day before: sports, a walk along the coast, your favourite classic film, a full-body massage, whatever. This does not include drinking binges, extreme sports or anything else which might leave you feeling bad the next day.
- Get a good night's sleep.

On the day

On the day, turn up in plenty of time, and have something to do while you wait. Don't be offended if you aren't introduced to the examiners, invited to join them for lunch or if you're kept waiting before the session begins. All of these are perfectly routine features of the viva process and reflect neither discourtesy nor inefficiency. You might, for instance, be kept waiting because some idiot has been illicitly using the viva room for an unofficial seminar, and has had to be evicted, leaving the examiners with the thrilling job of rearranging all the furniture.

At the start of the viva, be polite and do your exercises for staying calm if you need to. If you aren't asked to do a presentation or an overview, don't fret: the mock session won't have been wasted, because it will have helped you to pull together your thoughts about the thesis in a way which will come in very useful during the viva.

The first question or two will probably be fairly light, and used for breaking the ice. With these and the subsequent questions, you need to remember the three golden rules (don't lie, don't try to be funny and don't panic and blurt out the truth) plus a couple of other things.

One thing is that the viva is quite a lot like fencing practice. The session is used to assess your fencing skills, so you are expected to defend yourself in a way which shows your skill in fencing. You are neither expected to let your opponent hit you every time, nor to attempt to kick your opponent in the groin and then pummel them to death. What matters is how you answer the questions, rather than whether you happen to know a correct answer. At this level, there often aren't any unambiguously correct answers.

Another thing to remember is that you don't need to reply instantly. You can buy yourself some thinking time by using tactics such as raising an eyebrow, saying 'Hmmm' in a thoughtful way, or saying 'That's an interesting question; I'll need to think about that for a moment.' There's also nothing wrong with asking the examiner to clarify something in the question (as long as you don't ask something silly, like the meaning of a term which is a central part of your discipline). When you've given your answer, there's nothing wrong with checking whether it's answering the question they intended.

One colleague scores vivas like a boxing match: for each question and response, he decides if the point goes to the student or the examiner. The point of the analogy is that, barring a rare knock-out blow (usually self-inflicted, such as a student admitting plagiarism, or blurting out by way of explanation, 'My supervisor made me do it!'), you 'win on points'. It doesn't matter if the examiners get in a few punches, as long as you get in more.

After the viva

After the viva, make sure that you don't vanish off the face of the earth; it's a good idea to borrow a friend's office to retire to, but a bad idea not to let anyone know that you're in there, so that the examiners have to scour the corridors looking for you. If you've failed, take the news calmly, be polite and read our section on what to do if things go wrong after giving a presentation (see p. 181) (in brief, go away and feel sorry for yourself for the rest of the day, then do some sensible advice-gathering and planning the next day – a fail is not the end of the world). Statistically speaking, though, you will probably be passed subject to some changes to the thesis. There is no point in arguing about the changes at this stage – argument would only show that you don't understand the way things work on a PhD. Instead, be grateful that you've passed subject to changes, thank the examiners and your supervisor politely and go off to celebrate. Don't worry about remembering all the changes; you should have arranged with your supervisor beforehand that they will make sure there is a clear written list which you can collect from them the next day. If you've passed without changes, then be sure to thank your supervisor – they will have earned it. You can now go out and have that large drink, or whatever form of celebration takes your fancy.

Many students are so overwhelmed by the viva that the full impact does not sink in for some time. One of our students had the following experience. The examiners began the viva with: 'Congratulations, Dr X'. She missed that. They asked interested questions for three hours, and then recommended pass with revisions. She missed that. En route to the department celebration, she stopped her supervisor and asked: 'What just happened?' Her supervisor reassured her: 'You passed.' She paused again: 'Are you sure?'

Handling revisions

The day after the viva, possibly nursing a hangover, you need to present yourself at your supervisor's door and work out precisely what needs to be done and by when. A surprising proportion of candidates give up at this stage. Doing corrections is not much fun, but it's a lot better than failing. Work out a clear timetable, with some contingency time, and get cracking on the corrections. If you want to have a break first, that's up to you, but don't put the corrections off; do them at the earliest possible opportunity and make sure your supervisor okays them. Write a covering letter detailing where you have made which changes and how – that makes it a lot easier for the examiners to check that you have done everything required. It's useful to present the changes in a table: the first column lists the revisions required by the examiners, in their language, one change per row; the second column details the action you've taken (including page numbers) or explains why you've taken an alternative course. In most institutions, minor changes will only need to go back to the main examiner, but major changes will need to be approved by the whole examination team, and a covering letter makes life easier for everyone involved in such situations.

During or after the viva, you need to get the examiners to be very specific about the changes they want. Which chapter, which section of the chapter, which paragraph in the section need to be changed? Can they give you an example of the change they mean? How is this different from what was addressed in section X of the dissertation? You need to show judgement and discretion – if they say something like 'This whole chapter is unclear' then there's a limit to how much precision anyone can give.

You also need to check that you know the date by which the corrections are due. Do not aim to have everything ready five minutes before the deadline; you will need to liaise with your supervisor about the revisions and give your supervisor a reasonable amount of time to check them before you hand them in. This is particularly important if you're near the end of your time as a registered PhD student. The last thing you want to do is to miss the deadline for the revisions because (a) your printer broke down at the last minute or (b) because your supervisor spotted a fatal flaw requiring days of work on your revisions when you finally handed them over for inspection the day before the deadline.

Doing the revisions can produce surprising feelings of revulsion for some students – it's a bit like washing up greasy plates in cold water the morning after a wild party when you have a massive hangover, or so we are reliably informed by friends who attend wild parties. It's worth knowing about this so that if you find yourself engaged in displacement activities rather than doing the corrections, then you can spot this and do something about it. The standard motivation techniques, plus strong support from friends, are helpful here.

Once the changes have been approved, you can plan for graduation. Most institutions allow you to have two guests at the ceremony, which normally means that the candidate's partner and one parent attend while the other parent remains in outer darkness – a source of potential annoyance, and one which it's wise to address as early as possible. Many candidates end up wishing they had better photos of themselves in the formal gowns; it's worth thinking about hiring the gown for a week instead of just a day, and then arranging some decent photos somewhere scenic (especially if you graduate in winter and it's pouring with rain outside on the day of the ceremony).

After all of this, you will probably never want to see your thesis again, and will be seriously tempted to burn it to ashes. Don't do that. The thesis is like a mask: where you see only the inside with all its imperfections, the rest of the world sees the glittering, burnished exterior. Yes, that's a somewhat over the top metaphor, but you've earned a bit of praise by the time you reach this stage.

The viva: hints, lists and things to remember

Despite the reputation of the viva, the truth is that, by the time you get there, you've already done the hard part. Remember: a viva is pass–fail. Most examiners are looking for a reason to pass the candidate. Your job is to make it easy for them. Perfection is not required. Competence is.

Personal presentation for the viva

Dressing for the viva is a form of expressive behaviour: the manner of dress indicates the candidate's role and attitudes. Therefore, candidates should dress in a way that shows respect for the examiners and for the gravity of the process. This means a degree of formality. A simple rule of thumb is to dress as one would for a professional job interview.

Flippancy in dress implies flippancy about the examination. The student in torn jeans and a dirty flannel shirt is conveying 'I can't be bothered'. One should also avoid gaffes that are likely to distract the examiners from your erudite and scintillating responses.

How to distract or annoy your examiners (examples from life)

- **Smell:** people tend to perspire when they are nervous, and nervous perspiration can exude a noxious odour. Sitting in an enclosed space for two or more hours with someone else's body odour is not particularly pleasant, and at worst it can provoke headaches and bad humour. So do take care over hygiene on the morning of your viva, and use an effective deodorant. Strong perfumes can be as distracting as body odour, so avoid those as well.
- **Wear something uncomfortable:** 'a degree of formality' need not mean a business suit and tie, especially if you never wear that sort of thing and it makes you uncomfortable. Watching a student tug nervously at jacket sleeves, or pluck at pockets on a jacket so new that the pockets are still tacked shut, or claw desperately at a tie which then dangles at an unnatural angle can be most distracting – both to the student and to the empathetic

examiners. If you mean to wear a tie (or any unfamiliar garment), then wear it repeatedly over a couple of weeks before the viva in order to habituate to it.

- **Wear something sexy:** tight T-shirts over bulging muscles, plunging necklines and short skirts belong in pubs and parties, not PhD vivas.
- **Forget the tissues:** coughs, splutters, sneezes and sniffles are not uncommon, and so are best anticipated. It's painful to everyone when the student has an incorrigible sniffle and no means to address it. Bring tissues and cough lozenges (the examiners should ensure that water is provided for you). Tissues are also useful when you spill your water into your lap. Useful, too, for wiping the sweat from your brow should nervous perspiration break out on your face.
- **Wear squeaky shoes:** squeaky shoes are like a persistent bad joke. One of us sat through a viva in which the student shuffled his feet under the table whenever he was thinking or nervous. The chirps, creaks and groans that came from his shoes were hilarious, functioning as an anxiety meter. The examiners struggled to suppress their laughter.

Presentation is something you want to sort out in advance, so that you can forget about it on the day. Good presentation gives the student confidence and sends the right signals to the examiners.

And don't forget your beauty sleep – a good night's sleep before a viva is disproportionately beneficial.

How to fail a viva

- Assume that the viva doesn't matter
- Answer any question about what you did with, 'My supervisor made me do it'
- Stick to one-word answers
- Display intransigence
- Display rampant cynicism
- Display flippancy
- Display a lack of interest
- Persist in an inability to describe your own work
- Persist in an inability to define fundamental terms
- Persist in an inability to talk about the papers you cite
- Call the examiner rude names

These are tried and true methods; we've seen students fail using them.

Also, don't waste time second-guessing the examiners. A professor in our acquaintance tells the story of a brilliant student who, having seen the professor write 'failure' in his notes, decided that failure was imminent and 'died' through the latter half of her viva. The professor couldn't understand the dramatic change in her previously flawless performance and asked about it afterwards. When she explained, he was horrified; he'd actually just been making a note to follow up on an interesting idea (about failure) in one of her answers.

How to impress your examiners

- Come prepared
- Listen; comprehend the questions and address them directly
- Make eye contact
- Show enthusiasm for your work
- See your work in the bigger picture
- Be able to refer directly to your text (highlight key passages) in answering questions
- Be able to refer directly to seminal texts by author and with accuracy
- Be able to articulate the nature and scale of your contribution
- Think forward – think beyond the research to further work and implications
- Be reflective – be able to articulate both what was good about your work and what could be improved, and how

These are tried and true methods as well. Students who show command of their material – both their own research and the prior work that frames and contributes to it – and who engage in the examination dialogue with knowledge, interest and courtesy are able to impress their examiners, even though they may also make some errors or sometimes answer falteringly. Examiners like lively and interesting examinations.

Fending off panic

- **Pause:** you're allowed time to think
- **Breathe deeply:** three deep, 'centring' breaths, making sure that you exhale slowly, usually help
- **Take a drink:** there's usually water on the table
- **Make quick notes** to yourself, especially if you have more than one point to make

If you don't understand the question or don't know the answer:

- Ask the examiner to repeat the question (chances are, they'll simplify it as they do so). This is best when you simply didn't take the question in.
- Rephrase the question back to the examiner: 'I think you're asking me about X' – and then answer it.
- Offer alternative interpretations: 'I'm not sure if you mean X or Y. Could you clarify?'
- It's much better to offer an interpretation of the question than to say 'I don't understand', but once or twice you can do that too.

Keep it simple, stupid. When you hear yourself saying the same thing for the third time, just *stop and smile*, or say, 'Sorry, I'm repeating myself.' We all get nervous. Once (but only once) in a viva, if you really can't help yourself, you're allowed to relax the stiff upper lip entirely and say something like, 'I'm sorry, I'm feeling very nervous, I just need a moment . . .' The examiners are likely to back off a bit and ask you a warm-up question before carrying on in earnest.

Questions examiners ask

- **Warm-up questions** to calm you down. Often of the form, 'So how did you come to research this subject?' Or, 'Can you summarize your core thesis for us?'
- **Confirmatory questions** to let you demonstrate your knowledge. Often in the form of asking you to reiterate or define something in your dissertation.
- **Deep confirmatory questions** to let you demonstrate that your knowledge is more than skin deep. These are usually follow-ups to confirmatory questions that take up some point in your answer. Just keep your head and continue to address the questions.
- **Calibration questions** to help the examiner check their own understanding of your work.
- **Scholarship questions** to let you demonstrate that you know the field as well as your own research.
- **Salvaging questions** – when you've written something badly, to let you show you do know what you're talking about after all.
- **Pushing the envelope questions** to see how far your knowledge goes.
- **'This is neat' questions** to give the examiner a chance to discuss your interesting ideas.
- **Redemptive, 'lesson learned' questions** to give you a chance to admit some awful blunder in your work so that the examiner can 'let you off' without worrying that you'll make it again. A typical example is, 'Would you take this approach again if you were pursuing this issue?' when a student has applied an inappropriate method that yielded little.
- **'This is a good student; how good?' questions** – a little 'sparring' to let you really show your stuff.
- **'Give me a reason to pass you' questions** – often, if the examiners continue asking about the same topic, it's because they're interested; if so, then cooperate actively with them, rather than trying to change the topic.

These are all moderately benign questions. If you arouse the examiners' anger or a suspicion that there is something wrong with your work, however, you may be asked some hard, sharp questions. The next section lists some classic 'killer' questions and suggests some ways of responding effectively to them.

Killer questions and how to survive them

In this section, Q = question, A = suggested answer, C = our comments on the question and/or answer.

Q: *How does your work relate to Jim Bloggs' recent paper?* (when you've never heard of Bloggs)
A: 'I'm not familiar with that paper. Does he take an X approach or a Y approach?'
C: Show something you do know that's relevant; then, when the examiner offers a *précis*: 'Ah, so it's like so-and-so's work?'

Q: *Isn't this obvious?*
A: 'Well, it may appear that way with hindsight, but there was surprisingly little work on this topic in the literature, and the question needed to be properly answered.'
C: Many dissertations codify what people think they already know but which has never been properly established. 'Obvious' can be good; it can make a contribution. Marian's *external* examiner asked her this and, fortunately, her *internal* examiner answered him that it was only obvious because he'd read her dissertation. You might try a modestly phrased version of this answer yourself if nobody offers it for you.

Q: *Isn't this just like Brown's work?*
A: 'It differs from Brown's work because . . .'
C: Everyone worries that someone else is going to 'gazump' them and publish exactly their work just before they do. Forget it. There will be something – a difference of approach, of technique, of sample – that distinguishes your work and protects your contribution. If you know Brown's work already, then you should have already identified how it differs from yours; if you don't, ask about Brown's work until the answers reveal a difference.

Q: *You use the term X in two different ways in Chapters 4 and 6. What do you mean?*
A 'In Chapter 4, I was using Smith's definition, which was most appropriate for that part of the thesis. In Chapter 6, I was using Brown's . . .'
C: Answer the question, giving a concise clarification. Make a note of what you say because you'll probably be asked to amend the text with the clarification when you do your corrections.

Q: *Why didn't you . . .?*
A: 'Because . . .'
C: This is why you re-read your thesis and have a mock viva. Re-reading your thesis will remind you of why you did things the way you did (and, conversely, tell you why you didn't use the other options). This will also give a

sanity check that you haven't missed anything obvious. If the suggestion is something little known in your field, then you can reply along the lines of, 'That's interesting, and it sounds as if it should be more widely known in this field.' You can then turn this into a discussion of methods in the field and an opportunity to talk about the things you *do* know about.

Some ways of addressing weakness

Sometimes, you just have to admit that you were wrong. Occasionally, just making the admission with humour is effective. (As with the student who, when asked if she would use the same (fruitless) survey technique again, said with feeling: 'Hell, no'.)

More often, it's safer to follow the three-point plan:

1 Reiterate why whatever you did was a justified choice at the outset
2 Explain, as simply as possible and without apology, that you understand why it failed
3 Make some alternative suggestions about what you'd do instead next time that would improve your chances of getting it right

No one expects doctoral research to flow smoothly without errors or hitches. Indeed, it is rare for any research to do so – research is opportunistic and (happily) full of surprises. What examiners expect is that students will respond to the errors and hitches with intelligence and by learning from them.

Generic viva questions

We haven't suggested answers to these, for obvious reasons. You may find it reassuring and useful to have a friend ask you these, and then see if you can answer them. The friend doesn't need to understand your answer; if you can answer swiftly, confidently and concisely, then you'll probably be fine. If you can't, then some time thinking about possible answers should prove very useful.

- How did you come to research this topic in this manner?
- What are the main achievements of your research?
- Which of the achievements is most important to you, and why?
- What has your thesis contributed to our knowledge in this field?
- What are the major theoretical strands in this area: what are the crucial ideas and who are the main contributors?
- What are the main issues (matters of debate or dispute) in this area?

- Where is your thesis 'placed' in terms of the existing theory and debate? How would the major researchers react to your ideas?
- Who, in your opinion, will be most interested in this work?
- What published research is closest to your work? Who are your main competitors, and how is your research distinguished from theirs?
- Why did you choose the particular research methodology that you used?
- Did you consider using any other research methodology?
- What were the crucial research decisions that you made?
- If you were doing this research again, what would you do differently?
- What do you see as the next steps in this research?
- What was the most interesting finding in your results?
- Isn't this all obvious?
- Were you surprised by any of your results (if so, why, and what was surprising)?
- What advice would you give a new student entering this area?
- What is your plan for publication?
- What haven't I asked you that I should have done, and what would your answer have been?

16

Sabotage and salvation
Or, developing habits for success

*Reputations • Destructive habits • Time, sensible planning and useful
displacement activities • Constructive habits • Professional etiquette:
respecting working relationships*

> *He wished to excel in every aspect of human potentiality, so he created simulacra
> of the sixteen muses.* [1]

So, we've established that there are lots of ways to climb a mountain. There are
also lots of ways to fall off the mountain if you're not paying attention.
Switching to our favourite metaphor, whether you're going to end up with a
beautifully-formed cabinet or a pile of firewood and sawdust depends largely
on how you manage yourself and your behaviour. Switching metaphor again,
think of the process as health care rather than disease control: prevention
is better than cure. And prevention is easier if you're brutally honest with
yourself. This chapter is about self-management, about learning to recognize
and avoid your behavioural enemies, including 'the enemy within', and about
professional etiquette.

We start with a fundamental concept: reputation. Then we walk through
three categories of behaviour: behavioural enemies (or self-destructive habits),
displacement activities (or ways of doing something constructive while gaining some 'mental space'), and constructive habits and their relationship to
professional etiquette.

---

[1] Wagner, K.E. (1979) *Nightwinds*. London: Coronet Books, p. 108.

Reputations

A note on reputations. What sort of researcher and colleague do you want to be known as? Most people would favour a characterization as widely respected, fair, honest, brilliant, kind, supportive and things of that sort, and there are people in the research community who fit that description. Unfortunately, there are also those known as exclusive, back-stabbing, corrupt or self-serving.

Your reputation is shaped by your accomplishments, your behaviour and your interactions. Good research which is well published contributes to your reputation, as does a record of effective collaboration, generous and successful PhD supervision and attracting grants which are then used for good research, well published. Those are the usual 'academic metrics'. Engagement in and contribution to the research community through things like programme committees for conferences, editorial boards for journals, policy consultations, external examination, refereeing, networking effectively, sharing information and mentoring also help. The positive side of a reputation within the research community is that it 'makes' your career.

The negative side of a reputation within the research community is that a bad reputation can destroy your career. It takes some time to build a sound reputation, but it only takes one or two unworthy acts to destroy one. The extreme case is academic fraud. The entire edifice of research is based on a foundation of basic starting points (data, methods, etc.) When you do some research, you start from what is already known in the field. If it turns out that one of those starting points is wrong because someone deliberately faked it, then the time you spent in your research was wasted. In some areas, such as medicine, delays in finding the answer can lead to people dying.

Such instances are extreme. More common instances involve grey areas – for instance, trying to claim more credit than is strictly justifiable, or making exaggerated claims. There are also personality issues, such as people who are needlessly aggressive or rude to colleagues. Although such bad habits can to some extent be outweighed by good-quality research, nobody actively wants to work with someone unpleasant and untrustworthy if there is an alternative. Such people tend to suffer what might be called passive damage to their careers. This takes the form of things which do *not* happen, particularly where a career marker involves invitations – for instance, invitations to join editorial boards, to give keynote talks at conferences or to collaborate on major research proposals. An interesting feature of this is that the people involved may be quite unaware that it is happening.

You'll find that managing your behaviour has a lot to do with establishing your good reputation, and that reputation recurs through the discussion in this chapter.

Destructive habits

PhDs are messy, personal and ill-specified. They involve putting your ideas on the line in a way that is more personal than writing essays or papers at undergraduate or masters level, and many students perceive that it's not just their ideas that are being judged, but their intellect and by implication their worth. PhDs involve intimate, intense, long-term relationships with supervisors, often without much choice or planning. People tend to learn what a PhD is and entails implicitly; the rules and requirements aren't specified very clearly (hence the need for books like this). As a result, perfectly capable and accomplished students experience stress, behave emotionally and often irrationally, and take things personally. Many develop destructive habits and thereby become their own worst enemy.

Learned helplessness

If you give animals electric shocks when they attempt to escape, in a situation where they can't escape, eventually they stop trying to escape, even when the situation changes and escape is possible. (Like Milgram's conformity experiment, the research behind this finding would probably not get past an ethics committee today, but is invaluable as an insight into apparently unlikely behaviour.)

PhD students are particularly prone to this feeling, and usually go through at least one phase of feeling that they are getting nowhere and that there is no point in keeping going. If this is an accurate description of how you're feeling, then pull yourself together long enough to eat some chocolate and acquire a self-help book (e.g. *Feel the Fear and Do It Anyway* by Susan Jeffers – see 'Some further reading'). Read the book, set yourself some manageable goals that are at least vaguely relevant and talk things through with someone who can give you sensible, supportive advice. Also, get some exercise away from your usual haunts, to help acquire a sense of perspective. Once you've done this, you should be sufficiently clear of the immediate doldrums to be able to plan a sensible way forward for yourself.

One of the advantages of well-designed research is that you should know precisely what you're doing at each stage of the research, and what you will do in response to each eventuality that might come along. The bad news is that this might involve knowing in advance that you will go through a long phase of data-crunching; the good news is that if you know this, you should know precisely how to crunch the data and what to do with the results when you finally get them. If you don't know this in advance, then you need to rethink your research design.

Expressive behaviour

Expressive behaviour often accompanies learned helplessness. Instrumental behaviour is behaviour which moves you toward your goals. Expressive behaviour is behaviour intended to demonstrate to others what sort of person you are. A student sitting in the library wading through the six key texts for their area of research is engaging in instrumental behaviour. The student sitting at the next table reading the same page of an irrelevant paper over and over again in a state of nervous collapse is going for expressive behaviour ('Look how hard I'm working! Please have mercy . . .'). The student who produces a thesis containing all the features that their external examiners love is also engaging in expressive behaviour, but of a much more useful sort. Unfortunately for some, examiners mark what you produce, not what sort of person you are; the brilliant piece of work by someone who hacked it together in a couple of days will be better received than a mediocre piece of work produced by someone who laboured over it for months.

Sometimes you can use expressive behaviour to help yourself *out* of negative feedback loops. For example, if there's a problematic, pesky, niggling idea that you can't get rid of (and you can't deal with right now), you can ritualistically hand the problem over to someone else (like your supervisor) and agree a date when you'll come to visit it again. Or you can put it symbolically in a box, tape the box shut and write 'do not open until . . .' across the tape. It's the same for useless self-judgements: symbolic, expressive actions like writing them on a piece of paper and then burning it, burying it, or tying it to a helium balloon and letting it go can actually help you move on.

Taking ages to get nowhere

There are several quite different reasons for taking ages to get (apparently) nowhere, with different implications.

- **Reason 1:** you are taking ages to get nowhere because you don't have the faintest idea what you are doing and where you are going. If you suspect this is the case, draw a diagram. It consists of an arrow going into a box. The arrow is your research question, the box is the data collection and analysis. Now draw arrows emerging from the box, with each arrow representing a different logically possible outcome from the data collection and analysis. For instance, the outcomes may be 'A is greater than B', 'A is smaller than B' and 'A and B are the same size'. You should be able to list all the possible outcomes and explain why each one tells you something useful and significant. (You should also remember this exercise from the chapter on 'Research design'.) You should also know exactly what form your data will take and how you are going to analyse it, right down to the level of what tables you will use to show your results. (You should not, however, have more than a shrewd suspicion of which particular answer you will find, otherwise the research is probably too trivial to bother with.) If you fail this test, then you're taking chances and may well end up getting nowhere. Redesigning your research is a good idea in such cases; it doesn't mean that you have to use quantitative methods or whatever your personal bugbear is, or that you have to abandon your area of research. It simply means that you have to revise your question so that it's guaranteed to reduce the problem space (i.e. eliminate a set of possibilities which had previously seemed plausible), rather than being a bet on a particular finding. Gambling with several years of your life is not usually a wise idea, and undertaking research only if you are sure that the results will confirm your initial beliefs is a very dodgy undertaking – what would you do if the data disagreed with your initial beliefs? Fiddle the data or face the prospect of changing your opinions?

- **Reason 2 (in no particular order):** you are taking ages to get nowhere simply because you are in the middle of a PhD or an MSc project. If you pass the diagram test and are more than a third of the way through your planned time, then this is likely to be the explanation. The 'second-year blues' are a fairly normal part of doing a PhD. Just get on with it.
- **Reason 3:** you are kidding yourself by confusing 'displacement activity' with 'productive activity'. This involves doing something that looks like work that isn't in the critical path to completing your PhD, and doesn't contribute to something that is in the critical path, and doesn't even contribute to something that contributes to something that is in the critical path. An example is given under 'expressive behaviour', above, and more constructive uses of displacement activity are discussed below. As with any unproductive activity, the first, most important, response should be: stop. Stop the activity. Stop reinforcing the negative feelings. Then choose a constructive activity instead, like getting someone else to help you set out an action plan with clear steps and specified checkpoints.

Isolation

Isolation and perceived isolation are problems for many (if not most, if not all) students, and especially for part-time students. Sometimes there are real barriers to interaction that need to be addressed (such as communication out of office hours, physical isolation or a lack of local expertise in your topic). The chapter on 'Networks' should help. We also isolate ourselves unnecessarily. Sometimes we have false expectations about what productive activity looks like (see Reason 3 above) and want to live the fantasy of the lone scholar in the ivory tower, even though what's really needed is a good critical conversation with someone who makes it necessary to externalize our thinking. Sometimes we have false expectations about other people's availability and interest. It's frustrating to hear students say things like: 'I didn't want to disturb you, because I know how busy you are' when we actually could have used an hour's distraction and a cup of coffee. Sometimes we have false expectations about ourselves, such as 'I work better alone'. The evidence is clear that, even though students do need time to work quietly by themselves, those who seek dialogue regularly (every week, if not every day), and engage in the community, succeed more reliably, more confidently and more promptly – because they're exposed to more learning opportunities, more perspectives and more scrutiny.

Other assorted bad habits

There are numerous other bad habits which afflict researchers, such as hiding from your supervisor (covered in the chapter on 'Supervision'), bad time management, failure to prioritize, procrastination and not bothering to become familiar with the tools of the trade. If you're to sort yourself out properly, you need to learn how to identify and correct bad habits. Most bad habits involve deceiving, kidding or obstructing yourself. You need to be brutally honest with yourself in diagnosing them. You need to stop the ones that are causing you harm, but that doesn't mean that you have to proceed to correcting all of them. Many habits, such as following an interest regardless of whether it looks like a good career move, are personal choices and you might decide that the positive side of the habit is well worth the price. Others, though, such as refusing to accept that you are wrong, are bad for you. You won't improve without change; you won't undergo change without pain. Learn to accept the pain as a friend and your life will be transformed.

Those of you who are worried about the long-term consequences of close familiarity with pain might be reassured to learn that there are ways of tackling research which involve a minimum risk of having to admit that you are wrong. Phrasing the research question in such a way that you have not committed yourself to any of the possible outcomes is a good example of this: whatever happens (short of a total shambles) you will have proof of your brilliance in identifying the right question in the first place.

Time, sensible planning and useful displacement activities

You need to accept that things take time. There are different sorts of time. One sort is elapsed time; another sort is task time. A lot of things take quite a short time for the action itself (task time) but involve a lot of waiting around until the action itself can begin (elapsed time). For instance, you're organizing something with someone else by email. The actual exchanges of information only take a total of five minutes at the keyboard, but the elapsed time to make the arrangements totals up to several days because you're having to wait for each other's replies. So, slow down a bit, stop rushing, and slow down a bit more. You will then waste less energy fretting and be in a better position to do some sensible planning.

Sensible planning is a very different activity from two familiar enemies, namely unproductive displacement activities and the wrong sort of expressive behaviour (i.e. the sort used to say 'I'm busy' in place of actually doing anything useful or instrumental). Sensible planning is often quite difficult to do when you're stressed out by life events and hassles. The best thing to do initially is to buy yourself some time, plan how to buy yourself some more time, and bootstrap up a bit at a time. How do you do that? Ironically, a good start is via displacement activities – the useful sort that help you relax and 'regroup'.

One of us was once given some very wise advice by their supervisor, namely that if you are going to engage in a displacement activity, you should make sure that it's a useful one. Useful displacement activities are essential to good research, but by definition involve effort with no visible output (at least none which relates directly to your PhD). They are *invisible support activities* whose importance lies in gaining you time to think (mental time). Examples range from sorting and tidying, to stocking up your stationery, to doing general background reading (as opposed to focused reading). You have to do these things. Order is important, stationery is essential and background reading expands the mind.

A long soaky bath

Once a week, instead of slumping despondently in front of the television, run yourself a long, hot bath. Lie in the bath with a wet cloth over your face. This will calm you down. It will also lead surprisingly often to your seeing your situation in clearer perspective, and realizing some better ways of handling things. The long, soaky bath is our proxy for the whole class of activities whose purpose is to empty the mind and relax the body.

Take a walk

Walking has amazing restorative powers. Instead of persisting in a destructive habit or a pattern of frustration, take a walk. The exercise is good: it increases your circulation and moves the limbs you've been sitting on for too many hours. The change of scenery is good: it gives your eyes a break, gives you a change of air and provides a different backdrop for your thinking. Often, a half-hour walk provides a new perspective, a few insights and a feeling of reinvigoration – enough to set you back onto a productive track.

Tidy and file

Most people don't tidy and file enough. Tidying and filing, if you do them in manageable doses, can be very soothing activities and can give you a feeling of control. They also reacquaint you with your own activity; sometimes they can remind you of forgotten papers, rekindle forgotten strands of thought or fill in some other gap. They also make a practical difference to your life – it's a lot easier to be efficient and to have some spare time if your tidying and filing are under control.

This applies to life debris as well as PhD material. Most of us have large amounts of clutter. Look through your belongings, get rid of the things that are neither useful, loved nor beautiful, and create some storage space and some 'swap space'. Swap space is another useful concept: it's space needed temporarily while you rearrange things. For instance, if you're tidying shelves, you'll need at least enough swap space for the contents of one shelf so that you can empty that shelf, clean it, and decide which contents to put where. Hardly anyone has enough swap space or storage space. Don't try to do all of this at once; have an evening per week or per month when you do a bit.

Read a book about something different from your PhD topic

This will help you to break out of the cycle of worry about your PhD, will help you to see things in perspective and will quite probably one day provide you with the key insight that changes your life.

There are some excellent books available on planning, time management and self-development. They will give you a lot of ideas about ways of organizing yourself in the medium term, and a fair few ideas about developing yourself as a person. What you will probably find is that you start off fired with good intentions, take on too much and gradually slip back into bad habits. One thing you can do about this is to start on a manageable scale, without trying to do too much. Another is to try a variety of approaches until you find some that work well for you. For some jobs, for instance, traditional time management doesn't work very well because the job involves too much unpredictable firefighting (i.e. dealing with serious immediate problems caused by people other than yourself). In such situations, what you have to do instead is priority management, which involves a different set of skills. Another thing that often happens is that you find that one way of structuring your time (e.g. planning the day as a series of time slots) just doesn't work for your personality, but that another (e.g. planning for the week, with the days as the units – an admin day, a research day etc.) works well for you.

General reading is highly advisable, since a lot of the best work comes from applying work from one area to another area. (One of us once supervised an undergraduate dissertation which took a nineteenth-century researcher's formalisms for describing the structure of Russian folk tales and applied them to the plots of computer games . . . excellent and highly entertaining work, with a lot of implications for the computer games industry, but not exactly the sort of thing which is likely to emerge from focused reading.) The trouble is that you can never tell in advance when something will be useful or where; the Russian folk tale idea derived from reading about the topic some 20 years previously. The good news is that when you do encounter a relevant area for this sort of cross-fertilization you can produce brilliant work for very little apparent effort.

Displacement activities can be useful or unproductive (i.e. instrumental or uselessly expressive). It's not the activity itself that makes the difference, but what you use it for, and for how long. If you use displacement activity to mask that you're stuck or confused, then it's destructive. If you use displacement activity briefly to buy yourself some planning and relaxation time, then it's useful. One way to work out which it is, is to consider how long you've been indulging in displacement activity, and how regularly. If you've done it briefly and moved on, you're probably fine. If you've been doing it for hours or days or it's becoming habitual, then you need to reassess, because you've probably been kidding yourself.

Constructive habits

It's easier to develop constructive habits if you understand fully that your PhD is not just your PhD, but also a socially-embedded activity that reflects more widely: on your supervisor, your department, your institution. You're in a complex relationship with your supervisor that is expected to change over time. But, whereas you'll be growing and changing significantly during your studies (at a rate comparable to that at which children develop), your supervisor will be growing and changing more subtly (at a rate comparable to that at which parents develop) – and will be less focused on their development than you are on yours.

Doing a PhD requires a balance between independence and guidance. On the one hand, you're expected to produce original work that is your own. On the other, you're expected to be guided by and to learn from your supervisor. Missing the balance either way (by ignoring your supervisor and insisting on doing everything by yourself without benefit of the available wisdom, or by relying too heavily on your supervisor and failing to take initiative or think independently) is problematic. The complexity of balance trickles into other issues, like intellectual property: students own their own work, but they rarely work in strict isolation, and so their work is often not just their own. Moreover, students often do work associated with projects or in collaboration with other people. Understanding these forms of interdependence is crucial to maintaining professional etiquette, that is, maintaining proper behaviour for a professional researcher. Professional etiquette is, in effect, a means of managing and protecting your professional reputation.

Communicate

Talk about your research. Talking about it forces you to 'put it out there', to express your ideas (and hence help you think through them), to articulate your concerns or issues (and hence help you assess them pragmatically) and to get your thinking scrutinized (and hence either reassure you that you're making sense or alert you early about errors, gaps or misconceptions). Talking about expectations and assumptions gives you a chance to calibrate yourself with others in your community – and may give others a chance to share tips and tricks.

Don't just talk; listen. Listening to other people's research can help you develop your critical skills and give you insights into what works and doesn't. Other students may have solved problems you're facing or are about to face. Just listen with a mite of scepticism; remember that most students are feeling vulnerable, and that makes some of them exaggerate their accomplishments and play down their anxieties and obstacles.

Make mistakes

You need to recognize that you can make mistakes during your PhD studies. Indeed, if you're not making mistakes, then you're probably not trying hard enough, because you're working within your comfort zone. The point is not to avoid mistakes entirely, but to learn from the ones you do make.

Part of the reality of mistakes is handling criticism. We are reminded of one student who, whenever one of her ideas was challenged would counter: 'Why do you hate me?'. The first rule of academic criticism is: don't take it personally. The second rule is: criticism is engagement. If your supervisor or a colleague criticizes your work, it suggests that they have engaged with it sufficiently to have an opinion. Appreciate the engagement and learn from the criticism. The third rule is: not all criticism requires a response. Assess the criticism. If you can learn from it, then use it. If it's ill-founded or unwarranted (and you're sure you're in a position to judge whether or not it is), then consider whether there is a problem with how you've tried to communicate your ideas. If you're convinced after due consideration that the criticism is inappropriate, then ignore it. The fourth rule is: give the sort of criticism you'd like to receive (clear, informative, well-founded, constructive).

Practise finesse

No one enjoys being criticized, pilloried or humiliated (whether or not it's warranted). Nevertheless, academia requires us to critique, challenge and oppose, and to do so articulately. The trick is to also do so with finesse, using non-aggressive forms of speech, so that the points are made and the insights are expressed without the recipient feeling assaulted personally. Often this is as simple as avoiding bald assertion or harsh statement. Ask a question, rather than make a statement. Ask for clarification, rather than making a challenge. This has the advantage of saving you from your own unnoticed assumptions and misconceptions, as well as giving your correspondent some 'room to move'. Behaviour counsellors often espouse the value of 'I statements': expressing a conflict in terms of its effect on you, rather than as an accusation against another. 'I'm confused when you use familiar terms in unfamiliar ways, and it would be helpful if you would define your usage when you're appropriating a familiar word to a specific technical meaning.' Or 'I'm distracted when you call me by the wrong name; please call me [the right name].' Everyone makes mistakes, and gentle correction saves face.

Give credit

You never lose by giving credit. You often gain.

- Understand the scope of your research and contribution: modesty pays
- Be scrupulous about giving credit where credit is due (e.g. when you publish papers)
- Be accurate in your use of other people's material (ideas, direct references, quotations, etc.) and attribute them correctly

Giving credit is instrumental in establishing your integrity, and expressive in showing your respect for others' contributions.

Keep an eye on the Big Picture

It's very easy to get 'bogged down' in detail, or to become utterly immersed in the task of the moment. Unfortunately, time is limited, and so you need to use your time effectively – which means strategically. That means that you need a strategy, you need to keep your eye on the Big Picture that links your research question to your research plan and your intended destination (see Chapter 8), that has you doing PhD research that is meaningful or purposeful for you. It means that you need to be able to 'see the wood for the trees' – and not just that, but also to know which wood you're in, and why.

Once you have a Big Picture, you need to keep it in mind, or at least to revisit it regularly. Monitor your work in terms of its contribution to your Big Picture. What's in the critical path? What isn't? Prioritize. This will also help you to avoid over-commitment, as long as you're honest with yourself about your capacity.

Professional etiquette: respecting working relationships

The basics of professional etiquette are comparable to the cardinal rules about dealing with your supervisor (see Chapter 4): being honest, articulate, informative, respectful and responsible. They are about observing your 'duty of care' to those involved directly or indirectly in your research (including yourself). They are founded in low-level, everyday behaviour: doing what you promise (reliability), delivering on time (punctuality) and leaving emotion to one side in intellectual discourse (objectivity). And they are anchored in the notion that you are not an island: you are part of a social system and are accountable for your decisions and actions.

One skill essential to developing effective working relationships that is often forgotten (especially by academics) is *listening*. Another is *tolerance*.

Scenarios

Here are some examples of 'sticky situations', drawn from life. Consider your reactions.

You are visiting a company which you hope will give you access to data for your research. They ask you to sign a non-disclosure agreement. What should you do?
Do you understand the implications of a non-disclosure agreement for your research? Are you empowered to sign such an agreement, or should you consult your supervisor or the contracts department of your university first?

There's a conference deadline on Monday. On Friday, you have a bright idea for a paper and you whip together a draft over the weekend. But you can't find your supervisor on Monday. What should you do?
What's the worst that could happen? Perhaps that you go ahead, and some half-baked paper gets accepted and published, with the result that you annoy your supervisor and establish a history of shoddy work . . .

Another student complains to you about his supervisor, accusing him of gross misconduct. The student is a bit of a clown, and you're not sure how much is exaggeration. On the other hand, the story he's telling is compelling and quite serious. What should you do?
What don't you know? What are the costs – to you, to this student, to his supervisor, to other students, to the department – of doing nothing, or of taking action? What response is both responsible and discreet?

You've been following your supervisor's guidance on a line of research, conducting studies that he sets out and that you flesh out together. You propose to write the work up for publication, but the supervisor objects. What should you do?

What don't you know? What might your supervisor's reasons be for objecting? Would you rather assume that your supervisor is an obstructive idiot, or ask some gentle questions before you make a fool of yourself?

You did some work as part of a project, hence part of a collaboration. You want to take the work further, extending the ideas a bit into a new paper. What should you do? Are there boundaries to collaboration? What would you want your collaborators to do if the positions were reversed?

There aren't cut-and-dried answers to these scenarios. Most of them depend on things that may not be immediately apparent, and so it's usually a good idea to consider what isn't expressed, or isn't evident that might have a bearing on what the situation really is or really means.

Common principles for professional etiquette

Three principles for protecting your reputation can be captured in terms of familiar sayings:

1 **The golden rule:** do unto others as you would have them do unto you. (In fact, you might interpret this within a double standard and judge your own behaviour by the highest standards, while maintaining tolerance for the shortcomings of others.)
2 **Prevention is better than cure:** establishing appropriate and explicit expectations in research interactions usually prevents misunderstandings later.
3 **What goes around, comes around:** when you enter a PhD programme, you're entering an established social network; researchers you meet in your and your supervisor's domain are likely to know your supervisor and each other. Conversations and actions do not occur in isolation from all that interconnection – what you say outside may well follow you home.

The good news is that there are huge advantages to behaving well, developing a reputation as a 'fair dealer' and interacting with others in your research community. What goes around, comes around: the good works that you do are likely to lead to positive responses such as shared information, useful invitations and happy collaborations.

17

What next?

Career goals • Academia or elsewhere? • Academic career types • Various other things • Identifying opportunities • Writing a CV • Applications and cover letters • Job interviews

> *This terror is not due altogether to the sinister nature of his recent disappearance, but was engendered by the whole nature of his lifework . . .* [1]

So there you are, through your viva, corrections finished to everyone's satisfaction and waiting for graduation day, without the thesis filling your life. At this point many students realize with growing unease that they haven't given much thought to the topic of what to do next with their lives. This chapter discusses some issues relating to that topic.

One issue is career structure within the academic world. We discuss this so that you can observe the lifestyle of people who have followed various career routes and then think about which of these routes, if any, might suit you. This should help you decide which jobs to apply for (though in practice your options will probably be a research assistantship or a lectureship – we include the Big Picture because it comes in useful for all sorts of other purposes).

Once you know which job to apply for, you need to know how to handle job interviews – what to do before interviews and during them. Most people take the perfectly understandable view that this involves thinking about what they have to offer; we describe a better strategy, and give various other hints and tips. We've phrased this in terms of applying for a lectureship, to help your

---

[1] Lovecraft, H.P. (1921–22) Herbert West – Reanimator, in *Omnibus 2: Dagon and Other Macabre Tales* (1985). London: Grafton Books, p. 158.

morale, and because if you can handle that then you should be able to handle interviews for other jobs, with appropriate changes to our advice.

Career goals

In order to make sense of academic careers, you need to understand what motivates successful researchers. According to Indiana Jones, the answer is 'Fortune and glory'. That, however, is fiction. The reality is more subtle. Successful researchers are driven by a need for two or more of three things: status, power and satisfaction of their curiosity. (You'll notice that money is not among them. If you're in it for the money, you'll probably choose business, industry or a more lucrative profession instead.)

Satisfaction of curiosity

Satisfaction of curiosity is an important theme in research – you can be paid (not well, but well enough) to be nosy. If you are shrewd, you can use this to get funding for things such as travel to exotic places to study the behaviour of holidaymakers on sunny beaches. Wise geologists are aware that some types of lava are only found in a few places, such as Hawaii. Researchers crop up in all sorts of unlikely-sounding places – for instance, digging holes through bits of frozen wasteland in the Arctic, sitting in the control tower of an airfield watching the air traffic controllers and on patrol with the local police, to mention just a few examples of things our colleagues have done. However, nobody will pay you for long if you just satisfy your curiosity and do nothing more; you also have to let the world know what you've found, which leads on to the other two goals (especially if what you've found is something significant and useful).

Status

Status in the academic world is not quite like status outside it. The status that really matters to a researcher is status in the research community. Research investigates areas – for instance, glacial geomorphology, prion structure, criminal behaviour among teenagers. Within each research area there are well-established conferences, journals, newsletters, etc. There is also a body of researchers who are working in that area, who form its research community. They will usually read the same journals as each other, attend the same conferences and so on. Within each research community there is a fairly clear pecking order, from beginners that no one has heard of, through moderately well-known researchers to the major authorities whose names and work are known and revered by everyone in the area. (The other researchers may not always agree with them, but they know them and acknowledge their status.)

Status in the research community does not derive from the prestige of your institution, or the impressiveness of your title (though these can help a bit). What matters is the quality of your work. If you're doing boring, routine work which produces no surprises, then the research community will be utterly unimpressed by your being Professor of Computer Science, Mathematics and Hard Concepts and will simply think that you don't deserve that post. If you're doing work which produces interesting findings and opens up new research directions for your colleagues, then you will be taken seriously, even if you're a research assistant at Fenlands College. Some academics actually make a deliberate choice to work in little-known places, on the grounds that a high-profile successful academic in such a place is more likely to be allowed to get on with their work in peace without being messed around by The System. Status of this sort is spread in various ways, but mainly through word of mouth and social networks. It is recognized at a formal level in various ways within the research community: for instance, being invited to give keynote talks at conferences, being appointed to journal editorships and positions on funding bodies (these are known in the lingo as 'esteem indicators').

Unfortunately, there can be quite massive mismatches between someone's status in their research community and their status in their home organization. As a broad generalization, this is more of a problem in new universities, where the administrative system is not used to dealing with research and equates status directly with position in the organization's official hierarchy. In such a situation, a professor with no standing in the research community will be treated as quite important, whereas a lecturer with a huge international reputation in the research community will be treated as a nonentity. This can feel quite surreal to the individual involved – being treated with deference at an international event one day and being harangued by minor administrators at work the next day – and can also become extremely annoying. For this reason, most researchers sooner or later start a dalliance with the concept of power.

Power

Power is extremely useful. For most researchers, the initially attractive aspect of power is the power to refuse to do things which are an annoying distraction (e.g. paperwork or teaching a topic about which the researcher has little knowledge and even less enthusiasm). Contrary to what Theory X managers believe, most researchers, if left to their own devices, would happily research for as many hours a day as they could manage. Having power allows researchers more time to get on with what they really enjoy, which is a seductive prospect.

Where does power come from? In the researcher's home institution, power does not come from status in the research community; it comes from the ability to influence things in a way which matters to the host institution. This may come from official roles – for instance, if you're on the funding panel for a major grant-giving body then some parts of your institution will be unlikely to want to antagonize you too much. Other parts of your institution, however, couldn't care less – for instance, the parts which are concerned only with teaching and to whom research funding bodies are of no interest whatsoever. For these and other reasons, therefore, a more potent source of power is money. If you bring large amounts of money into the institution, then you will be viewed as a valuable asset. The more money you bring in, the more valuable you will be, and the better your chances of being treated well. Money in the accounts today is visibly useful to an organization in a way which the prospect of money tomorrow from a funding body is not. If that cash flow is being threatened because you are annoyed with the way that someone in administration is treating you, and you are thinking of moving somewhere where you will be better treated, then that person in administration is likely to receive a word from someone in the hierarchy, and the problem is likely to go away.

So far, all well and good. However, what happens when you're bringing in lots of money and become locked in conflict with someone else in the institution who is bringing in even more money? The answer is that you will probably lose. On a more virtuous level, what happens if you realize that your work can make the world a better place, but there aren't enough hours in the day for you to do all the things that are needed? The answer to both these questions is 'more power'. The prospect of having a few research assistants and perhaps a small research centre, possibly with just one or two colleagues, starts to become appealing, and you begin to flirt with the concept that having an empire is not an inherently Bad Thing. You realize that having an imposing title, a large office and numerous underlings allows you to deal with petty bureaucrats in the institution more effectively, and to get on with the important things in life, such as research. You become aware that you have reached a new phase of your career, for which you will need new skills and values. You begin to understand how much von Clausewitz was misunderstood, and start to read his classic text *On War* (in the original, in case you missed anything in the translated version). You wonder what was so wrong anyway about displaying the severed heads of your enemies on stakes in a prominent place . . .

Academia or elsewhere?

This chapter has an unashamedly academic focus, largely just to keep things simple. But there is a much bigger world out there. Some of the most interesting research is done outside academia, where timeframes, resources, funding and priorities are structured around The Market or around social or political priorities, rather than around arcane systems of status and reputation. One of the big distinguishing questions is to do with autonomy: how important is it to you to set your own research agenda, to choose your own projects, to ask questions in ways that you design? A second is to do with outcomes: how important is it to you to publish, to have direct and public credit for your research contributions, or to see your ideas implemented in concrete and practical ways? A third is to do with resources: who controls the key resources you need to do your work (this is crucial in big equipment disciplines such as astrophysics), and what level of funding does your research require. Another is to do with communities: what sort of people excite you, and where do they work?

Sometimes it's not a strict choice: people can keep a foot in each camp, either working in industry and maintaining collaboration with academia, or vice versa. This is heavily dependent on the discipline and the organizations involved. And of course it's usually easier for more senior researchers to structure their work in interesting ways. Some companies and public organizations encourage employees to take the initiative, to publish and to collaborate. Others see that as frivolous distraction from the real business. Others are neutral, tolerating such activity as long as it doesn't interfere with the 'real work' or the organization's priorities. Some welcome initiative, innovation and discovery – but keep it strictly private, so that they can exploit the intellectual property. It's up to you to work out what sort of environment suits your needs.

Depending on your local discipline and local culture, stepping out of academia for a while can have a varying impact on your ability to step back in later. For example, in the UK in computing, time spent in industry is a decided advantage, providing real-world experience and industry contacts, and lending practical credibility. In other cases, time spent in industry is time not building an academic career and hence putting you at a disadvantage. Similarly, the worth of time in academia can be interpreted variably. In some cases it is a decided advantage, lending authority and credibility. In others, it is viewed as self-indulgent time away from 'the real world'. Find out what the case is in your context. And consider not just 'how can I get a job now' but also 'where do I want to be in 10 years or 20?'.

Whether you choose academia or elsewhere, the basics of 'selling' yourself are the same: finding out about potential employers (both in terms of who has jobs and what sorts of employers you want to work for), and assessing the fit between what you want from a job, what you can actually offer and what they want from an employee.

Do your reconnaissance; it's dangerous to make choices without assessing accurately the 'lie of the land'. Different organizations operate in different ways, and you need to discover the structures, priorities and cultures of each. Unfounded assumptions are rife on both sides and lead to silly misunderstandings. For example, one of us was courted by a major American computer company, and went through two days of successive half-hour interviews, each of which started: 'This isn't quite like the ivory tower you're used to, we don't concentrate on one project at a time here' (one then had to explain that running a research centre was rather different from that fairy tale model of academic research).

Academic career types

In Heroic Times, the hero was traditionally offered a choice by Fate when at an impressionable age. The choice was between a short, brilliant life and a long, unremarkable one. The legends which survived were invariably the ones where the hero chose the short, brilliant life. This may be because heroes were all predictable when it came to that choice, or perhaps it's simply that legends about people leading long, unremarkable lives did not have a great deal of staying power.

Anyway, the relevance of this to the would-be researcher is that there is a similar choice in academia. At a certain point in your career you have to make a decision. It's not quite the same as for heroes, but it's similar. After being a lecturer long enough to notch up the appropriate points on your CV, you can either take the route of becoming primarily a researcher or primarily an administrator and teacher. The former is usually the glamorous route; the latter is normally the route followed by invaluable people who hold institutions together, and who are usually overworked, badly treated and unappreciated until their stress rating reaches the point where they take early retirement. This is not particularly fair, and we do not greatly approve of it. One crumb of consolation for those who take the worthy, unglamorous road is that they might some day become a head of department, perhaps a dean, maybe even a vice-chancellor, and have the prospect of wielding a fair quantity of legitimate power over those who took the other road. A nasty chewy bit in that crumb of consolation, however, will be the discovery that eminent research professors with high-profile research groups can wield a large quantity of less officially recognized power, and can play dirty organizational politics just as well as anyone else. So it goes.

There are various classic career patterns for academic researchers. None is right or wrong *per se*, though each has its advantages and disadvantages.

The empire builder

One classic route is through the various formal levels of academic seniority towards a research empire of your own. You start off by doing a PhD then work as a postdoctoral research assistant for a few years, get a lectureship and work at that level for a few years, get a few grants on which you're principal investigator, become a Reader for a couple of years and then get a chair (i.e. become a professor). In the process of becoming a professor, you will have built up the start of an empire (research assistants and PhD students of your own); after becoming a professor, you will build up a research group, perhaps a research centre with lecturers, research assistants and PhD students attached to it, possibly a research institute. You have gradually shifted the balance of your activity from researching to research entrepreneurship – that is, to directing and managing research. This will make you a considerable power broker in your department, since you will be bringing large amounts of prestige and money in, so a wise head of department will not antagonize you. Most people who follow this route will not want to be a head of department; it's too much hassle, with no research reward. They might possibly take on the role for a couple of years just so they have it on their CV (it can come in handy, and can also make the point to any subsequent head of department that there is someone else who is perfectly capable of running the place if the newcomer gets any silly ideas about throwing their weight about). There is much to be said for this route if you want to get things done, and to wield some power; the drawbacks are the politics and the administrative effort involved. If these are not for you, you might consider something less fraught, such as the wandering scholar route.

The wandering scholar

Wandering scholars may wander geographically, or in academic discipline, or both. This has a long and honourable history. In the Middle Ages, scholars would move from university to university around Europe (having Latin as a common language made this considerably easier). During the Napoleonic Wars, it was considered completely unremarkable for eminent British scientists to give visiting lectures in France, even while the two countries were at war. This tradition is still very much alive, and good research groups are often populated by bright researchers from around the world. For practical reasons, people following this route usually don't build up substantial formal empires, though they may build up formidable reputations. A word of warning, though: it's easy to build up a formidable reputation if you wander about geographically, as long as you publish your work in respected venues within your chosen research area – the journals and conferences that everyone reads and attends. However, without substance, publications, and critical mass, all you accumulate is stamps in your passport. It's very difficult to build up a formidable reputation if you wander about between research *topics*. It takes time to establish a reputation (a rule of thumb is three years from starting a piece of research to seeing it in print in a reasonable journal and even longer in a high-status journal), and if you change fields frequently, then you won't be able to do this. One apparent exception to this generalization occurs if you use your wandering between areas as a way of building up a substantial body of expertise in related areas, then settle down in one area and apply concepts from other areas. That can be extremely productive, but does have an initial cost attached.

The geographically wandering scholar approach is a good way of working with the brightest minds in your area (and building your own reputation, if you have something good to offer), as well as seeing the world. However, if you have commitments which make this route difficult, or you dislike travel, then you may wish to consider a non-wandering career, described here as the hermit scholar approach.

Hermit scholars

Hermit scholars are, in fact, usually not celibate and usually do not live a life of austere contemplation in caves, but the mediaeval metaphor was too tempting to abandon. The term is used here to describe someone who conducts their own research, without a formal research group around them in their base institution (although often with a substantial network of collaborations externally) and whose research remains within a single theme. This is a perfectly respectable route and has quite a few advantages to offer, if played correctly. It can also be quite as social as the other routes, because of the nature of fame in academia, described above. People working in this tradition are quite likely to collaborate with researchers from other institutions around the world, and can build up a formidable reputation because of their in-depth knowledge of their chosen area.

Various other things

The classic fast track for research involves something along the lines of a first at Cambridge in something prestigious like mathematics, followed by a PhD with someone who has an outstanding reputation, followed by some postdoctoral work somewhere prestigious, and then a progression along the lines described above. Someone following this track will usually become more and more specialized in one or at most two areas as they progress.

However, it's important to remember that this is just one route. Another important fast track route can be described as a delayed-action fast track. It involves becoming expert in one area, then transferring concepts from that area to solve problems in a new area (the classic example here is John Maynard Smith's importation of game theory into evolutionary ecology). It is also important to remember that the race is not always to the fast: research reputations are built on quality of research, not speed of promotion. Becoming a professor by the age of 40 is a sign of achievement, but is not much use to the world if you don't come up with any particularly interesting research after becoming a professor. It also won't cut much ice with the rest of the research community – it's the content of your research which matters to the research community, not how quickly you climbed up the slippery pole.

It's also worth mentioning at this point that the research community is a strange place as regards status symbols. Students tend to worry a lot about what class of degree they will get. This is sensible at one level, since you are unlikely to be accepted for a PhD unless you have an upper second or first. After that point, though, other researchers won't be particularly interested in the class of your degree. Another oddity is that, as you proceed up the research pecking order, the field of your first and subsequent degrees will become less and less important. This is particularly apparent in broad fields such as psychology, where it is quite normal for researchers to have started off in other fields such as mathematics, statistics or musicology before the direction of their research interests led them into a psychology department. Many borderlines between disciplines are debatable at best, and debated at worst – for instance, fields such as cognitive modelling, artificial intelligence and human-computer interaction are on the borderline between psychology and computer science, and it is often a matter of chance whether a researcher in these areas happens to be located in a psychology department or a computer science department.

Identifying opportunities

'Chance favours the prepared mind': some of the best job opportunities come from unexpected places, and you need to be open to re-thinking your ideas about what the ideal job looks like. Good job hunters are proactive. Look in the obvious places: newspapers or trade publications (particularly the ones with issues or sections devoted to advertising academic posts; find out where your intended employers advertise); employment agencies, job sites online or headhunters (both face-to-face and online); personnel sites of individual institutions. Consult the career counsellors at your institution and get their help.

Also look in the less obvious places: mailing lists, bulletin boards, announcements of grants (suggesting who might soon be advertising for post-docs). If you can anticipate the conditions leading to job opportunities, you can investigate those, rather than waiting for jobs to be announced.

But the single best way of identifying opportunities is to network. Tell your network that you're looking for a job. Employers are happier to hire a 'known quantity' – including someone recommended by someone whose judgement they trust. Use your personal as well as your professional networks – you never know who knows whom, and who might just make a connection. Ask your mentors (e.g. your supervisor, an academic who has taken an interest in your career, a colleague in industry who has provided guidance) to compile a list of half a dozen or so names of people who might have jobs (or know someone who has jobs), and ask if you can use your mentor's name in introducing yourself. Write letters: 'Dear Prof Eminence, Dr Rising Star suggested that I write to you . . .' The reputation of the mentor will draw attention and add interest to your introduction. But do expect at least one of the recipients to get in touch with the mentor to ask questions.

Writing a CV

The main purpose of a CV is to get you 'across the threshold', typically to get you an interview. What story do you want to tell about yourself; what do you want to emphasize? The story will change with the purpose, and so the CV will change for each use as well. Think about CVs as 'effective or ineffective' rather than as 'good or bad'. Read other people's CVs and consider what they say to you about the person, and why.

Key features of an effective CV are:

- Continuity
- Evidence of development and progression
- Consistency
- Accuracy
- Accessibility

The private 'repository' CV versus the selective, purpose-written CV

A good strategy is to keep one, private, up-to-date 'repository' CV containing anything that might possibly be useful, from publications through to course attendance. Things like key projects, seminars in other institutions, doctoral events, consultancy work, refereeing, conference organization, awards (including studentships) and so on, can be relevant, so keep track of them. (Remember those annual reports all through the PhD? – you can use them as a good opportunity to update your repository CV, or you can use your repository CV as a good source to complete the reports.)

Then make strategic selections from the collection to tailor a CV for a specific use. Use a structure that reflects the purpose (e.g. one that maps onto the job requirements).

CV design choices: write it to be read

Imagine that your CV is one of 50 – or 500 – submitted for a position. Most selection panels first skim-read CVs in order to identify those worthy of further scrutiny. *Write your CV to be skimmed.*

Interview panels are trying to divine what sort of candidate you are. They will read CVs strategically to glean particular sorts of information (e.g. specific skills, particular experiences, evidence of team work, evidence of individual initiative), to look for 'danger signs' (e.g. lots of chopping and changing, inconsistencies, significant omissions), to examine continuity and to look for indications of development or excellence. *Write your CV to be scrutinized in detail.*

When you design your CV, you make choices about selection of information, emphasis and style of presentation.

Selection

What you choose to include can give your interviewers something to ask about. But *anything* you include is open to discussion. Don't include things you'd rather avoid discussing or that might be misunderstood. Think carefully about whether you really want to include personal information (e.g. marital status) or religious or political affiliations, and even consider what your hobbies say about you before you decide to include them. Sometimes this 'peripheral' information can make all the difference – either for or against you – so make sure that what's there is how you want to be seen. Also consider what your omissions may say about you, especially omissions that relate to the purpose for which you're preparing the CV.

Emphasis

Choices you make about things like how you record dates, how you describe previous jobs and how you report your education can convey what you think is important. For example, when you're listing your degrees, do you prioritize the subject or the institution?

Style

The way you present your information can show that you understand what the employer values. For example, if you're going for an academic post, it's a good idea to present your publications in a stratified way that reflects different levels of refereeing and quality control (i.e. status): books (indicate clearly if you're an author or an editor), book chapters (indicate if the chapter was invited or edited), refereed journal publications, refereed conference publications, other lesser publications. If you're going for an industry post, it's a good idea to make accessible the technical qualifications that relate to the post and to emphasize any indicators of customer or market awareness.

Academic CVs tend to be different from industrial CVs. There are times when you need to emphasize your technical qualifications and times when you need to show what a versatile and well-rounded person you are. The trick is to understand enough about the context into which you're sending your CV, in order to emphasize the appropriate things.

CVs change over time, as people develop. CV design choices will change over time, too. Choices that are appropriate for an early career CV will be less appropriate for a mature career CV, and vice versa.

Writing for the skim-reader

- Make every word count. Don't use 'Curriculum Vitae' as your major heading – it's a waste of words. Your name should be the principal heading.
- The first page is crucial. Imagine that someone is trying to review half a dozen candidates and has spread the six CVs on the desk as an *aide mémoire*. A good first page can make you more memorable, more impressive, more accessible. What you put on the first page should reflect what you think is most important for the purpose.
- Be thoughtful in your use of typographic design; good design can help make important information accessible. White space and highlighting 'guide the eye' – make sure the eye is guided to important information. If you just scan down the emboldened words, what do you read? Indenting and spacing can help group information. For example, ex-dented dates can make it easy to scan for continuity.

Writing for the scrutinizer

- Proofread! Then get someone else to proofread!
- The use of narrative trades off with scan-ability. Hence, use narrative sparingly and strategically, offering one or two lines to amplify or describe (e.g. indicating the significance of your doctoral work or highlighting the skills and responsibilities embodied in a previous job).
- Review your CV in the context of particular questions. Does it show continuity of activity? Are there any periods unaccounted for? Can the reader relate jobs to skills or outcomes in some way? Take questions from the job specification: what evidence does the CV provide that you meet the selection criteria?

What to avoid

- **Never lie in a CV**: but make the most of your history, selecting and highlighting relevant and important information. Don't call attention to things you'd prefer not to discuss. (If you lie, there's the horrible risk that you might get the job and then have to try teaching several courses on topics about which you know nothing. Or get fired when your employer finds out you lied.)
- **Focus on content, not dressing**: don't get fancy or cute, it almost always backfires. Conveying information is the goal, not impressing with your decorative flair.
- **Don't leave gaps**: if you do, employers will assume that you're concealing something, such as a spell in prison. If you were unemployed, then it's better to say so than to leave a gap; say something about how you used that time to prepare for the next job.

Applications and cover letters

People tend to talk a lot about CVs and overlook the application and cover letter, which are equally important. They are all part of soliciting an 'invitation to the ball'.

Why must you fill out an application when you've already provided a CV? Because selection panels receive lots (tens and hundreds) of applications and have an obligation to assess them fairly and comparably. The application form puts everyone's information into standard format. It also tells you what criteria are important to the organization. Do ensure that the information you put on the application form matches the information in your CV.

What's the cover letter for? It's an opportunity to match your CV to the organization's needs (the 'person specification') explicitly. Good cover letters are always written for the specific application and echo language from the information for applicants as a way of highlighting the candidate's pertinent and distinguishing characteristics. The cover letter is an opportunity to convey your unique voice in a way that's more difficult in more standardized forms. Cover letters can count, either to your benefit if they are good, or to your detriment if they are bland or formulaic.

Job interviews

Some day, unless you do something very wrong or very silly, you will find yourself sweating outside an interview room, waiting to be interviewed for that all-important job. (They all appear all-important at the time – the first lectureship, the first permanent contract, the senior lectureship that shows you've made your mark, the readership that shows you've made your mark, the chair that shows you've made your mark and so forth.) So, what do you do to help your chances of getting that job?

As usual, it's worth stepping back and having a careful think. This is one context where the virtual cup of coffee is a better idea than an actual cup of caffeine-laden mocha. People get very stressed about interviews, and unfortunately caffeine isn't good for lowering stress levels. You need to think about things such as whether you really want that job. When you're near the end of a PhD/contract/course of medication for stress-related illness, it's easy to grab for any straw that passes near your bit of the torrent, and to persuade yourself that the job you're applying for is exactly what you need to make your life perfect. There are some very nice jobs out there, but they're a minority, and are usually guarded with limpet-like tenacity by the incumbents (and who can blame them?). So, have a long hard think. If you realize that you're desperately clutching at a straw, then bear this in mind when you go for interview, and treat the interview as a chance to practise your technique.

This has various advantages:

- You will be less stressed, which is helpful in itself
- You will get some useful interview practice
- You will probably perform considerably better than usual, which is useful in itself and also practice for the future (there is, in fact, a real risk that you will be offered the job)

Preparation

A moment spent in reconnaissance is seldom wasted, to quote the sponsor of one of the earliest major scientific expeditions. Reading the information for candidates (department description, job description, person specification, etc.) is a good start. It doesn't do any harm to know the department personally; you can do this via things like giving a seminar there, or striking up friendships with members at conferences. Doing reconnaissance has two major advantages: (a) it gives you a better basis for deciding if the job is one you want and (b) panels treat candidates who've 'done their homework' as more serious, more competent and more willing to integrate into the department.

In theory, the interview process starts with a fat first-class letter arriving in the post at your home address inviting you to interview. The fat first-class letter (or fat email) will contain information about how to get to the place, and about the time and the format of the interview, and about any other tasks you're expected to perform. In practice, some institutions may try more creative approaches such as emailing you at your work address or telephoning you. Most places now tell you that because of cost they won't notify unsuccessful candidates. It's a good idea, if you're reasonably sure you're appointable and you haven't heard anything after a decent interval, to check politely with the relevant part of the institution (usually the personnel department) to see whether you've been shortlisted.

If you're applying for a postdoctoral research post, then you need to use the grapevine and read between the lines of CVs on websites to find out what your potential bosses are like to work with. Will they work you like a dog, leave your name off publications and ditch you as soon as the funding runs out? Are they pleasant people who will look after you, give you first authorship of a paper or two and do what they can to look after you once the funding ends – for instance, by finding more money for a follow-on project?

Find out what the institution is like, and specifically how the department you're applying to presents itself. Check out its website and prospectus. What courses does it teach, how many staff does it have, how many students does it have (so you can work out staff–student ratios and therefore workloads)? Is there anything distinctive about its curriculum or teaching style? What are its research strengths? Who are the research leaders? How much have they published? Who is in the department – and who among those are you likely to work or want to collaborate with?

Once you've done this, then you will have a better idea of what line to take for your application. More importantly, you'll have a better idea of whether you want the job in the first place. A closing note well worth remembering is that the job application process is two-way. You don't have to take the first job you're offered; you don't have to fit in with the requirements of the prospective employers if they're clearly inflexible and unreasonable people. It's your life, not theirs.

Practicalia

What to wear

Academic dress conventions are usually fairly relaxed compared to the rest of the world during the working week, but interviews are different. Go back to the viva chapter and the advice there. The panel will assume that what you wear to interview is your idea of what you would wear to a formal occasion. As with academic language and other expressive behaviours, you need to think functionally. What is the function of interview clothing? One function is simply to show that you have reasonable social skills and can be dragged out to help liaise with outside bodies if need be. This is sometimes referred to by expressions such as, 'They wear a good suit', meaning that they can look reasonably professional and presentable in a fairly formal context. For instance, if some people are needed to show moderately important visitors around, are you presentable enough to be turned loose? If you dress like the village idiot, then the answer is likely to be 'no', and that's one less possible use for you in the organization's scheme of things (and therefore, one less tick in the boxes that record your good points).

Some minor details, in no particular order:

- Some interview panel members look to see whether your shoes are immaculate, or scruffy and tatty. If the latter, then they'll suspect you of being the sort of person who does bad work and then tries to dress it up.
- Most interviewees wear dark clothes. The reason for this will become apparent the first time you spill a drink in your lap two minutes before the interview, or have to sprint across a muddy car park to get to the interview room in time.
- One game played by some panel members in boring interviews is spotting which interviewees are wearing a tie/suit/dress for the first time in a couple of years. It's usually a fairly easy game (especially if the labels are still attached). If you're about to be interviewed, and plan to dress formally, then practise beforehand so the clothes don't distract you.

What to carry

Figure out what you need to take with you. Maps and directions. An easy-to-read watch. Plenty of cash (often useful when things don't go to plan). Something sustaining and un-messy to eat, like a granola bar. The interview and job details. Your documentation, suitably indexed for easy reference. Copies of any papers or other supporting material you might want to share with the panel. An extra shirt, tie or pair of tights (as appropriate), in case of accidents. Protection against adverse weather. A pleasant novel or some other good book to distract yourself with. If you put a phone in your bag, you'll need to remember to turn it off before the interview.

Getting there

Usually, the convention is to do presentations in the morning and interviews in the afternoon. The candidates who come from furthest away are usually given the latest slots, to take some of the pressure off them in terms of travel. You will usually be sent a map, or directed to a website containing travel information.

There's no single right answer about whether to use public or private transport. Whichever you use, allow plenty of time for things going wrong and take plenty of cash. That way, if you have a disaster, you might well be able to rescue the situation. For example, if the train breaks down a stop too soon, get a taxi (which is why we recommend cash). If you spill tea down your best shirt, buy a new one. If the journey looks like being really horrible, then consider travelling the day before and staying at a hotel overnight.

When you reach the site, it's a good idea to make your way to the contact point as soon as possible, to check that it really is where it appears on the map. Some universities have two sites at opposite ends of the town, for instance, and these regularly have trouble with candidates going to the wrong site. Identify yourself to the secretary handling the interviews, to let them know that you've arrived. Then do something to relax: take a walk around (if you're not restricted by local security measures), or park yourself in a corner and meditate, or read the good book that you brought with you for just this sort of situation.

You're likely to be offered a drink. If you're asked how you like your coffee, don't say, 'Whatever is least trouble' since that is an unhelpful reply. If they haven't told you where the toilets are, then find out; either use your initiative, or ask in a polite, unapologetic tone. You can then do important things such as checking whether you have oil stains on your shirt, hair sticking up at the back of your head and so forth. It's also useful for when the coffee works its way through your system shortly before the interview starts.

Your presentation

It is common practice to ask candidates to do something in addition to the interview: to give a lecture on a specified topic to a specified audience, to give a research seminar, to prepare teaching material, to critique existing material, to provide an example of published work, to set out a research agenda and so on. These tasks are important: they give you a chance to demonstrate skill and raise interest, and they give the panel a chance to examine some concrete evidence of the claims you make in your application and/or CV. They also give you a hint about the sort of activity the panel considers important. Presentations in particular allow potential employers to 'see you in action'.

The value of this practice for detecting good candidates is questionable, but it's surprisingly good at detecting some of the loons you would not want in your department at any price. (Not all of them, unfortunately, but some, and that's better than nothing.) Very often, the presentation (and any questions afterwards) is when the rest of the department gets a chance to look over the candidates, and often one of them is designated to report the department's impressions to the interview panel. Things to bear in mind:

- Remember the cabinet-making metaphor – what skills do you need to demonstrate in your talk?
- Are you demonstrating all of the essential and most of the desirable skills from the job/person specification that came with the job details?
- What would encourage you about a candidate if you were on the interview panel?
- Have backups – if using PowerPoint or equivalent, then have overhead projector slides as backups and be prepared to use a whiteboard if all else fails.
- Do as many practice sessions as it takes to get the talk down to the right length, days before the interview. Give the talk to an empty room if you have to (though feedback from more experienced colleagues is very useful).
- Think about what the sensible, obvious approach to the topic is. That's what everyone else will be using. Then think about a sensible, non-obvious approach which they won't be using, preferably one that shows you are more mature and far-seeing than the competition.
- Show some personality: if not passion, then at least enthusiasm and engagement.

Your interview

The interview panel will have a make-up determined by a variety of factors. The roles usually include some or more of the following:

- Someone from personnel to see that procedures are duly followed
- Someone external to see that the level of appointment is appropriate and that the panel isn't appointing someone underqualified out of desperation
- Someone from the department, who might have some idea what you're talking about

- Someone else from the department, to pad the department's vote and reduce the risk of the panel appointing someone disastrous as a result of its ignorance of the department's field of interest
- Yet another person from the department who disagrees with the first two, wants to appoint someone with diametrically different skills and who is too senior to keep away
- One or two senior people like the dean who want to keep an eye on what's going on and make sure the department is fitting in with the master plan
- Someone reliable and sane who wears a good suit and has stood in at short notice for one of the above, to make up the numbers

The panel will usually operate more or less in turn, and will usually ask you the same questions that they ask the other candidates. If one of the other candidates has some odd characteristics, then you may in the interests of comparability be asked the same question that the panel will ask them. The results can sometimes seem rather odd to the candidates who have not got a complex and obscure status regarding their nationality and work permits, for instance. If you're thrown by the question, you can always try asking the panel to expand on it a bit, on the grounds that you're not quite sure what they're trying to ascertain.

The panel will (in theory) have agreed on their sequence and their questions beforehand. They will also (in theory) have a copy of the 'essential and desirable characteristics' list in front of them, and will tick off one by one the characteristics which you appear to have, with varying degrees of discretion.

Some panels then simply count the number of ticks and use that as a basis for appointment, which can lead to some scary decisions (hence the way that departments like to make sure they have the right people on the panel). There are all sorts of legal implications if a panel appoints someone who appears to be less qualified than an unsuccessful candidate, which is the reason for some of the more odd-looking decisions. The great bonus about this, from your point of view, is that if you're clearly much better than the internal candidate, then you have a good chance of getting the job.

You need to make very sure that you get as many things ticked as possible: read the list of 'essential and desirable characteristics' with care, and refer explicitly to particular characteristics if you think that the panel might not realize that you have those characteristics. Don't assume that they will have read your CV in detail; err on the side of spelling things out explicitly. Anyone senior enough to be on the interview panel will usually have a ludicrous workload, and can be excused for forgetting that you're the candidate who worked for six months with the Bristol research group.

At interview, you will be concerned with showing the panel how wonderful you are, with a view to furthering your career. The panel will probably not give a damn about that. They will be concerned with their own agenda. This includes things like the following.

Departmental members

- Finding someone who can help out with teaching the SOD2001 module which nobody on the current departmental team can teach
- Finding someone to teach pretty much anything to the first-year students
- Finding someone to teach the complicated stuff to the final-year students and the MSc students
- Finding a good safe pair of hands who can help with departmental firefighting
- Finding someone who can strengthen the next research review or quality audit
- Finding an ally for their long-running power struggle with another member of the department
- Finding someone pleasant to lessen the baleful presence of Professor Jones and Dr West
- Making sure they don't appoint anyone like Professor Jones and Dr West

Other panel members

- Making sure the proprieties are observed and the forms are filled in correctly
- Making sure the institution can't be sued by dissatisfied candidates
- Making sure the department doesn't appoint someone dreadful out of rampant cronyism, like they did with Professor Jones
- Making sure the department doesn't appoint the first person who looks vaguely suitable out of sheer desperation from lack of staff, like they did with Dr West
- Getting the whole business over with as soon as possible because there's too much else to do
- Having a leisurely break from the ludicrous volume of routine admin tasks

The departmental agenda is usually the more important one from your point of view, and can be summed up in one question: what can this person do to make our lives better? If you come across as someone who can clearly fit one or more of the department's needs, then that's a very important step. If you ascertain what the department wants (e.g. by reading the information for candidates) then that makes life a lot easier for you.

Knowing your enemy

As ever, knowing your enemy is extremely important. If you're keen on research, then the standard researcher is one of your enemies, as the lists below should make clear.

The standard researcher criteria for a good job are:

- Little or no teaching

- Little or no admin
- Few or no committee meetings
- As much autonomy as possible

These differ subtly from the criteria which most departments use to describe a good candidate:

- Willing to do a reasonable amount of teaching
- Willing to shoulder their share of the admin
- Willing to help out with those boring committee meetings
- A team player

The positive way to view this is to look at the phrasing in the departmental criteria. In a fair department you will be expected to do your share of everything. That's not unreasonable. In an unfair department you will be expected to do too much of everything. In a pathological department you will be expected to do things which are a total waste of your time and expertise, and which damage your career and health. How can you as a novice tell which category your prospective department falls into? You probably can't. That's why you have a supervisor, and wonderful people to whom you can turn for advice.

Questions they might ask

Classics include the following.

'Did you have a good journey?' which means, 'You're probably feeling nervous; let's start gently.' It does not mean, 'We would dearly love to hear about the roadworks at junction 14.'

'Would you like to tell us about yourself?' can be asked for various reasons, such as reminding the overworked panel whether you are the one from Southampton, or giving you a chance to describe yourself more coherently than you did on your CV. Whatever the reason, this is a good chance to summarize why you fit well with the essential and desirable skills.

'Why did you apply for this job?' can mean either, 'Why are you so clearly desperate to flee your present job?' or, 'Do you actually want this specific job, or would you settle for the first job that came along?' You need to be careful about the first of these, since you don't want to look like a vindictive failure. It's better in such cases to use a neutral phrasing which acknowledges that the present post is not for you, and that you've decided to move on. For the second meaning, you need to phrase your reply to show a well-informed appreciation of the good things about the department, and to show how you can help it.

'Where do you see yourself five years from now?' is a cliché, but a good one. It shows two main things, namely whether you're the sort of person who plans ahead, and what your schemes are for using the department to further your career. If you're either short of planning skills or moving in a direction which will leave a trail of havoc through the department, then your chances of being appointed will probably dwindle.

'What would you teach if appointed?' Possible answers include the following, ranging from dreadful to good:

- 'Me? Teach?'
- 'I hadn't really thought about that.'
- 'Something to do with human factors.'
- 'Human-computer interaction; quantitative methods.'
- 'I've taught system analysis and design at all levels from HND to MSc, so I could teach your SOD1001, SOD2001, SOD3001 and SOD4001 modules. I could also . . .'

Interviews are usually time limited, so use the time well and don't waste it on content-free answers. Marshall your evidence. Follow up general statements ('I like working in collaboration') with reasons ('because it's a chance to combine strengths and be surprised by different perspectives') and concrete examples ('My collaboration with M.R. Wonderful on the meaning extraction project that won a best paper award'). A job interview is a like a *viva voce* examination about you, so you'd better have mastered the topic. (Unlike the candidate we interviewed who, when asked to tell us about his thesis, replied, 'I didn't prepare about that!')

Questions you can ask

There are various questions you can ask. These are useful for two purposes. One is to find out things that you need to know, the other is to demonstrate to the panel that you're bright enough to ask the right questions and shrewd enough not to ask the wrong ones. There are plenty of things that you need to know (for instance, how likely is it that you will have an enormous teaching load dumped on you?) but which nobody in their senses is going to tell you; if you ask questions along these lines then you show yourself as someone who does not understand the rules of the game. What you can ask is how the department would support you in doing the things that you really want to do, for example: 'I'm writing a grant proposal for detailed studies on how people read commercial websites. If the grant is awarded, will the department provide dedicated space for an eye-tracking lab?'

A better way of finding answers to these questions is via the grapevine. Questions which demonstrate that you have the right stuff will vary depending on the precise job, but if your question demonstrates a clear understanding of the department's teaching and research, then you probably won't go far wrong.

Once you've been offered the job, you can ask post-offer questions. This is where you negotiate, wrestle, wheel and deal with your potential employer. There's a trade-off here between getting what you want in the short term and antagonizing your employer in the long term. It's reasonable to ask for clarification about exactly what's on offer, in terms of responsibilities, infrastructure (office, labs, equipment) support (secretarial and technical support, as well as things like travel funding) and flexibility when opportunities arise (like the award of a grant). It's also reasonable to negotiate conditions particular to your needs ('So you'll arrange my schedule to release Mondays so that I can continue my productive collaboration with Prof Smart?'). It's usually easier to do this after an offer is made and before it has been accepted, than after you've taken the post. There's also a certain grudging respect for those bold enough to ask for justified resources commensurate with the post. Employers' amenability to negotiation tends to be proportional to the seniority (and salary) of the candidate. Just don't expect that the answer will always be yes. If there are particular things you want to be able to do (such as publish papers and attend conferences), then you need to ensure that they are either in the job description or accommodated in the terms and conditions. If they're not, then ask about them.

Ideally, find a 'home' that uses your strengths and puts you in an environment that compensates for your weaknesses. Find a setting which will allow you to grow and develop: hence, one that includes expertise, stimulating people and a lively community, a measure of flexibility and regard for initiative.

18

Closing thoughts

You cannot be just without knowledge. [1]

We began with the metaphor of cabinet-making, and that's how we'll end, with some thoughts about how cabinet-making maps onto the PhD.

The first thought is that you should follow your heart. Would you start an apprenticeship as a cabinet-maker if you weren't really interested in cabinet-making? On the same principle, why spend several years of your life doing a PhD on a subject which doesn't excite you?

The next thought is also about following your heart, in a different way. During a PhD which lasts several years there will probably be some rough times in your life. Reduce the stress by keeping the PhD in perspective. It's just about learning how to make a professional-quality cabinet; it's not about having to produce a cabinet so astonishing that it will be the prize exhibit of the world's leading furniture museum. Similarly, blood comes first: if one of life's assorted tragedies hits you, you can always take leave of absence from a PhD for a while, but you can't take leave of absence from a loved one, or your health. It's just an apprenticeship.

Learning will be painful at first: it always is. Accept that as part of the process and you will learn, and the pain will stop being an issue as it turns into growth. The great experts go on learning through their careers, and the learning involves humility – accepting that they don't know it all – and experimentation, and making mistakes, and learning from them.

During your time on the PhD, there will be plenty of occasions when you undergo doubt. When in doubt along the way, ask someone wise for advice. The apprentice who asks the expert about how to proceed is a better apprentice than the one who doesn't recognize when they are out of their depth, and who damages a prime piece of timber through ignorance. Similarly, you'll have to make choices, both practical and ethical. When you have to make a choice,

---

[1] Lavery, B. (ed.) (2007) *The Royal Navy Officer's Pocket-Book, 1944.* London: Conway, p. 16.

make one that you can look back on with a clear conscience in later years, when you are an expert and you are passing on your wisdom to the next generation of apprentices.

That concludes this book; we hope you've found it useful and enjoyable.

Some useful terms

Only yesterday I learnt, to my surprise, that you trice puddings athwart the starboard gumbrils, when sailing by and large. [1]

Standard terms are well described in the standard textbooks. This section concentrates on non-standard terms which you may find useful and terms which are not as widely known as they should be. We have also included some terms which you may be guiltily aware that you're not sure about, even though you know you should be – for instance, what is the difference between a journal and a magazine, and how do these relate to periodicals?

big name: someone with a considerable reputation in the research community. Also known as 'an authority'.

Big Picture: the vision or strategy for your research. In a larger sense, the vision or strategy for your career.

blood in the water: unnecessary indication of serious weakness in your work.

bounced (of paper submitted to a conference or journal): euphemism for 'rejected'.

buzzword: fashionable but usually content-free word. If you're working in an area which is currently popular in the media (e.g. biotechnology or nanotechnology) then you need to make it clear in your writing that you understand the area thoroughly and are not just waving buzzwords around without understanding.

cabinet-making: the thesis is like the 'master piece' produced by apprentices in The Past. It is the piece of work which demonstrates that you have attained mastery of your chosen field. Like the apprentice, you need to make sure that your chosen piece of work, your thesis, gives you the opportunity to demonstrate the whole range of skills that you should have.

chair: professorship.

critical depth: what you're trying to demonstrate with a PhD, a healthy, 'mindful' scepticism that allows you to question assumptions and reasoning, and to consider the value of questions, evidence, techniques, claims – in short, of research – even-handedly and systematically.

cup of coffee: this is shorthand for an informal chat with someone. It usually does take place over a cup of coffee – the best departments are well aware of

[1] O'Brian, P. (1981) *The Ionian Mission*. London: HarperCollins, p. 83.

the importance of coffee rooms as places for informal exchange of information and for introducing PhD students to tacit information about the academic world.

duty of care: this is the core concept underpinning research ethics. You have an obligation to consider the impact of your research on any of those involved in or affected by it, including (but not limited to) your participants, other researchers, those who fund your research and those who might use its outputs.

eyeballing the data: this is an informal term for having a look at the raw data. This is a good idea if you're doing statistical analysis – if the results from the analysis don't look consistent with your impression from eyeballing the data, then there's a chance that you've made a mistake with the analysis. It's surprisingly easy to make mistakes, so eyeballing the data is a good habit.

field, the: has two meanings, which may be confusing for beginners. Sense 1: a discipline, or area of research. Sense 2: place, somewhere outside the lab/ department, where data collection is conducted.

funded research project: if you want money to do some research, you can apply to various bodies for money (for instance, various research councils). Such funding bids range from a few hundred pounds for travel or equipment up to millions of pounds to set up a research institute. One common form of funded research project involves hiring a research assistant for one or two years to carry out the research specified in the funding bid. Bids of this sort bring money into universities and are an important part of research.

Good Thing: from the book *1066 and All That.* This is an ironic reference to things which are currently fashionable, with the implication that before long they will be out of fashion and replaced by some other fad.

Great Departmental Annual Report: most departments publish reports on their teaching and/or research at various intervals. This is usually because they are required to do so by some higher authority, such as the faculty or university, rather than because they want to. These reports are usually a thorough irritation to everyone involved, not least because they usually want information from you in a format which is as inconvenient as possible. They will also probably want to know the exact dates of any conferences at which you presented a paper, and the ISBN or ISSN for any publications. If you haven't kept records of these, then The System will probably hound you mercilessly until you track them down. The moral is to keep neat and complete records of publications (or, failing that, complete records – just putting all the paperwork from the conference in a folder to sort through later will probably be adequate).

harmless: a low-key insult. Describes something which is devoid of any particular good or bad features, but which will attract so little attention because of its mediocrity that it will do no harm to the world (e.g. 'a harmless paper').

inaugural: formal lecture given to colleagues and invited guests by a newly appointed professor, to mark their appointment.

inflating your *p* value: using an unnecessarily large sample size, so that a weak effect is statistically magnified to an unjustified extent. In some fields, weak effects are extremely important; however, in most fields the majority of weak effects are trivial and not worth bothering with.

journal: a learned periodical, aimed at a particular discipline. Differs from a magazine in several ways. Journals are intended for specialists, not general readers, and normally journal articles are written by academics, not journalists. More prestigious academically than magazines, having one of your articles published in a good journal is a sign of professional achievement.

named candidate: when you're writing a funding bid (to ask for money for a research project), some funding bodies like to know that you have already lined someone up to do the work if you get the money – it can be difficult to find someone with suitable skills for a specialist area of research, and a surprising number of projects fail because nobody suitable could be found to do the work. The named candidate is the person lined up to do the work; wise researchers are usually on the lookout for potential named candidates, such as PhD students who appear to know the unwritten rules.

operationalize: mapping from what we want to know to what we can investigate empirically, that is, to what we can observe in the world. It's important to realize that things we capture – recordings, descriptions, categorizations, measures – are not the whole phenomenon, and getting the mapping wrong leads to invalid conclusions.

Past, The: we've capitalized this to mark ironic humour. People tend to think of The Past as a fairly homogeneous time of slow changes, whereas the reality is rather different. In the case of the PhD, for instance, the nature of the doctorate has been changing at a noticeable rate throughout living memory, and probably throughout history. This misconception of The Past can be a serious issue if a central part of your thesis involves claims of unprecedented changes in some area within the last few years; fortunately, a full discussion of this is outside the scope of this glossary.

periodical: a publication which comes out periodically, usually several times a year, such as a journal or a magazine, and in contrast to one-off publications such as books.

PhD: formal abbreviation for Latin *philosophiae doctor* (doctor of philosophy). Highest regular university degree, usually given to a candidate who has successfully presented a written thesis on a research topic and passed a *viva voce* examination. There are also other doctoral qualifications with different abbreviations in disciplines such as theology. As usual, conventions vary across institutions and disciplines. People with a PhD can call themselves 'doctor', a rich source of argument with medical doctors, with each side viewing the other as interlopers.

practicalia: low-level practical things, like making sure you have enough paperclips, or getting a form filled in by the deadline.

professor: academic title; the top academic (as opposed to administrative) title. You do not need to have a doctorate to be a professor, though it is usual. Becoming a professor is equivalent to becoming one of the senior elders in a traditional clan society. Becoming a professor before 40 is usually viewed as a sign of a bright young thing.

protocol: the 'script' for an empirical study which specifies the design in full operational detail.

questionnaire: usually refers to a collection of poorly validated questions assembled without much thought about how they will be analysed, and with even less attention to the literature on good practice in data collection and in surveys. Much favoured by those who believe that it is better to collect large amounts of meaningless data than the right amount of meaningful data.

research metrics and assessment exercises: in the name of quality control, The System periodically asks universities to present data about their publications and other research activities. The better a university's research, the more money it is given by The System. What does 'better' mean? Good question. Shrewd departments have a fair idea of what will count as 'better' and will encourage it (usually papers in top journals and substantial income generation from research are in this category).

Reader: academic rank intermediate between lecturer and professor, specializing in research rather than administration. Usually Readers go on to be a professor fairly soon. We have spelled the term with a capital 'R' to reduce confusion and the scope for witticisms.

reducing the problem space: eliminating plausible but wrong possibilities so you can narrow down the set of possibilities which might be correct.

research assistant: a person who is employed to carry out research on a funded research project. Most PhD students go on to work as a postdoctoral research assistant for a few years after graduating, as a useful way of gaining experience. Once tellingly described as a 'research grunt' by a cynical colleague in that role (an allusion to the US Marine Corps which will probably be lost on most readers, but which might bring amusement to some).

research community: research in any given area involves a number of researchers; usually this number is surprisingly small, since fields tend to subdivide into manageably small subfields. All of the big names, and most of the leading researchers, will usually know each other, at least by name and reputation; they will normally meet at conferences each year. The usual career path is to find a research area which interests you and then to build a reputation within that research community.

research fellow: means different things in different institutions, ranging from a research assistant with a PhD to a very senior and very prestigious research post at a prestigious university.

rhetoric: the art of communication and persuasion.

rigour: the systematic pursuit of validity – and vigilance against bias – through disciplined practice and reasoning.

sample size: usually a very large number, selected for no obvious reason, and without reference to the various statistical tests which can be used to show when diminishing returns have been reached and when there is no point in collecting more data.

sanity check: a test, usually informal, to check that a claim or a finding is not obviously silly. Useful when you're using statistical software for the first time and there's a risk of an error producing output which is in the correct format but which is completely wrong.

significant: has a specialized statistical meaning, which can lead to serious misunderstandings for students who are unaware of this and who use the word in the loose, popular sense. In statistics, 'significant' means 'the likelihood of this happening by random chance is at most 1 in 20'; this is normally accompanied by naming the statistical test which was used. 'Highly significant' and 'very highly significant' involve the same principle, but with odds of 1 in 100 and 1 in 1000 respectively.

significant absence: something whose absence tells you something significant. In a Sherlock Holmes story, the main clue is that the watchdog did not bark when the criminal entered the premises. This absence of barking was significant, and showed that the dog knew the criminal. If the dog had been a friendly creature that never barked at anyone, then the absence of barking would not have been a significant absence. Academic significant absences usually take the form of no reputable published accounts of a particular phenomenon or effect. Learning to spot significant absences takes time, but is an invaluable skill.

System, The: ironic reference to the image, widespread among students and supervisors alike, of the higher reaches of the university as being an unholy hybrid spawned by the imaginations of Kafka, Lovecraft, Orwell and Stalin.

tacit knowledge: in the broad sense, knowledge which is not usually mentioned explicitly, whether because it is taken for granted, or because it is about a sensitive topic. Much expertise consists of tacit knowledge, and acquiring it is an important part of doing a PhD This topic usually isn't addressed in PhD training courses or books, and is usually left to the supervisor, if indeed anyone thinks explicitly about it at all.

there is a literature on that: a middle-key insult that means, 'That topic has been thoroughly studied by a large number of people, and you have clearly failed to do your homework and discover it; also, you have just wasted a chunk of your life reinventing the wheel.'

viva: short for Latin *viva voce*. A live interrogation, usually by external examiners, to test your knowledge of your chosen subject. The final stage of a PhD may also be used on MSc and undergraduate students on occasion. In some countries, the viva takes place as a public event open to anyone who feels like coming along to the lecture hall where it is held; in The Past, as a further aid to students' nerves, vivas were held in Latin, so if you're feeling worried about your own viva, then count yourself lucky that you aren't having it in sixteenth-century Paris.

voice: somewhere between style and viewpoint. For instance, the voice in which a paper is written may be austere, or informal, and/or authoritative. The same word is used in a different sense in traditional grammar.

Some further reading

. . . he was no more consistent than other men, and in spite of his liberal principles and his dislike of constituted authority he was capable of petulant tyranny when confronted with a slime-draught early in the morning. [1]

This section consists, like the rest of this book, mainly of things that don't usually appear in other books on this topic (some of which may seem improbable), and is intended to complement the standard-issue 'further reading' sections rather than to duplicate or supplant them.

Phil Agre, on 'Networking the network':

http://polaris.gseis.ucla.edu/pagre/network.html

Phil Agre has a site full of interesting material. This part is our favourite.

Richard Bolles, on what you want to be when you grow up:

Bolles, R.N. (2009) *What Colour is Your Parachute?: A Practical Manual for Job-hunters and Career Changers*. Berkeley, CA: Ten Speed Press.

There's a reason that this book has been around in various editions for 30 years. It has lots of excellent exercises to help you work out exactly what you want from life, however, it was written by an ordained Episcopal priest, previously canon pastor of Grace Cathedral in San Francisco, and so it has a certain coloration.

Judith Butcher, on copy-editing:

Butcher, J., Drake, C. and Leach, M. (2006) *Butcher's Copy-editing: The Cambridge Handbook for Editors, Copy-editors and Proofreaders*, 4th edn. Cambridge: Cambridge University Press.

The classic book on copy-editing; invaluable for doing a professional job when the proofs come back with a note asking you to check them within two working days.

Tony Buzan, on producing mindmaps:

Buzan, T. (1997) *The Mindmap Book*. London: BBC Books.

[1] O'Brian, P. (1981) *The Ionian Mission*. London: HarperCollins, pp. 70–1.

Mindmaps are a handy way of taking notes or making brain dumps.

Alan Chalmers, on the philosophy of science:

Chalmers, A.F. (1999) *What is This Thing Called Science?* 3rd edn. Maidenhead: Open University Press.

A useful and digestible introduction to the philosophy of science, just the thing for the bathtub or a train ride.

Chris Chatfield, on statistics:

Chatfield, C. (1995) *Problem Solving: A Statistician's Guide*, 2nd edn. London: Chapman & Hall/CRC.

Chatfield gives a thoughtful, accessible introduction to thinking about real data and from that sorting out strategies for statistical analysis. The book is concerned with solving problems rather than just using techniques.

Edward de Bono, on creative thinking:

de Bono, E. (1999) *de Bono's Thinking Course*. London: BBC Books.

We may not love de Bono, but you might, and he's a cultural reference that comes in handy.

Lyn DuPré, on improving your writing:

DuPré, L. (1998) *BUGS in Writing, Revised Edition: A Guide to Debugging Your Prose*. Reading, MA.: Addison-Wesley.

A practical, nuts-and-bolts guide to English usage that combines wit with mastery.

Ben Goldacre, on the nature of evidence:

Goldacre, B. (2008) *Bad Science*. London: Fourth Estate.

Goldacre offers a highly amusing and well-written critique of how evidence is used and abused – including how evidence is distorted in the service of marketing. This book is consistent with our chapters about evidence and critical thinking – but funnier.

Stephen Jay Gould's books of essays:
Useful for helping students to appreciate the scholarship of previous centuries in context, rather than as a quaint collection of mistaken and discarded beliefs.

Sir Ernest Gowers, on effective writing:

Gowers, E. (revised by Greenbaum, S. and Whitcut, J.) (2003) *The Complete Plain Words*. Harmondsworth: Penguin.

The classic advice on writing: 'Keep it simple, stupid.'

Herodotus:

Herodotus, Marincola, J.M. and De Selincourt, A. (1996 edition) *The Histories*. Harmondsworth: Penguin.

A wonderful example of uncritical but scrupulously accurate reporting. We often use Herodotus as a contrast to Thucydides for purposes such as explaining the difference between a literature report (Herodotus) and a literature review (Thucydides).

Darrell Huff, on statistics:

Huff, D. (2003 reissue) *How to Lie with Statistics*. London: W.W. Norton.

Once celebrated as 'blasphemy against the religion of statistics', this delightfully readable book is a classic on the use and abuse of statistics. Huff is a salutary reminder to *pay attention to the evidence*.

Susan Jeffers, on dealing with frustration, indecision and self-doubt:

Jeffers, S. (2007) *Feel the Fear and Do It Anyway*, 20th anniversary edn. London: Vermillion/Random House.

This is one of a slew of self-help books, the sort of thing you read over a coffee and, if the moment is right, use constructively. If you're really keen, there's a whole industry that goes along with the book; visit www.susanjeffers.com.

John Malouff, on problem-solving techniques:

Malouff, J. (2008) *Over Fifty Problem Solving Strategies Explained*, www.une.edu.au/bcss/psychology/john-malouff/problem-solving.php.

This is a compendium of problem strategies gathered from a variety of sources.

Kenneth May, on using a card index:

May, K.O. (1973) *Bibliography and Research Manual of the History of Mathematics*. Toronto: University of Toronto Press.

Pages 2–27 offer a system for maintaining a card index.

Scott McCloud, on comics:

McCloud, S. (1993) *Understanding Comics: The Invisible Art*. New York: Harper Perennial.

A sideways introduction to storytelling and rhetoric.

David Patterson, on 'How to have a bad career in research/academia':

www.cs.berkeley.edu/%7Epattrsn/talks/BadCareer.pdf.

These are slides from a talk by David Patterson offering advice that is wickedly and memorably to the point.

Estelle M. Philips and Derek S. Pugh, on how to get a PhD:

Philips, E.M. and Pugh, D.S. (2005) *How to Get a PhD: A Handbook for Students and their Supervisors*, 4rd edn. Maidenhead: Open University Press.

There's a good reason why this book has sold so many copies year after year. It's an excellent overview of the PhD process – indeed, we have always considered our book as a complement to Philips and Pugh.

George Pólya, on reasoning and problem solving:

Pólya, G. (1971) *How to Solve It: A New Aspect of Mathematical Method*. Princeton, NJ: Princeton University Press.

Although an introduction to mathematical problem-solving might seem irrelevant, it's not. Good research is about good reasoning, and Pólya's book is a fine excuse to explore and reflect on strategies for problem-solving.

Robert Rosenthal and Ralph Rosnow, on human-participants studies:

Rosenthal, R. and Rosnow, R.L. (2008) *Essentials of Behavioural Research: Methods and Data Analysis*, 3rd edn. New York: McGraw-Hill.

There are numerous textbooks and reference works on research methods involving human participants. If you were only to read one, this would be a safe choice. But it would take you a long time.

Donald Schön, on reflective practice:

Schön, D. (1984) *The Reflective Practitioner: How Professionals Think in Action*. London: Temple Smith.

Schön promotes critical self-reflection and articulates that professional excellence arises from 'reflection in practice', a continual feedback loop of experience, learning and practice. A useful (and highly influential) perspective.

The **Skeptic's Encyclopedia**, on reasoning and evidence:

http://skepdic.com/contents.html

Very useful for practice in reasoning, logic and use of evidence.

William Strunk Jnr. and E.B. White, on writing right (sorry, we couldn't resist that one):

Strunk, W. and White, E.B. (1979) *The Elements of Style*. New York: Macmillan.

This is a fundamental guide to English usage. Every writer should have it, and should have read it.

Robert H. Thouless, on reasoning and thought:

Thouless, R.H. (1995) *Straight and Crooked Thinking*. London: Macmillan.

This is a book about argument and intellectual engagement set in the context of human emotion and psychology. It articulates a range of pitfalls in argumentation. Students would do well to use the appendix on 'Thirty-eight dishonest tricks which are commonly used in argument' as a checklist for debugging their dissertations.

Thucydides, on rigorous thinking:

Thucydides, Warner, R. and Finley, M.I. (1954) *History of the Peloponnesian War.* Harmondsworth: Penguin.

Most students have a certain degree of condescension towards work done before they were born, and this can lead to dangerous habits and sloppy scholarship. Thucydides' writing and reasoning (for instance, his analysis of the size and significance of the Trojan War) help students understand how much there is to gain from treating the literature seriously, however old it is.

Edward Tufte, on visual presentation of data:

Tufte, E.R. (2001) *The Visual Display of Quantitative Information,* 2nd edn. Cheshire, CT: Graphics Press.

The canon on visual design for graphical presentation of numerical data. Elegant, lavish, lucid, diverting and informative.

The urban legends FAQ:

http://www.urbanlegends.com/afu.faq/

Generally entertaining (though often gruesome); good for teaching students caution when deciding which statements need to be checked and which statements are known by everyone to be true.

Vitae, on an establishment view of PhDs and early research careers:

http://www.vitae.ac.uk/

'Vitae is a national [UK] organization championing the personal, professional and career development of doctoral researchers and research staff in higher education institutions and research institutes.' Actually, the site has all sorts of useful material, do look.

Wikipedia sections on rhetoric and on logical fallacies:

http://en2.wikipedia.org/wiki/Rhetoric http://en.wikipedia.org/wiki/Fallacy

Most students have room for improvement as regards seeing errors either in their own reasoning or in the texts they are using. The Wikipedia site is one of several modern sites which provide accessible introductions to this via understanding rhetoric and logical fallacies.

Index

Related books from Open University Press
Purchase from www.openup.co.uk or order through your local bookseller

WRITING FOR ACADEMIC JOURNALS
SECOND EDITION
Rowena Murray

Academics are expected to write but seldom consider and discuss the nature of academic writing. As a result, the practice is shrouded in mystery. Writing for Academic Journals makes explicit much of what is normally opaque and it should be among the first ports of call for any academic who is contemplating getting published. This new edition achieves the near-impossible: improving on what was already acknowledged as a first-rate compendium.
> Professor Ronald Barnett, Institute of Education, University of London, UK

Our experience is that Rowena's practical approach works for busy academic staff. Not only does it enable them to increase their publication output and meet deadlines, but it boosts enthusiasm for writing and stimulates creative thinking.
> Kate Morss, Director, Queen Margaret University College, Edinburgh, UK

This book unravels the process of writing academic papers. It tells readers what good papers look like and how they can be written.

Busy academics must develop productive writing practices quickly. No one has time for trial and error. To pass external tests of research output we must write to a high standard while juggling other professional tasks. This may mean changing our writing behaviours.

Writing for Academic Journals, Second Edition, has been comprehensively updated to include the most recent research and theory in order to provide new knowledge on writing across the disciplines. Drawing on her extensive experience of running writing workshops and working closely with academics on developing writing, Rowena Murray offers practical and tested strategies for good academic writing.

Contents
Preface – Acknowledgements – Introduction: Beyond reason and vanity – Why write for academic journals? – Targeting a journal – Finding time to write – Finding a topic and developing an argument – Outlining – Drafting – Revising the draft – Dialogue and feedback – Responding to reviewers' feedback – Bibliography – Index

2009   228pp
978-0-335-23458-5 Paperback

HOW TO SURVIVE YOUR DOCTORATE

Jane Matthiesen and Mario Binder

If you are doing, thinking about doing, or know someone who is doing a doctorate, then this is the survival kit you need! Rather than focusing on the technical side of the doctorate, this book looks at all the other crucial skills that are part of everyday doctoral life. This candid book provides real insight into what it's like to do a doctorate and offers practical advice on:

- The application process
- Sources of financial support
- Motivational issues
- Student-supervisor relationships
- Departmental and university politics
- Publishing, conferences and networking
- Career strategies

Written by recent doctoral graduates, the book also includes real examples and case studies from current doctoral students and recent graduates across a range of disciplines and universities. By demystifying the doctoral process *How to Survive Your Doctorate* prepares you for life as a doctoral student like no other book. See for yourself and be a survivor!

Contents

List of figures – List of tables – Acknowledgements – Introduction – Getting started – Managing the self – Dealing with your supervisor – Sidelines of a doctorate – Finances – Politics – Alternative routes to a doctorate – Career paths and strategies – Getting out: the viva and beyond – References – Index

2009   208pp
978-0-335-23444-8 Paperback   978-0-335-23443-1 Hardback